Caryl Churchill

Light Shining in Buckinghamshire

Pluto  Plays

A Note on the Author

Caryl Churchill has written for stage, radio and television. Among her stage plays are *Owners* 1972; *Objections to Sex and Violence* 1974; *Traps* (also to be published by Pluto Press in 1978); *Vinegar Tom* (for the *Monstrous Regiment*) and *Light Shining in Buckinghamshire* (for Joint Stock) all written in 1976.

Light Shining in Buckinghamshire

You great Curmudgeons, you hang a man for stealing, when you yourselves have stolen from your brethren all land and creatures. *More Light Shining in Buckinghamshire*, a Digger pamphlet 1649

A revolutionary belief in the millenium went through the middle ages and broke out strongly in England at the time of the civil war. Soldiers fought the king in the belief that Christ would come and establish heaven on earth. What was established instead was an authoritarian parliament, the massacre of the Irish, the development of capitalism.

For a short time when the king had been defeated anything seemed possible, and the play shows the amazed excitement of people taking hold of their own lives, and their gradual betrayal as those who led them realised that freedom could not be had without property being destroyed. At the Putney debates Cromwell and Ireton argued for property; Gerrard Winstanley led Diggers to take over the common land: 'There can be no universal liberty till this universal community be established.' The Levellers and Diggers were crushed by the Army, and many turned in desperation to the remaining belief in the millenium, that Christ would come to do what they had failed in. The last long scene of the play is a meeting of Ranters, whose ecstatic and anarchic belief in economic and sexual freedom was the last desperate burst of revolutionary feeling before the restoration.

The simple 'Cavaliers and Roundheads' history taught at school hides the complexity of the aims and conflicts of those to the left of Parliament. We are told of a step forward to today's democracy but not of a revolution that didn't happen; we are told of Charles and Cromwell but not of the thousands of men and women who tried to change their lives. Though nobody now expects Christ to make heaven on earth, their voices are surprisingly close to us.

A Note on the Production

First of all, Max Stafford-Clark and I read and talked till we had found a subject in the millenial movement in the civil war. There was then a three-week workshop with the actors in which, through talk, reading, games and improvisation, we tried to get closer to the issues and the people. During the next six weeks I wrote a script, and went on working on it with the company during the five-week rehearsal period.

It is hard to explain exactly the relationship between the workshop and the text. The play is not improvised: it is a written text and the actors did not make up its lines. But many of the characters and scenes were based on ideas that came from improvisation at the workshop and during rehearsal. I could give endless examples of how something said or done by one of the actors is directly connected to something in the text. Just as important, though harder to define, was the effect on the writing of the way the actors worked, their accuracy and commitment. I worked very closely with Max, and though I wrote the text the play is something we both imagined.

The characters Claxton and Cobbe are loosely based on Laurence Clarkson, or Claxton, and Abiezer Coppe, or Cobbe, two Ranters whose writings have survived; the others are fictional, except for those in the Putney debates, which is a much-condensed transcript of three days of debate among Army officers and soldiers' delegates which took place in 1647.

The characters are not played by the same actors each time they appear. The audience should not have to worry exactly which character they are seeing. Each scene can be taken as a separate event rather than part of a story. This seems to reflect better the reality of large events like war and revolution where many people share the same kind of experience. I recommend other productions to distribute parts in the same way, since the play was constructed with this in mind; and there would be difficulties if each character was played by one actor – for instance, Briggs's friend in the recruiting scene is by implication Claxton, from the reference to the baby, yet in the last scene Briggs and Claxton meet as strangers. When different actors play the parts what comes over is a large event involving many people, whose characters resonate in a way they wouldn't if they were more clearly defined.

The play was performed with a table and six chairs, which were used as needed in each scene. When any chairs were not used they were put on either side of the stage, and actors who were not in a scene sat at the side and watched the action. They moved the furniture themselves. Props were carefully chosen and minimal.

The play opened at the Traverse Theatre, Edinburgh, in September 1976, and was then on tour and at the Royal Court Theatre Upstairs.

Actors in the workshop:

Ian Charleson

Jenny Cryst

Linda Goddard

Carole Hayman

Will Knightley

Colin McCormack

Anne Raitt

David Rintoul

Actors in the play:

Janet Chappell

Linda Goddard

Bob Hamilton

Will Knightley

Colin McCormack

Nigel Terry

When Janet Chappell had to leave the cast her parts were played by Carole Hayman.

Directed by Max Stafford-Clark

Designed by Sue Plummer

Lighting by Steve Whitson

Music by Colin Sell

Scenes;	Parts played by:
COBBE PRAYS	Nigel
THE VICAR TALKS TO HIS SERVANT	Colin and Bob
MARGARET BROTHERTON IS TRIED	Janet, Colin and Will
STAR RECRUITS	Bob as Star, Will as Briggs, Colin as Friend, and the rest
BROTHERTON MEETS THE MAN	Janet and Bob
BRIGGS JOINS UP	Colin as Star, Nigel as Briggs
HOSKINS INTERRUPTS THE PREACHER	Nigel, Linda, and the rest
CLAXTON BRINGS HOSKINS HOME	Linda as Wife, Janet as Hoskins, Will
COBBE'S VISION	Bob announcing, Colin as Cobbe
TWO WOMEN LOOK IN A MIRROR	Janet and Linda
BRIGGS RECALLS A BATTLE	Nigel
THE PUTNEY DEBATES	Nigel as Rainborough, Bob as Sexby, Linda as Rich, Janet as Wildman, Colin as Cromwell, Will as Ireton
CLAXTON EXPLAINS	Will
BRIGGS WRITES A LETTER	Bob and Colin
THE WAR IN IRELAND	Colin
THE VICAR WELCOMES THE NEW LANDLORD	Will and Nigel
A WOMAN LEAVES HER BABY	Linda and Janet
A BUTCHER TALKS TO HIS CUSTOMERS	Bob

LOCKYER'S FUNERAL	Nigel
THE MEETING	Janet as Hoskins, Linda as Brotherton, Colin as Cobbe, Will as Claxton, Nigel as Briggs, Bob as the Drunk
AFTER	Same as the meeting

Documentary material:

Fear, and the pit . . . Isaiah 24, xvii–xx

A Fiery Flying Roll Abiezer Coppe 1649*

All Seems Beautiful . . . Song of Myself Walt Whitman

The Putney Debates 1647

The True Levellers Standard Advanced Gerrard Winstanley, 1649

The English Soldier's Standard to Repair to 1649

The Moderate, a Leveller newspaper, 1649

The sleep of the labouring man . . . Ecclesiastes 5

* The correct date is 1649 though the date 1647 is given in the text as this seemed the best place for the scene. It seemed unnecessarily confusing for the audience to go forward to 1649 then back to 1647 for the Putney debates.

List of characters in order of appearance:

Cobbe

Vicar

Servant

1st JP

2nd JP

Margaret Brotherton

Star

Briggs

Friend

Man

Preacher

Hoskins

Claxton

Claxton's Wife

1st Woman

2nd Woman

Colonel Thomas Rainborough

Edward Sexby

Colonel Nathaniel Rich

John Wildman

Oliver Cromwell

General Ireton

Winstanley

Butcher

Drunk

ACT I

All (*Sing Isaiah 24 xvii–xx*)

> Fear, and the pit, and the snare are upon thee, O inhabitant of the earth.
>
> And it shall come to pass that he who fleeth from the noise of the fear shall fall into the pit; and he that cometh out of the midst of the pit shall be taken in the snare; for the windows from on high are open, and the foundations of the earth do shake.
>
> The earth is utterly broken down, the earth is clean dissolved, the earth is moved exceedingly.
>
> The earth shall reel to and fro like a drunkard, and shall be removed like a cottage; and the transgression thereof shall be heavy upon it; and it shall fall and not rise again.

COBBE PRAYS

Cobbe Forgive my sins of the night and already this new day. Oh prevent me today from all the sins I will note – action, word, thought or faint motion less than any of these – or commit unknowing despite my strict guard set. Sloth not rising when mother called, the air so cold, lay five minutes of sin till she called again. Break me, God, to welcome your cold. Lust when the girl gave meat last night, not keeping my eyes on my plate but followed her hand. Repented last night with groans to you, O God, and still dreamt. Guard me today. Let me not go to hell, hot nor cold hell, let me be one of your elect. What is worst, I am not praying to you about the worst sin. I sin in my fear of praying about that sin, I sin in denying my fear. But you cut through that mesh, knowing. Why is it not enough to use your name in prayer, oh God, oh Lord Jesus Christ, amen, this is prayer, oh God, no swearing. Rich men of Antichrist on horses swear, king's officers say 'dammee' laughing. The beggar swore when they whipped him through the street and my heart leapt at each curse, a curse for each lash. Is he damned? Would I be? At table last night when father said grace I wanted to seize the table and turn it over so the white cloth slid, silver, glass, capon, claret, comfits overturned. I wanted to shout your name and damn my family and myself eating so quietly when what is going on outside our gate? Words come out of my mouth like toads, I swear toads, toads will sit on me in hell. And what light on my father, still no light? Not to honour my father is sin, and sin to honour a greedy, cruel, hypocritical – – Is it sin to kneel here till he leave the house? I cannot go down to him. It is sin to go down. I will wait till I hear the door. To avoid his blessing.

THE VICAR TALKS TO HIS SERVANT (CLAXTON)

The VICAR *sits at table, with wine and oranges.*

Vicar How's the baby today? Any better?

Servant No, sir.

Vicar You saw who were missing again from morning service.

Servant Sir.

Vicar No better – no worse, I hope?

Servant Yes, sir.

Vicar Good, good. The sermon would have done them good. It wasn't my own, you could probably tell. The Bishop's naturally more gifted. But it's no good having it read in every parish if nobody compels the tenants to hear it. It's the ones who weren't there that I was talking to. 'From whence come wars and fightings among you?' From their lusts, from greed and envy and pride, which are from the devil, that's where the wars come from. When you said yes, you meant no worse?

Servant No sir.

Vicar Worse.

Servant Sir.

Vicar God tries you severely in your children. It must have been a comfort this morning to have the Bishop himself encourage you to suffer. 'Be afflicted and mourn and weep.' That is the way to heaven.

Servant Sir.

He pours more wine.

Vicar Why we have this war is because men want heaven now. If God meant us to have heaven on earth, why did he throw us out of paradise? They're fighting God himself, do they know that? They must be brought before the magistrates and forced to come next Sunday, and I'll tell them in my own words. Thank you, a little. This is a godly estate and they will be evicted if they don't submit.

He gives SERVANT *an orange.*

Still we must pray your baby is spared this time. Take it an orange.

He drinks and takes an orange.

Servant Thank you, sir.

Vicar And if it is not spared, we must submit. We all have to suffer in this life.

He drinks.

MARGARET BROTHERTON IS TRIED

She is barely audible.

1st JP Is this the last?

2nd JP One more.

1st JP It's a long list.

2nd JP Hard times.

1st JP Soft hearts. Yours.

2nd JP Step forward please.

1st JP I still say he should have been hanged.

2nd JP He'll die in jail. Name?

Brotherton Margaret Brotherton.

1st JP That's no example, nobody sees it.

2nd JP Margaret Brotherton. Begging. Guilty or not guilty?

Brotherton I don't know what you mean . . .

1st JP You're not of this parish?

2nd JP Where do you come from?

Brotherton Last week I was at Aston Clinton, and before that from Northampton.

1st JP I don't want to be told every place you've ever been. Where were you born?

Brotherton Long Buckby.

1st JP If you belong fifty miles away what are you doing here?

2nd JP Have you relations here? Friends you could stay with?

1st JP Tell us about your third cousin's wife's brother who has work for you. No? Or have you been told you get something for nothing here?

2nd JP It's only our own poor who get help from this parish.

1st JP And we don't give money. So you can't drink it. It's your system of poor relief that brings them – they hear there's free bread and cheese, free fuel, there's no parish for miles that does that.

2nd JP We can't help every vagrant in the country.

1st JP You must go back to where you were born.

2nd JP If her parents didn't come from there they won't take her.

1st JP Her father's parish.

2nd JP She's never been there.

1st JP The parish she last lived in.

2nd JP They turned her out for begging.

1st JP Exactly, and so do we.

2nd JP Why aren't you married?

Brotherton . . .

1st JP Can we please agree on a sentence.

2nd JP First offence. Let's be lenient.

1st JP It's only fair to warn you in advance that the next council meeting may reconsider the whole question of poor relief.

2nd JP Margaret Brotherton, we find you guilty of vagrancy and sentence you to be stripped to the waist and beaten to the bounds of this parish and returned parish by parish to . . .

1st JP Where she was born.

2nd JP To the parish where you were born. Next please.

STAR RECRUITS

A prayer meeting.

Star Christ watch over this meeting and grant that your kingdom will come, amen.

All Amen.

Star Life is hard, brothers, and how will it get better? I tell you, life in Babylon is hard and Babylon must be destroyed. In Babylon you are slaves. Babylon is the kingdom of Antichrist. The kingdom of popery. The kingdom of the king. And it must be destroyed. Because then will come the kingdom of Jerusalem. And in Jerusalem you will be free. That is why you will join as soldiers. To destroy Antichrist. To fight with parliament for Jerusalem. To fight with Christ's saints for Christ's kingdom. Because when parliament has defeated Antichrist then Christ will come. Christ will come in person, God and man, and will rule over England for one thousand years. And the saints will reign with him. And who are the saints? You are. The poor people of this country. When Christ came, did he come to the rich? No. He came to the poor. He is coming to you again. If you prepare for him by defeating Antichrist which is the royalists. If you join the army now you will be one of the saints. You will rule with Jesus a thousand years. We have just had another bad harvest.* But, it is written, when Jesus comes 'the floors shall be full of wheat and the vats overflow with wine'. Why did Jesus Christ purchase the earth with his blood? He purchased it for the saints. For you. It will all be yours. You are poor now. You are despised now. But the gentlemen who look down on you will soon find out that the inhabitants of Jerusalem are commonwealth men. Now is the moment. It will be too late when Christ comes to say you want to be saved. Some will be cast into the pit, into the burning lake, into the unquenchable fire. And some will be clothed in white linen and ride white horses and rule with King Jesus in Jerusalem shining with jasper and chrysolite. So give now, give what you can to Christ now to pay his soldiers. Christ will pay you back in diamonds. Join now for a soldier of Christ and you will march out of this town to Jerusalem. Who are you? What are you? I know you all and you know me. You are nobody here. You have nothing. But the moment you join the army you will have everything. You will be as important as anybody in England. You will be Christ's Saints.*

†**Briggs** Going for a soldier?

Friend What soldier? What side?

Briggs Parliament, inne, Mr Star?

Friend He's a gentleman, inne, Mr Star?

Briggs Parliament's gentlemen. But parliament's for us.

Friend What's the pay?

* dialogue simultaneous with † to † pp. 4–5.

Briggs More than I'm getting now. And they give you a musket.

Friend For yourself?

Briggs To use it. Heard about the baby.

Friend Ah.

Briggs Wife all right? Thinking of going.

Friend What about . . .

Briggs Send them money. And where I am now, I'll be out again in the winter like last year. I'm not having that. You keep an eye on them. Won't be long.

Friend Christ's coming anyway.

Briggs You reckon?

Friend Something's going on.†

1st Friend And when will Christ come?

Star When will Christ come? 'From the abomination that maketh desolate, there shall be one thousand, two hundred and ninety days.' Now a day is taken for a year. And that brings us to sixteen hundred and fifty. Yes, sixteen hundred and fifty. So we haven't much time. Jerusalem in England in sixteen fifty. Don't leave it too late. Join the army today and be sure of your place in Jerusalem.

Now I've a list here of names that have joined already. Twenty-three saints that live in this town. Whose name is next on the list of saints?

Briggs What's the pay?

Star The pay is eightpence a day. Better than labouring. And it's every day. Not day labour. Not just the days you fight. Every day.

Briggs And keep?

Star Keep is taken out. But you're given a musket. Shall I take your name?

Three LISTENERS *speak out.*

1st I won't go to fight. But there's three of us could pay for a musket among the three.

2nd I've got four silver spoons. They'd pay for something.

3rd You can have a buckle I was given.

Briggs I'll give my name. Briggs. Thomas Briggs.

BROTHERTON MEETS THE MAN

She has several bags. He has a bottle.

Brotherton Went up the road about a mile then I come back. There's a dog not tied up. So I started back where I slept last night. But that was into the wind. So I'm stopping here. It's not my shoes. I've got better shoes for walking in my bag. My sister's shoes that's dead. They wouldn't fit you. How much you got?

Man Drunk it all.

Brotherton I'm not asking.

He gives her the bottle.

Man It doesn't matter not eating if you can drink. Doesn't matter not drinking if you can sleep. But you can't sleep in this wind.

He takes the bottle back.

Brotherton What you got there?

Man I thought my hands were cold but they're warm to yours.

Brotherton What you got?

Man Look, here, that's my Bible. That's my father's name, that's my name. Two and a half acres. I had to sell my knife. I sold my knife.

Brotherton How much you got now then?

Man Tenpence.

Brotherton That's a long time till you got nothing. Then you can sell the Bible.

Man No, I need that.

Brotherton What I've got, look. The shoes. A bottle, that's a good bottle. I had another one that was no good. I don't often throw something out but I won't carry anything I don't like. A piece of cloth. You can wrap it round. It's got lots of uses. I could sell you that. You can't see what's in here. That's more of my sister's things that's dead. There's a piece of rope. You could have that for a halfpenny.

Man Your face is cold. Your neck's cold. Your back's no warmer. The wind goes right through.

Brotherton You can have the rope and the cloth both for a halfpenny.

Man Come and lie down. Out of the wind. I'll give you a halfpenny after.

Brotherton No. With tenpence, we can get indoors for that.

Man Wouldn't last long.

Brotherton Last more than one day. Even one day's good.

Man If only I knew when Christ was coming.

Brotherton You think he's coming?

Man He must. If only the money would last till the world ends then it would be all right. It's warm in heaven.

Brotherton If he comes tomorrow and you've not drunk your money. Sitting here with tenpence in the cold. Christ laugh at you for that.

BRIGGS JOINS UP

STAR *eats.*

Star You keep your hat on. New style catching on.

Briggs Yes sir. I mean, yes, I do.

Star As a sign you're as good as me?

Briggs Yes. Nothing personal Mr Star. Before God only.

Star Parson seen you like that?

Briggs He said I was a scorpion, sir. Mr Star. I mean, he said I was a scorpion.

Star A hat's all right for a soldier. It shows courage.

Pause, while STAR *eats.*

You know what I'm eating?

Briggs Your dinner?

Star What it is.

Briggs Meat?

Star The name of it.

Briggs Beef? Mutton? I can't tell from here.

Star Sheep. Or, if it was, cow, but it's sheep. Now what language is that, beef, mutton?

Briggs It's not language –

Star Beef and mutton is Norman words. The Saxon raised the animal. Sheep. Cow. The Norman ate the meat. Boeuf, mouton. Even the laws of this country aren't written in English.

Briggs So I've come.

Star You haven't got a horse, I know, so I can't put you in the horse, though there's more thinking men there with hats on and writing their grievances down on paper. But you'll find plenty to talk about in the foot. Eight-pence a day and we deduct food and clothing. Cheese and hard biscuit. Anything else?

Briggs You don't know how long it's going to be?

Star Till we win.

Briggs That's what I mean. How long till we win?

Star What we're fighting for . . . We've known each other all our lives. Our paths never cross. But you know me as an honest dealer. I've been leant on many times to keep up the price of corn when it could be down. And I'd be a richer man. The hunger now is no fault of mine. You're a Saxon. I'm a Saxon. Our fathers were conquered six hundred years ago by William the Norman. His colonels are our lords. His cavalry are our knights. His common foot soldiers are our squires. When you join this army you are fighting a foreign enemy. You are fighting an invasion of your own soil. Parliament is Saxon. The Army is Saxon. Jesus Christ is Saxon. The Royalists are Normans and the Normans are Antichrist. We are fighting to be free men and own our own land. So we fight as long as it takes. In the meantime there's no looting. No raping. No driving off of cattle or firing ricks. We're not antichristian royalists. We're Christ's saints. It's an army that values godliness. There's no swearing. The men don't like swearing. They like reading their Bibles. They like singing hymns. They like talk. We don't discourage talk. Your officers are not all gentlemen, they're men like you.

Briggs Bacon. Is bacon Norman?

Star Pork, Briggs. Pig. Very good.

Briggs And Jacob the younger brother is the Saxon herds the pigs. And Esau the older brother is the Norman eats the pork.

Star Very good, Briggs. Excellent. Now one thing. You wear your hat. Will you take orders?
Briggs If they're not against God.
Star They can't be against God in God's army.

HOSKINS INTERRUPTS THE PREACHER

Preacher My text today is from Psalm one hundred and forty-nine.
> 'Sing unto the Lord a new song and his praise in the congregation of saints.
> Let the high praises of God be in their mouth and a two-edged sword in their hand.
> To bind their kings with chains and their nobles with fetters of iron.'

All and Hoskins Amen, amen.
Preacher It is no sin to take up arms against the king. It is no sin if we fight singing praises to God, if we fight to bind an unjust king with chains.
All Amen.
Preacher For it is written: 'The saints of the most High shall take the kingdom and possess the kingdom forever, even forever and ever.'
Hoskins Forever and ever, amen.
All Amen.
Preacher The saints will take the kingdom. And who are the saints?
Hoskins We all are.
Preacher The saints are those whom God has chosen from all eternity to be his people. For he has chosen a certain number of particular men to be his elect. None can be added to them and none can be taken away. And others he has chosen to be eternally damned. As John tells us in Relevation: 'Whosoever was not written in the book of life was cast into the lake of fire.' So it is God's saints, chosen before their birth, written in the book of life, who will bind the king and the nobles and take the kingdom which will last forever.
All Amen.
Hoskins But no one is damned. We can all bind the king.
Preacher Who are the saints? They are not the same people who rule in this world.
Hoskins Amen to that.
All Amen.
Preacher When Christ first came to earth he came to the poor. And it is to the poor, to you, to tailors, cobblers, chapmen, ploughmen, that he is coming again. He will not set up a kingdom like we have now, a kingdom of Antichrist, a kingdom of a king, nobles and gentry. In Christ's kingdom no worldly honour counts. A noble can be damned and a beggar saved.
All Amen.

Preacher All that counts is whether God has chosen you. Look into your hearts and see whether God has chosen you or – –

Hoskins He's chosen me. He's chosen everyone.

Preacher Or whether you are given over to the devil. For those that are not saved will be cast into the pit. 'And he that cometh out of the midst. of the pit shall be taken in the snare.'

Hoskins There is no pit, there is no snare.

Preacher For now is the time spoken of in Isaiah, 'the earth is utterly broken down, the earth is clean dissolved'.

Hoskins God would not send us into the pit. Christ saves us from that.

Preacher 'And it shall come to pass in that day, that the Lord shall punish the host of the high ones that are on high, and the kings of the earth upon the earth.'

Hoskins Yes he will cast them down but he will not damn them eternally.

Preacher Why are you speaking? I let it pass but you are too loud. Women can't speak in church.

Hoskins God speaks in me.

Preacher For St Paul says, 'I suffer not a woman to teach, nor to usurp authority over the man, but to be in silence.'

Hoskins A text? a text is it? do you want a text?

Preacher 'For Adam was first formed then Eve. And Adam was not deceived but the woman being deceived was in the transgression.

Hoskins Joel. Chapter two. Verse twenty-eight. 'And it shall come to pass that I will pour out my spirit upon all flesh; and your sons and your daughters shall prophecy, and your old men shall dream dreams and your young men shall see visions. And also upon the servants and upon the hand-maids in those days will I pour out my spirit.'

Preacher It has got about that I allow answers to my sermons. But this is taking the freedom to speak too far. If anyone can call out whenever they like it will be complete confusion. I allow answers to my sermon if they are sober and godly and if the speaker has the courtesy to wait – –

Hoskins You say most of us are damned. You say we are chosen to be damned before we are born.

Preacher I said to wait till the end of the sermon, and I do not allow women to speak at all since it is forbidden.

Hoskins How can God choose us from all eternity to be saved or damned when there's nothing we've done?

Preacher I will answer this question because it is a common one and others, who have the grace to wait, may be asking it within themselves. But I am not answering you. How can some people be damned before they are born? Sin is the cause of damnation, but the reason God does not choose to save some people from sin and damnation is his free will and pleasure, not our own.

All Amen.

Hoskins God's pleasure? that we burn? what sort of God takes pleasure in pain?

Preacher And those few that are saved are saved not by their own virtue though if they are the elect they will by their very nature try to live virtuously, but by God's grace and mercy – –

Hoskins No, it's not just a few. Not just a few elect go to heaven. He thinks most people are bad. The king thinks most people are bad. He's against the king but he's saying the same.

Preacher Get her out.

Two of the congregation throw HOSKINS *out.*

Hoskins In his kingdom of heaven there's going to be a few in bliss and the rest of us in hell. What's the difference from what we've got now? You are all saved. Yes, you are all saved. Not one of you is damned – –

Preacher Woman, you are certainly damned.

CLAXTON BRINGS HOSKINS HOME

WIFE *is bathing* HOSKINS'*s bruised head.*

Wife What you go there for?

Claxton When they beat her, you know . . . I couldn't . . .

Wife But who did it?

Claxton They chased her down the hill from the church and when she fell over . . . I couldn't stop them. I came up after.

Wife But what you go there for?

Claxton Just to see.

Wife It's not proper church.

Claxton Just to see.

Wife Parson won't like it.

Claxton Parson needn't.

Wife I'm not going there if they beat women.

Claxton No but they let you speak.

Wife No but they beat her.

Claxton No but men. They let men speak.

Wife Did you speak?

Claxton Don't want to work for parson.

Wife What then?

Claxton I don't know, I don't know.

WIFE *finishes bathing* HOSKINS'*s head.*

Hoskins Thank you.

Wife Better?

Hoskins Yes thank you.

Wife Where you from?

Hoskins Near Leicester.

Wife What are you doing here then?

Hoskins Travelling.

Wife Are you married? Or are you on your own?

Hoskins No, I'm never on my own.

Claxton Who are you with then?

Hoskins Different men sometimes. But it's not like you think. Well it is like you think. But then nothing's like you think. Who I'm with is Jesus Christ.

Claxton How do you live?

Hoskins Sometimes people give me money. They give me for preaching. I'm not a beggar.

Claxton Didn't say that.

Hoskins Steal though if I can. Its only the rich go to hell. Did you know that?

Claxton I think they do.

Hoskins And we don't, did you know that?

Wife You don't live anywhere?

Hoskins I'm not the only one.

Wife No one look after you?

Hoskins Jesus God.

Wife Are your parents living?

Hoskins You know how Jesus says forsake your parents. Anyone who hath forsaken houses, or brethren, or sisters, or father, or mother or wife . . . or children, or lands, for my sake. See.

Claxton No need to go that far.

Hoskins Well, it's the times. Christ will be here soon so what's it matter.

Claxton Do you believe that?

Hoskins I do.

Wife But women can't preach. We bear children in pain, that's why. And they die. For our sin, Eve's sin. That's why we have pain. We're not clean. We have to obey. The man, whatever he's like. If he beat us that's why. We have blood, we're shameful, our bodies are worse than a man's. All bodies are evil but ours is worst. That's why we can't speak.

Hoskins Well I can.

Wife You haven't had children.

Hoskins That's all wrong what you said. We're not – –

Wife Have you had a child?

Hoskins No but – –

Wife Then you don't know. We wouldn't be punished if it wasn't for something.

Hoskins We're not – –

Wife And then they die. You don't know.

Hoskins They die because how we live. My brothers did. Died of hunger more than fever. My mother kept boiling up the same bones.

Wife Go home. Go home.

Hoskins No, I'm out with God. You want to get out too.

Wife No. No we don't.

Claxton Sometimes I read in Revelation. Because people say now is the last
days. 'And I saw a new heaven and a new earth: for the first heaven and
the first earth were passed away. And there was no more sea.' Why no
more sea? I never seen the sea. But England's got a fine navy and we
trade by sea and go to new countries, so why no more sea? Now I think
this is why. I can explain this. I see into it. I have something from God.
The sea is water. And salt water, not like a stream or a well, you can't
drink it. And you can't breathe it. Because it's water. But fish can breathe
it. But men can't live in it.

Wife What are you talking about?

Claxton What it's saying, seems to me. Fish can live in it. Men can't. Now
men can't live here either. How we live is like the sea. We can't breathe.
Our squire, he's like a fish. Looks like a fish too, if you saw him. And
parson. Parson can breathe. He swims about, waggles his tail. Bitter
water and he lives in it. Bailiff. Justices. Hangman. Lawyer. Mayor. All
the gentry. Swimming about. We can't live in it. We drown. I'm a
drowned man.

Wife Stop it, you can't do it, you're making a fool – –

Hoskins No, it's good.

Claxton Octopus is a kind of fish with lots of arms grasping and full of black
stink. Sharks eat you. Whales, you're lost inside them, they're so big,
they swallow you up and never notice. They live in it.

Wife Stop it.

Claxton We can't live. We are dead. Bitter water. There shall be a new heaven.
And a new earth. And no more sea.

Wife No, don't start. Don't speak. I can't.

COBBE'S VISION

One of the Actors (*announces a pamphlet by Abiezer Coppe*) A fiery flying roll:
being a word from the Lord to all the great ones of the earth, whom this
may concern: being the last warning piece at the dreadful day of Judge-
ment. For now the Lord is come to first, warn, second, advise and warn,
third, charge, fourth, judge and sentence the great ones. As also most
compassionately informing, and most lovingly and pathetically advising
and-warning London. And all by his most excellent majesty, dwelling in
and shining through Auxilium Patris, alias Coppe. Imprinted in London,
at the beginning of that notable day, wherein the secrets of all hearts are
laid open. Sixteen hundred and forty-seven.

Cobbe All my strength, my forces, were utterly routed, my house I dwelt in
fired, my father and mother forsook me, and the wife of my bosom
loathed me, and I was utterly plagued and sunk into nothing, into the
bowels of the still Eternity (my mother's womb) out of which I came

naked, and whereto I returned again naked. And lying a while there, rapt up in silence, at length (the body's outward form being all this while awake) I heard with my outward ear (to my apprehension) a most terrible thunderclap, and after that a second. And upon the second, which was exceeding terrible, I saw a great body of light like the light of the sun, and red as fire, in the form (as it were) of a drum, whereupon with exceeding trembling and amazement on the flesh, and with joy unspeakable in the spirit, I clapped my hands, and cried out, Amen, Halelujah, Halelujah, Amen. And so lay trembling sweating and smoking (for the space of half an hour). At length with a loud voice I (inwardly) cried out, Lord what wilt thou do with me? My most excellent majesty and eternal glory in me answered and said, fear not. I will take thee up into my everlasting kingdom. But first you must drink a bitter cup, a bitter cup, a bitter cup. Whereupon I was thrown into the belly of hell (and take what you can of it in these expressions, though the matter is beyond expression) I was among all the devils in hell, even in their most hideous crew.

And under all this terror and amazement, a tiny spark of transcendent, unspeakable glory, survived, and sustained itself, triumphing, exulting and exalting itself above all the fiends. And I heard a voice saying, 'Go to London, to London, that great city, and tell them I am coming.'

TWO WOMEN LOOK IN A MIRROR

1ST WOMAN *comes in with a broken mirror.* 2ND WOMAN *is mending.*

1st Woman Look, look, you must come quick.

2nd Woman What you got there?

1st Woman Look. Who's that? That's you. That's you and me.

2nd Woman Is that me? Where you get it?

1st Woman Up the house.

2nd Woman What? with him away? It's all locked up.

1st Woman I went in the front door.

2nd Woman The front door?

1st Woman Nothing happened to me. You can take things – –

2nd Woman That's his things. That's stealing. You'll be killed for that.

1st Woman No, not any more, it's all ours now, so we won't burn the corn because that's our corn now and we're not going to let the cattle out because they're ours too.

2nd Woman You been in his rooms?

1st Woman I been upstairs. In the bedrooms.

2nd Woman I been in the kitchen.

1st Woman I lay on the bed. White linen sheets. Three wool blankets.

2nd Woman Did you take one?

1st Woman I didn't know what to take, there's so much.

2nd Woman Oh if everyone's taking something I want a blanket. But what when he comes back?

1st Woman He'll never come back. We're burning his papers, that's the Norman papers that give him his lands. That's like him burnt. There's no one over us. There's pictures of him and his grandfather and his great great – a long row of pictures and we pulled them down.

2nd Woman But he won't miss a blanket.

1st Woman There's an even bigger mirror that we didn't break. I'll show you where. You see your whole body at once. You see yourself standing in that room. They must know what they look like all the time. And now we do.

BRIGGS RECALLS A BATTLE

Briggs The noise was very loud, the shouting and the cannon behind us, and it was dark from the clouds of smoke blowing over so you couldn't see more than a few yards, so that when I hit this boy across the face with my musket I was suddenly frightened as he went under that he was on my own side; but another man was on me and I hit at him and I didn't know who I was fighting till the smoke cleared and I saw men I knew and a tree I'd stood under before the shooting began. But after I was wounded, lying with my head downhill, watching men take bodies off the field, I didn't know which was our side and which was them, but then I saw it didn't matter because what we were fighting was not each other but Antichrist and even the soldiers on the other side would be made free and be glad when they saw the paradise we'd won, so that the dead on both sides died for that, to free us of that darkness and confusion we'd lived in and bring us all into the quiet and sunlight. And even when they moved me the pain was less than the joy.

ALL *sing from 'Song of the Open Road' by Walt Whitman.*

All   All seems beautiful to me.
I can repeat over to men and women, You have done such good to me,
I would do the same to you,
I will recruit for myself and you as I go,
I will scatter myself among men and women as I go,
I will toss a new gladness and roughness among them.
Whoever denies me it shall not trouble me,
Whoever accepts me he or she shall be blessed and shall bless me.

THE PUTNEY DEBATES

Rainborough The Putney debates, October the twenty-eighth, sixteen forty-seven. I am Colonel Thomas Rainborough, a Leveller.

Sexby Edward Sexby, private soldier, elected representative or agitator from Fairfax's regiment of horse.

Rich Colonel Nathaniel Rich.

Wildman John Wildman, civilian, writer of Leveller pamphlets who has assisted the agitators in drawing up their proposals.

Cromwell Oliver Cromwell.

Ireton Commissary General Henry Ireton.

Cromwell If anyone has anything to say concerning the public business, he has liberty to speak.

Sexby Lieutenant General Cromwell, Commissary General Ireton, we have been by providence put upon strange things, such as the ancientist here doth scarce remember. And yet we have found little fruit of our endeavours. Truly our miseries and our fellow soldiers' cry out for present help. We, the agents of the common soldiers, have drawn up an Agreement of the People. We declare:

First: That the people of England being very unequally distributed for the election of their deputies in parliament ought to be proportioned according to the number of inhabitants.

Second: That this present parliament be dissolved.

Third: That the people choose a parliament once in two years.

Fourth: That the power of representatives of this nation is inferior only to theirs who choose them, and the people make the following reservations:

First: That matters of religion are not at all entrusted by us to any human power.

Second: That impressing us to serve in wars is against our freedom.

Third: That no person be at any time questioned for anything said or done in the late wars.

These things we declare to be our native rights and are resolved to maintain them with our utmost possibilities.

Cromwell These things you have offered, they are new to us. This is the first time we have had a view of them. Truly this paper does contain very great alterations of the very government of the kingdom. If we could leap out of one condition into another, I suppose there would not be much dispute. But how do we know another company of men shall not put out a paper as plausible as this? And not only another, and another, but many of this kind. And what do you think the consequence of that would be? Would it not be confusion? Would it not be utter confusion? As well as the consequences we must consider the ways and means: whether the people are prepared to go along with it and whether the great difficulties in our way are likely to be overcome. But I shall speak to nothing but that that tends to uniting us in one. And I am confident you do not bring this paper in peremptoriness of mind, but to receive amendments. First there is the question what commitments lie upon us. We have in time of danger issued several declarations; we have been required by parliament to declare particularly what we meant, and have done so in proposals drawn up by Commissary General Ireton. So before we consider this paper we must consider how far we are free.

Wildman I was yesterday at a meeting with divers country gentlemen and soldiers and the agitators of the regiments and I declared my agreement with them. They believe that if an obligation is not just, then it is an act of honesty not to keep it.

Ireton If anyone is free to break any obligation he has entered into, this is a principle that would take away all government. Men would think themselves not obliged by any law they thought not a good law. They would not think themselves obliged to stand by the authority of your paper. There are plausible things in the paper and things very good in it. If we were free from all other commitments I should concur with it further than I can.

Rainborough Every honest man is bound in duty to God to decline an obligation when he sees it to be evil: he is obliged to discharge his duty to God. There are two other objections: one is division: I think we are utterly undone if we divide. Another things is difficulties. Truly I think parliament were very indiscreet to contest with the king if they did not consider first that they should go through difficulties; and I think there was no man that entered into this war that did not engage to go through difficulties. Truly I think let the difficulties be round about you, death before you, the sea behind you, and you are convinced the thing is just, you are bound in conscience to carry it on, and I think at the last day it can never be answered to God that you did not do it.

Cromwell Truly I am very glad that this gentleman is here. We shall enjoy his company longer than I thought we should have done – –

Rainborough If I should not be kicked out.

Cromwell – And it shall not be long enough. We are almost all soldiers. All considerations of not fearing difficulties do wonderfully please us. I do not think any man here wants courage to do that which becomes an honest man and an Englishman to do. And I do not think it was offered by anyone that though a commitment were never so unrighteous it ought to be kept. But perhaps we are upon commitments here that we cannot with honesty break.

Wildman There is a principle much spreading and much to my trouble: that though a commitment appear to be unjust, yet a person must sit down and suffer under it. To me this is very dangerous, and I see it spreading in the army again. The chief thing in the agreement is to secure the rights and freedoms of the people, which was declared by the army to be absolutely insisted on.

Ireton I am far from holding that if a man have committed himself to a thing that is evil, that he is bound to perform what he hath promised. But covenants freely made must be kept. Take away that, I do not know what ground there is of anything you call any man's right. I would know what you gentlemen account the right to anything you have in England; anything of estate, land or goods, what right you have to it. If you resort only to the Law of Nature, I have as much right to take hold of anything I desire as you. Therefore when I hear men speak of laying aside all commitments I tremble at the boundless and endless consequences of it.

Wildman You take away the substance of the question. Our sense was that an unjust commitment is rather to be broken than kept.

Ireton But this leads to the end of all government: if you think something is unjust you are not to obey; and if it tend to your loss it is no doubt unjust and you are to oppose it!

Rainborough One word, here is the consideration now: do we not engage for the parliament and for the liberties of the people of England? That which is dear to me is my freedom, it is that I would enjoy and I will enjoy it if I can.

Ireton These gentlemen think their own agreement is so infallibly just and right, that anyone who doesn't agree to it is about a thing unlawful.

Rich If we do not set upon the work presently we are undone. Since the agreement is ready to our hands, I desire that you would read it and debate it.

Ireton I think because it is so much insisted on we should read the paper.

Wildman Twenty-ninth of October.

Ireton Let us hear the first article again.

Sexby That the people of England being very unequally distributed for the election of their deputies − −

Ireton 'The people of England.' This makes me think that the meaning is that every man that is an inhabitant is to have an equal vote in the election. But if it only means the people that had the election before, I have nothing to say against it. Do those that brought it know whether they mean all that had a former right, or those that had no right before are to come in?

Rainborough All inhabitants that have not lost their birthright should have an equal vote in elections. For really I think that the poorest he in England hath a life to live as the greatest he; therefore truly sir, I think it's clear, that every man that is to live under a government ought first by his own consent to put himself under it.

Ireton I think no person hath a right to an interest in the disposing of the affairs of this kingdom that hath not a permanent fixed interest in this kingdom. We talk of birthright. Men may justly have by their birthright, by their being born in England, that we should not seclude them out of England, that we should not refuse to give them air and place and ground and the freedom of the highways. That I think is due to a man by birth. But that by a man's being born here he shall have a share in that power that shall dispose of the lands here, I do not think it sufficient ground.

Rainborough Truly sir, I am of the same opinion I was. I do not find anything in the law of God that a lord shall choose twenty members, and a gentleman but two, or a poor man shall choose none. I find no such thing in the law of nature or the law of nations. But I do find that all Englishmen must be subject to English law, and the foundation of the law lies in the people. Every man in England ought not to be exempted from the choice of those who are to make laws for him to live under, and for him, for aught I know, to lose his life by.

Ireton All the main thing that I speak for is because I would have an eye to property. Let every man consider that he do not go that way to take away all property. Now I wish we may consider of what right you will claim that all the people should have a right to elections. Is it by right of nature? Then I think you must deny all property too. If you say one man hath an equal right with another to the choosing of him that will govern him, by the same right of nature he hath the same right in any goods he sees – he hath a freedom to the land, to take the ground, to till it. I would fain have any man show me their bounds, where you will end.

Rainborough Sir, to say that because a man pleads that every man hath a voice, that it destroys all property – this is to forget the law of God. That there's property, the law of God says it, else why hath God made that law, Thou shalt not steal? I am a poor man, therefore I must be oppressed: if I have no interest in the kingdom, I must suffer all their laws be they right or wrong. Nay thus: a gentleman lives in a country and hath three or four lordships, as some men have (God knows how they got them); and when a parliament is called he must be a parliament man; and it may be he sees some poor men, they live near this man, he can crush them – I have known an invasion to turn poor men out of doors; and I would know whether rich men do not do this, and keep them under the greatest tyranny that was ever thought of in the world. And I wish you would not make the world believe we are for anarchy.

Cromwell Really, sir, this is not right. No man says you have a mind to anarchy, but that the consequence of this rule tends to anarchy. I am confident on 't, we should not be so hot with one another.

Rainborough I know that some particular men we debate with believe we are for anarchy.

Ireton I must clear myself as to that point. I cannot allow myself to lay the least scandal upon anyone. And I don't know why the gentleman should take so much offence. We speak to the paper not to persons. Now the main answer against my objection was that there was a divine law, Thou shalt not steal. But we cannot prove property in a thing by divine law any more than prove we have an interest in choosing members for parliament by divine law. Our right of sending members to parliament descends from other things and so does our right to property.

Rainborough I would fain know what we have fought for. For our laws and liberties? And this is the old law of England – and that which enslaves the people of England – that they should be bound by laws in which they have no voice! And for my part, I look upon the people of England so, that wherein they have not voices in the choosing of their governors they are not bound to obey them.

Ireton I did not say we should not have any enlargement at all of those who are to be the electors. But if you admit any man that hath breath and being, it may come to destroy property thus: you may have such men chosen as have no local or permanent interest. Why may not those men vote against all property? Show me what you will stop at.

Rich There is weight in the objection, for you have five to one in this kingdom that have no permanent interest. Some men have ten, some twenty servants. If the master and servant be equal electors, the majority may by law destroy property. But certainly there may be some other way thought of, that there may be a representative of the poor as well as the rich.

Rainborough I think it is a fine gilded pill.

Wildman Our case is that we have been under slavery. That's acknowledged by all. Our very laws were made by our conquerors. We are now engaged for our freedom. The question is: Whether any person can justly be bound by law, who doth not give his consent?

Ireton Yes, and I will make it clear. If a foreigner will have liberty to dwell here, he may very well be content to submit to the law of the land. If any man will receive protection from this people, he ought to be subject to those laws. If this man do think himself unsatisfied to be subject to this law, he may go into another kingdom.

Wildman The gentleman here said five parts of the nation are now excluded and would then have a voice in elections. At present one part makes hewers of wood and drawers of water of the other five, so the greater part of the nation is enslaved. I do not hear any justification given but that it is the present law of the kingdom.

Rainborough What shall become of those men that have laid themselves out for the parliament in this present war, that have ruined themselves by fighting? They are Englishmen. They have now no voice in elections.

Rich All I urged was that I think it worthy consideration whether they should have an equal voice. However, I think we have been a great while upon this point. If we stay but three days until you satisfy one another the king will come and decide who will be hanged first.

Sexby October the thirtieth.

Rainborough If we can agree where the liberty of the people lies, that will do all.

Ireton I cannot consent so far. When I see the hand of God destroying king, and lords, and commons too, when I see God hath done it, I shall, I hope, comfortably acquiesce in it. But before that, I cannot give my consent to it because it is not good. The law of God doth not give me property, nor the law of nature, but property is of human constitution. I have a property and this I shall enjoy.

Sexby I see that though liberty was our end, there is a degeneration from it. We have ventured our lives and it was all for this: to recover our birthrights as Englishmen; and by the arguments urged there is none. There are many thousands of us soldiers that have ventured our lives; we have had little property in the kingdom, yet we have had a birthright. But it seems now, except a man hath a fixed estate in the kingdom, he hath no right in this kingdom. I wonder we were so much deceived. If we had not a right to the kingdom, we were mere mercenary soldiers. I shall tell you in a word my resolution. I am resolved to give my birthright to none. If this thing be denied the poor, that with so much pressing after they have sought, it will be the greatest scandal. It was said that if those in low condition were given their birthright it would be the destruction of this kingdom. I think the poor and meaner of this kingdom have been the means of preservation of this kingdom. Their lives have not been held dear for purchasing the good of the kingdom. And now they demand the birthright for which they fought. They are as free from anarchy and confusion as any, and they have the law of God and the law of their conscience with them. When men come to understand these things, they will not lose that which they have contended for.

Ireton I am very sorry we are come to this point, that from reasoning one to another we should come to express our resolutions. Now let us consider where our difference lies. We all agree you should be governed by elected representatives. But I think we ought to keep to that constitution which we have now, because there is so much justice and reason and prudence in it. And if you merely on pretence of your birthright pretend that this constitution shall not stand in your way, it is the same principle to me, say I, as if for your better satisfaction you shall take hold of anything that another man calls his own.

Rainborough Sir, I see it is impossible to have liberty without all property being taken away. If you will say it, it must be so. But I would fain know what the soldier hath fought for all this while.

Ireton I will tell you – –

Rainborough He hath fought to enslave himself, to give power to men of riches, men of estates, to make himself a perpetual slave. We find none must be pressed for the army that have property. When these gentlemen fall out among themselves, they shall press the poor scrubs to come and kill one another for them.

Ireton I will tell you what the soldier of this kingdom hath fought for. The danger that we stood in was that one man's will must be a law. The people have this right, that they should not be governed but by the representative of those that have the interest of the kingdom. In this way liberty may be had and property not be destroyed.

Rich I hope it is not denied that any wise discreet man that hath preserved

England is worthy of a voice in the government of it. The electorate should be amended in that sense and I think they will desire no more liberty.

Cromwell I confess I was most dissatisfied with that I heard Mr Sexby speak of any man here, because it did savour so much of will. But let us not spend so much time in debates. Everyone here would be willing that the representation be made better than it is. If we may but resolve on a committee, things may be done.

Wildman I wonder that should be thought wilfulness in one man that is reason in another. I have not heard anything that doth satisfy me. I am not at all against a committee's meeting. But I think it is no fault in any man to refuse to sell his birthright.

Sexby I am sorry that my zeal to what I apprehend is good should be so ill resented. Do you not think it were a sad and miserable condition that we have fought all this time for nothing? All here, both great and small, do think that we fought for something. Many of us fought for those ends which, we since saw, were not those which caused us to venture all in the ship with you. It had been good in you to have advertised us of it, and I believe you would have had fewer under your command to have commanded. Concerning my making rents and divisions in this way. As an individual I could lie down and be trodden there; but truly I am sent by a regiment, and if I should not speak, guilt shall lie upon me. I shall be loath to make a rent and division, but unless I see this put to a vote, I despair of an issue.

Rich I see you have a long dispute. I see both parties at a stand; and if we dispute here, both are lost.

Cromwell If you put this paper to the vote without any qualifications it will not pass freely. If we would have no difference when we vote on the paper, it must be put with due qualifications. I have not heard Commissary General Ireton answered, not in a tittle. To bring this paper nearer a general satisfaction and bring us all to an understanding, I move for a committee.

INTERVAL

ACT II

DIGGERS

One of the Actors (*announces*) Information of Henry Sanders, Walton-upon-Thames, April the sixteenth, sixteen hundred and forty-nine.

One Everard, Gerrard Winstanley, and three more, all living at Cobham, came to St George's Hill in Surrey and began to dig, and sowed the ground with parsnips and carrots and beans. By Friday last they were increased in number to twenty or thirty. They invite all to come in and help them, and promise them meat, drink and clothes.

Winstanley (*announces*) The true Levellers' standard advanced, sixteen hundred and forty-nine:

A declaration to the powers of England and to all the powers of the world, showing the cause why the common people of England have begun to dig up, manure and sow corn upon George Hill in Surrey. Take notice that England is not a free people till the poor that have no land have a free allowance to dig and labour the commons. It is the sword that brought in property and holds it up, and everyone upon recovery of the conquest ought to return into freedom again, or what benefit have the common people got by the victory over the king?

All men have stood for freedom; and now the common enemy has gone you are all like men in a mist, seeking for freedom, and know not where it is: and those of the richer sort of you that see it are afraid to own it. For freedom is the man that will turn the world upside down, therefore no wonder he hath enemies.

True freedom lies where a man receives his nourishment and that is in the use of the earth. A man had better have no body than have no food for it. True freedom lies in the true enjoyment of the earth. True religion and undefiled is to let every one quietly have earth to manure. There can be no universal liberty till this universal community be established.

1st Actor (*announces*) A Bill of Account of the most remarkable sufferings that the Diggers have met with since they began to dig the commons for the poor on George Hill in Surrey.

2nd Actor We were fetched by above a hundred people who took away our spades, and some of them we never had again, and taken to prison at Walton.

3rd Actor The dragonly enemy pulled down a house we had built and cut our spades to pieces.

4th Actor One of us had his head sore wounded, and a boy beaten. Some of us were beaten by the gentlemen, the sheriff looking on, and afterwards five were taken to White Lion prison and kept there about five weeks.

5th Actor We had all our corn spoilt, for the enemy was so mad that they tumbled the earth up and down and would suffer no corn to grow.

6th Actor Next day two soldiers and two or three men sent by the parson pulled down another house and turned an old man and his wife out of doors to lie in the field on a cold night.

1st Actor It is understood the General gave his consent that the soldiers should come to help beat off the Diggers, and it is true the soldiers came with the gentlemen and caused others to pull down our houses; but I think the soldiers were sorry to see what was done.

CLAXTON EXPLAINS

Claxton Wherever I go I leave men behind surprised I no longer agree with them. But I can't stop. Ever since the day I walked over the hill to Wendover to hear the new preacher for the first time. And though I'd thought of going for weeks, the day I went I didn't think at all, I just put on my coat and started walking. I felt quite calm, as if nothing was happening, as if it was an easy thing to do, not something I'd laid awake over all night, so that I wondered if it even mattered to me. But as I walked I found my heart was pounding and my breath got short going up the hill. My body knew I was doing something amazing. I knew I was in the midst of something, I was doing it, not standing still worrying about it, I was simply walking over the hill to another preacher. I'd found everything in my life hard. But now it seemed everything must be this simple. I felt alone. I felt certain. I felt myself moving faster and faster, more and more certainly towards God. And I am alone, because my wife can't follow me. I send her money when I can. But my body is given to other women now for I have come to see that there is no sin but what man thinks is sin. So we can't be free from sin till we can commit it purely, as if it were no sin. Sometimes I lie or steal to show myself there is no lie or theft but in the mind, and I find it all so easy that I am called the Captain of the Rant, and still my heart pounds and my mouth is dry and I rush on towards the infinite nothing that is God.

BRIGGS WRITES A LETTER

Star Writing more letters? Our children grow up without us. Is there still no news of your wife? Do you think of leaving the army to look for her? Because if you don't go to Ireland, there's not much to do in the army now.

Briggs Enough.

Star You make a mistake about Ireland. I understood two years ago, when the men didn't have their back pay, I was with you then. But now it's different. You were agitator of the regiment then and you still – –

Briggs I still am agitator of the regiment.

Star – Still think you're agitator of the regiment. I know that was a remark-able time for you. To be chosen out of so many. To stand up before the greatest in the country and be heard out. It's a council of officers now, you know that. You know an agitator means nothing. But you won't let it go. You keep on and on. The other men don't admire you for it.

Briggs We're demanding the council be set up like before. You know that. With two agitators from each regiment.

Star I know you won't get it. Everyone knows. The other men laugh. You'd far better go home. Or if you still want to serve the cause of the saints, sign for Ireland. Cromwell himself is going, that says something. It's the same war we fought here. We'll be united again. We'll crush the papists just as we did in England. Antichrist will be exterminated.

Briggs But don't you see, the Irish – –

Star What, Briggs?

Briggs The Irish are fighting the same – –

Star The Irish are traitors. What?

Briggs Nothing.

Star Show me the letter.

Briggs What?

Star Show me the letter.

Briggs Can't we even write a letter now without an officer looking it over?

Star It's not to your family.

Briggs No. What then?

Star It's a plot.

Briggs It's a list of proposals.

Star It's mutiny.

Briggs It's a list of proposals. I've made them often enough.

Star You have, yes, and nobody reads them now. You draw up a third agree-ment of the people, and a fourth, and a tenth. It's a waste of time.

Briggs I waste a few hours then. A few days. If I don't get what I fought for, the whole seven years has been wasted. What's a few weeks.

Star Show me the letter.

Briggs No.

Star It wasn't an order. You have not refused to obey my order. But I won't be able to save you from mutiny if that's what you're set on.

Briggs So we can't write now. We can't speak.

Star There's officers above me. Some of them think free talk doesn't go with discipline. I've always liked talk. I'd be sad to see us lose that privilege.

Briggs It's not a privilege. It's a right.

Star If it's a right, Briggs, why was Arnold shot at Ware? Why were five troopers cashiered for petitioning the council of officers?

Briggs Shall I tell you why?

Star It's not because I knew you before. The whole company is my friends. My rank leaves us equal before God. And yet my orders have been obeyed, because they have been seen for what they are, good orders. But lately I am talked of by my superiors – –

Briggs Shall I tell you why the Levellers have been shot? Because now the officers have all the power, the army is as great a tyrant as the king was.

Star I can choose to act as if no one is below me. I hope I do. But I can't pretend no one is above me. I have superior officers and I must obey. I don't think you want me removed.

Briggs You should join us against them.

Star If everyone says and does what he likes, what army is it? What discipline is there? In army or government. There must be some obedience. With consent, I would say, yes, but then you must consent, or – what? If every man is his own commander? There was a time when we all wanted the same. The army was united. I gave orders from God and you all heard the same orders from God in you. We fought as one man. But now we begin to be thousands of separate men.

Briggs God is not with this army.

Star It is the army of saints.

Briggs And God's saints shot Robert Lockyer for mutiny. By martial law. In time of peace. For demanding what God demanded we fight for.

Star If the army splits up – –

Briggs It has done.

Star If you Levellers split off into conspiracies away from the main army – –

Briggs It's you who've split off.

Star You risk the King's party getting back again.

Briggs Would that be worse?

Star Briggs. We can still be a united army. Remember how we marched on London, singing the fall of Babylon?

Briggs It's you who mutiny. Against God. Against the people.

Star Briggs.

Briggs It's Cromwell mutinies.

Star Briggs.

Briggs If I was Irish I'd be your enemy. And I am.

Star Briggs.

Briggs Sir.

THE WAR IN IRELAND

One of the Actors (*announces*) Soldier's standard to repair to, addressed to the army, April sixteen hundred and forty-nine.

Whatever they may tell you or however they may flatter you, there's danger lies at the bottom of this business for Ireland. Consider to what end you should hazard your lives against the Irish: have you not been fighting in England these seven years for rights and liberties you are yet deluded of? and will you go on to kill, slay and murder men, to make your officers as absolute lords and masters over Ireland as you have made them over England? If you intend not this, it concerns you in the first place to see that evil reformed here. Sending forces into Ireland is for nothing else but to make way by the blood of the army to extending their territories of power and tyranny. For the cause of the Irish natives in seeking their just freedoms, immunities and liberties is exactly the same with our cause here.

THE VICAR WELCOMES THE NEW LANDLORD

Vicar Mr Star. I wonder if I am the first to welcome you as the new squire.

Star And the last I hope. I'm no squire.

Vicar You've bought the land, that's all I meant.

Star I have bought the land, yes. Parliament is selling the confiscated land to parliament men. That does not make me the squire. Just as the country is better run by parliament than by the King, so estates will be better managed by parliament men than by royalists. You don't agree.

Vicar It's not for a parson to say about running an estate.

Star No, but you bury the tenants when they starve. You'll have fewer to bury. This country can grow enough to feed every single person. Instead of importing corn we could grow enough to export it if all the land was efficiently made profitable. The price of corn will come down in a few years. Agricultural writers recommend growing clover on barren land. I will have the common ploughed and planted with clover.

Vicar An excellent idea.

Star Nettles and thistles cleared, and a great crop.

Vicar And the little huts cleared, the squatters' huts.

Star Squatters?

Vicar On the common. These last two years. Everyone hopes that now the estate is properly managed again they will be moved on. They are not local people.

Star I haven't been down to the common. Well I'll speak to them. All over England waste land is being reclaimed. Even the fens. Many years ago before the war, Oliver Cromwell himself led tenants in protest against enclosing the fens. But now he sees, now we all see, that it is more important to provide corn for the nation than for a few tenants to fish and trap water-birds.

Vicar Yes indeed. Yes indeed.

Star When I say enclose the commons, I don't mean in the old sense, as the old squire did. I mean to grow corn. To make efficient use of the land. To bring down the price of corn. I'm sure the tenants will understand when I explain it to them.

Vicar They will do as they're told. I'm sure you'll have no trouble collecting the arrears of rent.

Star I know one of the reasons they haven't paid is because they've had soldiers billetted in every cottage. So of course I'll give them time to pay.

There is some talk of landlords reducing rents by as much as the tenants have paid out on the soldiers.

Vicar I have heard talk of that.

Star I hope very much they're not counting on it. It would make me responsible for the keep for six years of twenty men and would beggar the estate.

Vicar I told them that. I told them the new squire wouldn't hear of it.

Star In their own interests. I couldn't afford seed corn. I need two new ploughs.

Vicar I'm sure they know their own interest. They'll pay.

Star I don' want to evict anyone.

Vicar No, indeed, give them time. Three months would be ample.

Star I thought six.

Vicar That's very generous. The tenants will certainly bless you.

Star I thought I would send for them all to drink my health and I'll drink theirs.

Vicar That is the custom with a new squire. It is what they expect.

Star Is it? It's what I thought I would do.

Vicar Well, I can only say I welcome all the changes you are making. And I hope you won't make a change so unwelcome to the whole parish as to turn me away after so many years. I know the tenants here are as good and peace-loving as any in England, and I know they'll join me in supporting you in your plans to make this estate prosperous. It's been an unhappy time but the war is over. We are all glad to be at peace and back to normal.

Star It will be hard work. For the tenants and for me. I don't shrink from that. It is to God's glory that this land will make a profit.

Vicar I'm sure it will.

Star Don't misunderstand me, Parson. Times have changed.

Vicar I'm not against change, Mr Star. So long as there's no harm done.

A WOMAN LEAVES HER BABY

Two women. 1ST WOMAN *is carrying a baby.*

1st Woman You'll laugh.

2nd Woman No?

1st Woman Now I'm here I can't do it.

2nd Woman Waiting for that.

1st Woman Don't. Don't go. Don't be angry.

2nd Woman We come all this way.

1st Woman We go back.

2nd Woman Why we bother?

1st Woman We go back, quick, never mind.

2nd Woman We come so they look after her.

1st Woman I can't.
2nd Woman I know but just put her down.
1st Woman Too soon.
2nd Woman Put her down. Just . . .

Silence.

2nd Woman She die if you keep her.
1st Woman I can't.

Silence.

2nd Woman What you do then? You got no milk. She not even crying now, see. That's not good. You en had one, I'm telling you, she dying.

Silence.

1st Woman If I drunk more water. Make more milk.
2nd Woman Not without food. Not how ill you are.

Silence.

1st Women What if nobody . . . ?
2nd Woman They will. It's a special house. It's a good town. The mayor himself. Picture inside on the wall with his chain. Mayor himself see her all right.
1st Woman Another day.
2nd Woman She'll be dead.
1st Woman If she was bigger.
2nd Woman You're not doing it for you. Do it for her. Wouldn't you die to have her live happy? Won't even put her down. It's for her.
1st Woman Could die. Can't put her down.
2nd Woman Don't talk. Do it. Do it.
1st Woman If she was still inside me.

A BUTCHER TALKS TO HIS CUSTOMERS

Butcher Two rabbits, madam, is two shillings, thank you. And sir? A capon? Was yesterday's veal good? Was it? Good. Tender was it? Juicy? Plenty of it? Fill your belly did it? Fill your belly? It can't have done, can it, or you wouldn't want a capon today. Nice capon here, make a fine dinner for half a dozen people. Giving your friends dinner tonight, sir? And another night they give you dinner. You're very generous and christian to each other. There's never a night you don't have dinner. Or do you eat it all yourself, sir? No? You look as if you do. You don't look hungry. You don't look as if you need a dinner. You look less like a man needing a dinner than anyone I've ever seen. What do you need it for? No, tell me. To stuff yourself, that's what for. To make fat. And shit. When it could put a little good flesh on children's bones. It could be the food of life. If it goes into you, it's stink and death. So you can't have it. No, I said you can't have it, take your money back. You're not having meat again this week. You had your meat yesterday. Bacon on Monday. Beef on Sunday. Mutton chops on Saturday. There's no more meat for you. Porridge. Bread. Turnips. No meat for you this week. Not this year. You've had your lifetime's meat. All of you. All of you that can buy meat. You've had your meat. You've had their meat. You've had their meat that can't buy any meat. You've stolen their meat. Are you going to give it back? Are you going to put your hand in your pocket and give them back the price of their meat? I said give them back their meat. You cram yourselves with their children's meat. You cram yourselves with their dead children.

LOCKYER'S FUNERAL

One of the Actors From *The Moderate*, a Leveller newspaper, April the twenty-ninth, sixteen forty-nine.

Mr Robert Lockyer, a Leveller leader, that was shot Friday last was this day brought through the heart of the city. The manner of his funeral was most remarkable, considering the person to be in no higher quality than a private trooper. The body was accompanied with many thousand citizens, who seemed much dejected. The trooper's horse was clothed all over with mourning and led by a footman (a funeral honour equal to a chief commander). The corpse was adorned with bundles of rosemary stained in blood, and the sword of the deceased with them. Most of this great number that attended the corpse had sea-green and black ribbons in their hats. By the time the corpse came to the new churchyard, some thousands of the higher sort, that said they would not endanger themselves to be publicly seen marching through the city, were there ready to attend it with the same colours of sea-green and black. Some people derided them with the name of Levellers. Others said that King Charles had not had half so many mourners to attend his corpse when interred, as this trooper. A few weeks later at Burford, the Levellers were finally crushed.

THE MEETING

A drinking place. The DRUNK *sits apart from the rest.*

Hoskins (*to* BRIGGS) Come on, plenty to drink. Can't you smile? He wasn't like this last night.
Brotherton What do I do?
Cobbe Anything you like. I worship you, more than the Virgin Mary.
Hoskins She was no virgin.
Claxton Christ was a bastard.
Hoskins Still is a bastard.

Brotherton I thought you said this was a prayer meeting.

Claxton This is it. This is my one flesh.

Cobbe (*to the* DRUNK) Drinking by yourself? Move in with us, come on. Yes, we need you. Get over there when I tell you or I'll break your arm. That was God telling you.

Claxton God's a great bully, I've noticed that. Do this. Do that. Shalt not. Drop you in the burning lake.

Hoskins Give us a sip. He won't give us a sip.

Claxton He's not very godly. He needs praying.

Hoskins Let us pray. Or whatever.

Silence.

Brotherton When's he coming?

Cobbe Who?

Brotherton The preacher

Cobbe You're the preacher.

Brotherton What? No. I can't.

Hoskins Don't frighten her.

Claxton Anyone has anything to say from God, just say it.

Silence.

Hoskins There was a preacher. But his head fell off.

Silence.

Claxton It's a fine shining day. Whatever troubles we have, the sky's not touched. A clear day. Let us not lose it. Let us remember the Levellers shot. Those at Burford. Will Thompson and his brother. Private Arnold shot at Ware.

Hoskins And the four prisoners in the tower just for writing . . .

Briggs Avenge Robert Lockyer.

Cobbe Lockyer's blood. Robert Lockyer's blood. Lockyer's wounds.

Brotherton I don't know these gentlemen. If they have money. Well if you haven't and you're in the common gaol, you're lucky if you don't die. But if they have money for the jailor he gives you a room. With a bed and a window. I was told by a man who'd spent all his money. If you've got money . . .

Cobbe Damn. Damn. Damn. Damn. Damn.

There's angels swear, angels with flowing hair, you'd think they were men, I've seen them. They say damn the churches, the bloody black clergy with their fat guts, damn their white hands. Damn the hellfire presbyterian hypocrites that call a thief a sinner, rot them in hell's jail. They say Christ's wounds, wounds, wounds, wounds. Stick your fingers in. Christ's arsehole. He had an arsehole. Christ shits on you rich. Christ shits. Shitting pissing spewing puking fucking Jesus Christ. Jesus fucking – –

Brotherton Is that from God?

Cobbe What did you say?

Brotherton Is that from God?

Cobbe It is, yes. What does he say to you? Does he speak to you? What do you answer? He'll come and speak to you soon enough. The day he comes he'll speak to all of us. He'll come right up to you like this. He wants an answer. What do you say? Nothing? He'll damn and ram you down in the black pit. Is there nothing in you? What are you? Nothing? (*To* BRIGGS) Is it nothing but a lifetime of false words, little games, devil's tricks, ways to get by in the world and keep safe? You're plastered over, thick shit mucky lies all over, and what's underneath? Where's your true word? Is there anyone left inside or are you shrivelled away to nothing? (*To each*) What will you say? Speak up. What do you answer God? What do you answer? Answer. What do you answer?

Hoskins I love you.

Cobbe There. There.

He sits down. BROTHERTON *laughs. Silence.*

Claxton I tell you justice. If every judge was hanged.

Hoskins I steal all I can. Rich steal from us. Everything they got's stolen. What's it mean 'Thou shalt not steal'? Not steal stolen goods?

Cobbe Riches is the cause of all wickedness. From the blood of Abel to those last Levellers shot. But God is coming, the mighty Leveller, Christ the chief of Levellers is at the door, and then we'll see levelling. Not sword levelling. Not man levelling. And they feared that. Now God is coming to level the hills and the valleys. Christ break the mountains.

Silence. HOSKINS *holds out an apple.*

Hoskins This is something stolen by a farmer. Then by a stallholder. Then by me. It come to me God's in it. If a man could be so perfect. Look at it.

She gives it to BRIGGS, *who looks at it, then passes it back to her. She gives it to* BROTHERTON.

Brotherton I always like an apple if I can get it. I haven't been to church for a long time. I don't know if this is a church. It's a drinking place. I always hide on Sunday. They notice you in the street if everyone's in church so I go in the woods on Sunday. I can't see God in this. If God was in it, he'd have us whipped.

Claxton It wouldn't have you whipped, it would bless you. It does bless you. Touch it again. It blesses you. And my hand. Touch my hand. What's the matter?

Brotherton Nobody touches me.

Claxton Why not?

Brotherton They don't touch, I don't know why, nobody touches. I don't count hitting. Nobody's touched me since . . .

Claxton Since what?

Brotherton You don't want to touch me. Don't bother. Pass it on. Pass it on.

Hoskins Nobody's touched you since what?

Brotherton It's not right.

Claxton What's not right? Touching or not touching?

Brotherton Both are not right. Pass it on.

Claxton They are, they're both, whichever you want, when you want, is right. Do you want me to touch your hand?

Brotherton No.

Claxton That's right. God's in that too. God's in us. This form that I am is the representative of the whole creation. You are the representative of the whole creation. God's in this apple. He's nowhere else but in the creation. This is where he is.

He gives it to COBBE.

Cobbe I charge at coaches in the street. I shout at the great ones with my hat on. I proclaim the day of the Lord throughout Southwark. And what do they hear? If they could see God in this apple as I do now, God in the bread that they will not give to the poor who cry out day and night, Bread, bread, bread for the Lord's sake, if they could see it they would rush to the prisons, and they would bow to the poor wretches that are their own flesh, and say, 'Your humble servants, we set you free.'

COBBE *gives it to the* DRUNK, *who eats it.*

Hoskins There's a man eats God. There's a communion.

Brotherton You don't often see someone eat. They eat when you're not looking.

Briggs Friends. I have nothing from God. I'm sitting here. Nothing. If anyone can speak to my condition.

Claxton You're a soldier?

Briggs I was.

Cobbe A Leveller?

Briggs I was.

Claxton And now?

Hoskins Well, a drink would be best.

Claxton You'll find something. I've been different things. When I was first a Seeker, everything shone. I thought the third age was coming, age of the spirit, age of the lily, everything shining, raindrops on the hedges shining in the sun, worlds of light. Well, we know how parliament betrayed us. Then how the army betrayed us. It was all a cheat.

Hoskins Preaching itself is a cheat.

Claxton And then I saw even the Seekers were wrong. Because while I was waiting for God, he was here already. So God was first in the king. Then in parliament. Then in the army. And now he has left all government. And shows himself naked. In us.

Briggs We were the army of saints.

Claxton Let it go. Move on. God moves so fast now.

Hoskins I try to be sad with you but I can't. King Jesus is coming in clouds of glory in a garment dyed red with blood, and the saints in white linen riding on white horses. It's for next year. Now is just a strange time between Antichrist going and Christ coming, so what do you expect in a time like this? There's been nothing like it before and there never will be again. So what's it matter now if we've no work and no food or can't get parliament like we want? It's only till next year. Then Christ will be here in his body like a man and he'll be like a king only you can talk to him. And he's a spirit too and that's in us and it's getting stronger and stronger. And that's why you see men and women shining now, everything sparkles because God's not far above us like he used to be when preachers stood in the way, he's started some great happening and we're in it now.

Claxton St Paul to Timothy, 'Let the woman learn in silence.'

Hoskins Jone Hoskins to St Paul, fuck off you silly old bugger.

They laugh and start getting food out.

CLAXTON *holds out food.*

Claxton Christ's body.

Brotherton I'm afraid I haven't anything.

Claxton There's plenty.

HOSKINS *holds out wine.*

Hoskins This is Christ's blood.

Claxton (*to* BROTHERTON) When did you last eat? Eat slowly now.

Briggs Christ will not come. I don't believe it. Everything I've learnt these seven years. He will not come in some bloody red robe and you all put on white frocks, that will not happen. All I've learnt, how to get things done, that wasn't for nothing. I don't believe this is the last days. England will still be here in hundreds of years. And people working so hard they can't grasp how it happens and can't take hold of their own lives, like us till we had this chance, and we're losing it now, as we sit here, every minute. Jesus Christ isn't going to change it.

Claxton He may not be coming in red.

Briggs He's not coming at all.

Claxton But in us – –

Briggs No, not at all.

Hoskins He's coming in clouds of glory and the saints – –

Briggs No, no, no.

Cobbe Do you think God would do all this for nothing? Think of the dead. For nothing? Why did he call me to warn London? What sort of God would he be if he didn't come now?

Briggs No God at all.

Claxton But in us. In us. I know there's no heaven or hell, not places to go, but in us. I know the Bible was written by man and most of it to trick us. I know there's no God or devil outside what's in creation. But in us. I know we can be perfect.

Briggs Then we must do it.

COBBE *takes off his coat and throws it at* BRIGGS's *feet.*

Cobbe My coat's yours. And I hope yours is mine. We'll all live together, one family, one marriage, one flesh in God. That's what we do.

Hoskins Yes, everything in common.

Cobbe All things common. Or the plague of God will consume whatever you have.

Claxton All goods in common, yes, and our bodies in common – –

Briggs No.

Hoskins Yes, we'll have no property in the flesh. My wife, that's property. My husband, that's property. All men are one flesh and I can lie with any man as my husband and that's no sin because all men are one man, all my husband's one flesh.

Cobbe I, the Lord, say once more, deliver deliver my money which you have to cripples, thieves, whores, or I will torment you day and night, saith the Lord.

Claxton We'll take the land, all the land, and Christ will come, wait, I have something from God, Christ will come in this sense. He will come in everyone becoming perfect so the landlords all repent stealing the land. Sin is only the dark side of God. So when his light blazes everywhere, their greed will vanish – and that's how evil will go into the pit. Nobody damned, nobody lost, nobody cast out. But Antichrist cast out of us so that we become perfect Christ.

Hoskins Perfect men, perfect Christ in the street, I've seen them.

Claxton The rich will be broken out of the hell they are, however they howl to stay there, and when they're out in the light they'll be glad. They'll join us pulling down the hedges.

Briggs The landlords where they were digging at Cobham called the army in. And the soldiers stood by while the diggers' houses were pulled down, their tools destroyed, the corn trampled so it won't grow, men beaten and dragged off to prison. The landlords gave the soldiers ten shillings for drink. Does that sound like the landlords joining us? Does that sound like heaven on earth? I've a friend wounded in Ireland and nearly mad. When they burned the church at Drogheda he heard a man inside crying out, 'God damn me, I burn, I burn.' Is that heaven on earth? Or is it hell?

Brotherton It's hell, life is hell, my life is hell. I can't get out but I'll pull them all in with me.

Hoskins No, wait, just wait, you'll see when Christ comes – –

Briggs He's never coming, damn him.

Cobbe How we know for certain that God is coming is because of the strange work he has set us on. Who can live through one day the way he used to? I've seen poor men all my life. Last week I met a poor man, the ugliest man I've ever seen, he had two little holes where his nose should be. I said to him, 'Are you poor?' And he said, 'Yes sir, very poor.' I began to shake and I said to him again, 'Are you poor?' 'Yes, very poor.' And a voice spoke inside me and said, 'It's a poor wretch, give him twopence.' But that was the voice of the whore of Babylon and I would not listen. And again, 'It's a poor wretch, give him sixpence, and that's enough for a knight to give one poor man and you a preacher without tithes and never know when you'll get a penny; think of your children; true love begins at home.' So I put my hand in my pocket and took out a shilling, and said, 'Give me sixpence and here's a shilling for you.' He said, 'I can't, I haven't a penny.' And I said, 'I'm sorry to hear that. I would have given you something if you could have changed my money.' And he said, 'God bless you.' So I was riding on when the voice spoke in me again, so that I rode back and told him I would leave sixpence for him in the next town at a house I thought he might know. But then, suddenly, the plague of God fell into my pocket and the rust of my silver rose against me, and I was cast into the lake of fire and brimstone. And all the money I had, every penny, I took out of my pocket and thrust into his hands. I hadn't eaten all day, I had nine more miles to ride, it was raining, the horse was lame, I was sure to need money before the night. And I rode away full of trembling joy, feeling the sparkles of a great glory round me. And then God made me turn my horse's head and I saw the poor wretch staring after me, and I was made to take off my hat and bow to him seven times. And I rode back to him again and said, 'Because I am a king I have done this, but you need not tell anyone.'

Hoskins ⎫
Claxton ⎬ Amen.

Briggs That man will die without his birthright. I've done all I can and it's not enough.

Claxton It's not over, there's more, God hasn't finished.

Briggs I'll tell you who's with God.

He nods at the DRUNK. HOSKINS *laughs, kisses him, gives him drink.*

Brotherton No I can't. I'm not one of you, I try, you're very kind, I'm not one of you, I'm not one flesh. I'm damned, I know it.

Cobbe You're in hell now but you can come out. Suddenly, suddenly you are out.

Brotherton I mustn't come in a place where God is. It's your fault bringing me here, I'm no good here, I can't be here − −

Cobbe We don't want any filthy plague holiness. We want base things. And the baseness confounds the false holiness into nothing. And then, only then, you're like a new-born child in the hands of eternity, picked up, put down, not knowing if you're clean or dirty, good or evil.

Brotherton No, I'm wicked, all women are wicked, and I'm – –

Hoskins It's a man wrote the Bible.

Claxton All damnation is, listen, all it is. Sin is not cast out but cast in, cast deep into God.

Brotherton No I don't want to.

Claxton As cloth is dyed in a vat to a new colour, the sin is changed in God s light into light itself.

Brotherton No.

Claxton That's all damnation is.

Brotherton Let me go.

Claxton It's only God.

Brotherton I must be punished.

Hoskins What have you done?

Brotherton Let me go.

Cobbe No, what did you do? God is in me, asking you, God is asking, I am perfect Christ asking why you damn yourself, why you hold yourself back from me?

Brotherton Don't touch me. I'm evil.

Briggs There's nothing you can have done.

Claxton There's no sin except what you think is sin.

Hoskins God makes it all, he makes us do it all, he can't make us sin. The men that crucified Christ, Christ made them do it.

Brotherton The devil, the devil's got me.

Cobbe A fart for the devil.

Hoskins Don't be frightened. We've got you.

Claxton Sin again, do the same sin as if it were no sin – –

Hoskins Sin to God's glory.

Claxton Then you'll be free from sin.

Cobbe You're in heaven, look, you're shining.

Brotherton No, how can I do it again? I did it then when I did it. It was a sin. I knew it was. I killed my baby. The same day it was born. I had a bag. I put it in the ditch. There wasn't any noise. The bag moved. I never went back that way.

Briggs That's not your sin. It's one more of theirs. Damn them.

Cobbe God bows to you. God worships you. Who did he come to earth for? For you. That's everyone's grief, we take it.

Brotherton He wasn't baptised. He's lost. I lost him.

Claxton Baptism is over.

Hoskins No, wait, sit down, listen – –

Claxton A baby doesn't need baptism to make him God, he is God. He's not born evil. He's born good. He's born God. When he died it was like a pail of water poured back in the ocean. He's lost to himself but all the water's God.

Cobbe Believe us.

Hoskins He's our fellow creature, and you're our fellow creature.

Claxton You're God, you, you're God, no one's more God than you if you could know it yourself, you're lovely, you're perfect – –

Brotherton No, I'm nobody's fellow creature.

Hoskins God now.

Cobbe Behold, I come quickly, saith the Lord.

Claxton God's going through everything.

Briggs Christ, don't waste those seven years we fought.

Claxton Everything's changing. Everything's moving. God's going right through everything.

Cobbe And God for your sin confounds you into unspeakable glory, your life, your self.

Hoskins God has you now.

Claxton Nothing we know will be the same.

Briggs Christ, help her.

Claxton We won't know our own faces. We won't know the words we speak. New words – –

Cobbe Believe us.

Briggs Be safe.

Hoskins God has you now.

Claxton Everything new, everything for the first time, everything starting – –

Brotherton Yes.

Briggs Be safe.

Brotherton Yes.

Briggs So it's over.

Brotherton Yes.

Hoskins There.

Briggs You can be touched. It's not so terrible. I'll tell you what I'll do. Avenge your baby and Robert Lockyer. I'll make Cromwell set England free. And how? Easy. Kill him. Killing's no murder. He wanted to free England. That's how he'll do it. Dead.

Cobbe God won't be stopped.

Drunk I'm God. I'm God.

Briggs Yes, amen, look who's God now.

Drunk I'm God. And I'm the devil. I'm the serpent. I'm in heaven now and I'm in hell.

Claxton Amen.

Cobbe You are God. Every poor man.

Drunk I'm in hell, I'm not afraid. I seen worse things. If the devil come at me I kick him up the arse.

Claxton And that's the devil gone.

Hoskins Amen, no devil.

Drunk I'm in heaven. And I go up to God. And I say, You great tosspot, I'm as good a man as you, as good a God as you.

Claxton And so are we all.

Hoskins And so is everyone in England.

Drunk Plenty of beer in heaven. Angels all drunk. Devils drunk. Devils and angels all fornicating.

Cobbe You are God, I am God, and I love you, God loves God.

Claxton Oh God, let me be God, be clear in me – –

Hoskins All the light now – –

Cobbe Sparks of glory under these ashes – –

Hoskins Light shining from us – –

Drunk And I say to God, get down below on to earth. Live in my cottage. Pay my rent. Look after my children, mind, they're hungry. And don't ever beat my wife or I'll strike you down.

> BROTHERTON *gets out some food.*

Brotherton I didn't give you – I kept it back – let me give you – –

Claxton Yes, yes, God's here, look, God now – –

Drunk And I say to God, Wait here in my house. You can have a drink while you're waiting. But wait. Wait. Wait till I come.

All (*sing Ecclesiastes 5, viii–x, xii*)

> If thou seest the oppression of the poor, and violent perverting of judgement and justice in a province, marvel not at the matter: for he that is higher than the highest regardeth; and there be higher than they.
>
> Moreover the profit of the earth is for all: the king himself is served by the field.
>
> He that loveth silver shan't be satisfied with silver; nor he that loveth abundance with increase: this is also vanity.
>
> The sleep of the labouring man is sweet, whether he eat little or much: but the abundance of the rich will not suffer him to sleep.

AFTER

Hoskins I think what happened was, Jesus Christ did come and nobody noticed. It was the time but we somehow missed it. I don't see how.

Cobbe It was for me, to stop me, they passed the Blasphemy Act. I was never God in the sense they asked me at my trial did I claim to be God. I could have answered no quite truthfully but I threw apples and pears round the council chamber, that seemed a good answer. Dr Higham. I changed my name after the restoration.

Brotherton Stole two loaves yesterday. They caught another woman. They thought she did it, took her away. Bastards won't catch me.

Drunk The day the king came back there was bread and cheese and beer given free. I went twice. Nobody noticed. Everyone was drunk the day the king came back.

Briggs I worked all right in a shop for a while. The mercer had been in the army, he put up with me. Then I started giving things away. If a boy stole, I couldn't say anything. So when I left I thought I must do something practical. I decided to bring the price of corn down. A few people eat far too much. So if a few people ate far too little that might balance. Then there would be enough corn and the price would come down. I gave up meat first, then cheese and eggs. I lived on a little porridge and vegetables, then I gave up the porridge and stopped cooking the vegetables. It was easier because I was living out. I ate what I could find but not berries and nuts because so many people want those and I do well with sorrell leaves and dandelion. But grass. It was hard to get my body to take grass. It got very ill. It wouldn't give in to grass. But I forced it on. And now it will. There's many kinds, rye grass, meadow grass, fescue. These two years I've been able to eat grass. Very sweet. People come to watch. They can, I can't stop them. I'm living in a field that belongs to a gentleman that comes sometimes, and sometimes he brings a friend to show. He's not unkind but I don't like to see him. I stand where I am stock still and wait till he's gone.

Claxton There's an end of outward preaching now. An end of perfection. There may be a time. I went to the Barbados. I sometimes hear from the world that I have forsaken. I see it fraught with tidings of the same clamour, strife and contention that abounded when I left it. I gave it the hearing and that's all. My great desire is to see and say nothing.

First published 1978 by Pluto Press Limited
Unit 10 Spencer Court, 7 Chalcot Road, London NW1 8LH

All rights whatsoever in this play are
strictly reserved and applications for
permission to perform it in whole or in part must be
made in advance, before rehearsals begin, to
Margaret Ramsay Limited, 14a Goodwin Court,
St Martin's Lane, London WC2
Other productions of the play may use their
own musical settings of the Bible and
Whitman quotations, but the music for the
orginal production may be obtained from
the composer, Colin Sell, c/o Pluto Press

ISBN 0 904383 74 1

Designed by Tom Sullivan
Cover designed by Kate Hepburn
Cover picture: contemporary
woodcut of the Ranters

Printed in Great Britain by Latimer Trend & Company Ltd Plymouth

Light Shining in Buckinghamshire

Today's Latin America

ROBERT J. ALEXANDER is presently professor of history at Rutgers University. He received his B.A., M.A., and Ph.D. degrees from Columbia University and has taught at Columbia University School of General Studies, Atlanta University, and the University of Puerto Rico. Among the organizations he has worked for are the Board of Economic Warfare (Brazilian desk), the Office of Inter-American Affairs, the Economic Cooperation Administration, and the International Cooperation Administration. An annual visitor to Latin America, he is the author of many books on the subject, among which are *The Peron Era*, *Communism in Latin America*, *The Bolivian National Revolution*, *The Struggle for Democracy in Latin America* (with Charles O. Porter), and *Prophets of the Revolution*.

TODAY'S
LATIN AMERICA

Robert J. Alexander

Anchor Books
Doubleday & Company, Inc.
Garden City, New York

C

Maps by Louise Jefferson; map of South America first published in *South America A to Z* by Robert S. Kane, Doubleday & Company, 1962. Copyright © 1962 by Robert S. Kane.

The Anchor Books edition is the first publication of *Today's Latin America*

Anchor Books edition: 1962

To Frances Patterson

Contents

Preface

Until recently Latin America has been largely unknown to most of us North Americans. Few of us have traveled there (except possibly to Mexico or Cuba) and our newspapers have only bothered to report Latin American news when it concerned a revolution or a *coup d'état*. Our government officials have tended to take the other American republics for granted and to pay attention to them when they presented this country with some kind of crisis which could not be avoided.

However, recent events in Latin America have served to focus more attention upon these nations. First, the regime of Guatemalan President Jacobo Arbenz engaged in violent campaigns against the United States and all that it stood for. After his overthrow in 1954 we had no sooner settled down to our usual complacency about our southern neighbors than the then vice-president of the United States, Richard Nixon, was spat upon and stoned in several countries while on a "good-will tour." Finally, with Fidel Castro's rise to power in Cuba this country was confronted with the development of a violently anti-Yankee totalitarian regime closely allied with our world-wide enemies, the Soviet Union and International Communism.

We can no longer afford the luxury of being ignorant about the twenty republics to the south of us. What happens in Havana, Brasília, or Buenos Aires is just as important to our national welfare and future as events transpiring in Paris or Berlin or New Delhi. It is high time that the average citizen of the United States began to have some idea of what the Latin American countries are like, and what political, economic, and social forces are at work in them.

I hope that the present little volume will make some contribution to the process of enlightening our fellow citizens concerning Latin America. I have tried to discuss all of the most salient aspects of life and society in these nations, and, if anything, I have probably generalized too frequently. There is no doubt that life and events in Latin America are complex. Indeed, anyone writing about Latin America should start out by warning his readers that any general statement made about the whole area will be untrue about some portion of it.

On the other hand, such generalization is necessary. The region does have certain characteristics which are very widespread, and all of the countries of the area share many similar problems. With caution it is possible to draw a panoramic picture of the area as a whole.

Since the purpose of the book has been to give as broad and deep a picture of contemporary Latin America as is possible within the compass of a relatively small number of pages, I have purposely not concentrated attention upon the matter which is of greatest immediate interest to most people in the United States, namely Fidel Castro. The basic problems, trends, and attitudes of present-day Latin America were there before Castro appeared on the scene; they may well remain long after he has departed. This is not to say that I have ignored Castro and the revolution which he has brought to Cuba and to the hemisphere generally. Where a discussion of these things is relevant, the reader will find it. However, I hope that he will find it in perspective, without a note of panic and without too much exaggeration.

If the reader's curiosity is aroused by what is written

here, he may go on to peruse some of the suggested readings which are to be found in the Bibliographical Note at the end of the book. He may also want to go more deeply into the problems of one or more particular countries. Many books are available about individual Latin American nations.

In writing this work I have drawn heavily upon my own personal acquaintanceship with the Latin American area, resulting from fifteen years of travel and study there, and from an even longer period of reading about it. Therefore, the generalizations here are usually my own responsibility. On the other hand, I have also drawn from a number of published sources, many of which are noted in the text. However, I have tried not to burden the reader with references.

Many people have helped with the preparation of this book. Thanks must go to Pyke Johnson, Jr., of Doubleday and Company, who first suggested it, and to James K. Page, Jr., who has handled it as editor. I must also mention Robert Carlsson, who helped to gather much of the statistical material presented here and to put it in tabular form. I likewise must thank Mrs. Emma Wenz, who has twice typed the manuscript. Many thoughtful suggestions were made by my mother, Mrs. R. S. Alexander, and by Mrs. J. B. Carman, both of whom read the original draft of the manuscript from the point of view of the observant layman.

Finally, as is the case with all writers who are also husbands and fathers, I owe an immeasurable debt to my wife, Joan P. Alexander, and my children, Meg and Tony, who allowed me to be diverted from more important matters in order to bring this book to a conclusion.

Robert J. Alexander

Rutgers University
New Brunswick, New Jersey
January 1962

Today's Latin America

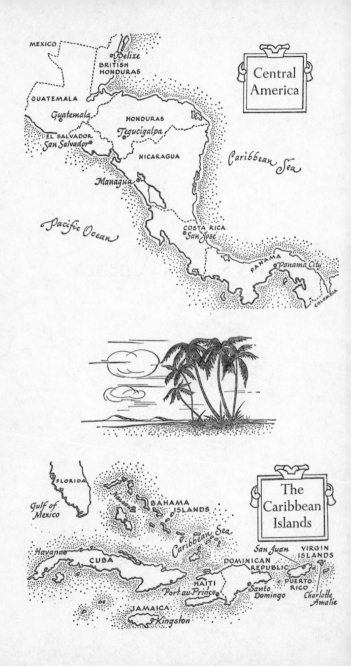

The Importance
of Latin America
in Today's World

Future historians will probaby observe that the most important revolution of the twentieth century was not the Bolshevik upheaval which began in Petrograd on November 7, 1917. Much more profound is the decline of the Europeans as masters of the world, and the emergence of those parts of the globe which were once the colonies or spoils of conquest of the European powers. The rise of the United States and the Soviet Union to a predominant position during the first half of our century may well prove to be but the opening phase of this tremendous upheaval. The second half of this period seems destined to see the power and influence of these two young giants diluted, while the nations which today we call "the undeveloped countries" emerge into the front rank.

The twenty republics of Latin America constitute an important segment of this emerging two-thirds of the human race. Occupying an area which constitutes about one-eighth of the earth's land area, possessing vast resources as yet largely untapped, and with a large and very rapidly growing population, this region has scarcely begun to play the role which it is destined to have upon the stage of human history.

THE EARLY IMPORTANCE OF LATIN AMERICA

Once before Latin America played an important part in the affairs of the world at large, but then only as a fountain of resources for the development of the various powers contending for domination of Europe, and hence, of the world. During the colonial period of Latin America's history, which included most of the sixteenth, seventeenth, and eighteenth centuries and went on into the first years of the nineteenth, it was a vast source of wealth for Europe. The Andean highlands of South America and the mountains of Mexico provided a constant stream of precious metals, and hence the sinews of war for Imperial Spain. The islands and coastlands of the Caribbean, as well as northeastern Brazil, provided rich agricultural lands for growing sugar, tobacco, and other products highly prized in Europe. The exploitation of these agricultural resources likewise provided a vast market for slaves, imported from Africa, and thus provided another source of wealth for the empires of the Old World.

In this period Latin America's role was a secondary and subordinate one, albeit very important, in which the Latin Americans themselves had little say about how they or their lands were used by their European masters.

During most of the nineteenth century Latin America's importance to the rest of the world seemed to decline. For many decades it was a relatively unimportant backwater, to which the rest of the world paid but little attention. Broken into a number of quarreling states, the area was the scene of innumerable wars, revolutions, and *coups d'état*. Its politics provided material for light comedy, its people became known to the outside world largely through ludicrous stereotypes.

But during these long decades a process which had gone

on throughout the colonial centuries continued and began to mature. This process was the forging of a new people or series of peoples, with characteristics all their own. The blood of the one-time conquering European became increasingly mixed with that of the Indian semiserf and the African slave. Through a slow and painful process a new and indigenous culture began to emerge. It borrowed from the Europeans but mixed these borrowings with elements of other races and of the American physical environment. Indigenous political and social institutions also were incubating, in spite of an apparently endless process of trying to copy those of Western Europe and the United States.

OUTSIDE INFLUENCES

During the later decades of the last century and the first few years of the present one, strong influences from abroad acted as a catalyst in Latin America and tended to bring about the emergence of the Latin American nations as an independent force, playing an increasingly autonomous and important role in world affairs. These influences were both economic and political.

The growing industries of Western Europe and the United States demanded larger amounts of raw materials, and their booming populations, with their rising standards of living, needed growing supplies of foodstuffs. One of the regions to which they turned to obtain these was Latin America. Argentina's wheat, Chile's nitrates and copper, the coffee of Brazil, Colombia, and half a dozen other countries, the bananas of several Caribbean republics, the diverse minerals of Mexico and Peru, the oil of Venezuela and various other Latin American nations, all became of vital importance to the industrial nations.

The exploitation of these resources for the benefit of Europe and North America brought profound changes to the Latin American nations. Modern methods of mining and of plantation agriculture were installed in their midst. Transportation facilities and public utilities were built to service the mines and the plantations. The rhythm of commercial activity quickened; new markets composed of miners, plantation workers, and small- and medium-sized merchants began to appear. Thousands of artisans' workshops sprang up to serve a part of these new markets.

These events had other important effects. They made Latin America much more dependent economically on the outside world than it had been before. The people who were working in the new mining or agricultural enterprises, or who were doing business with these enterprises, became accustomed to the use of many manufactured goods which they could get only from abroad. So in return for the minerals and agricultural raw materials and foodstuffs streaming to Europe and North America, an increasingly large number of industrial products began to flow back from those areas to Latin America.

The two world wars and the Great Depression of the early 1930s added another major ingredient to this increasingly complex Latin American economy: the modern factory. Because they cut the area off from the markets for its export products and from its sources of supply for manufactured goods, these events forced the Latin American countries to try to make for themselves many of the things which they had become accustomed to using and had hitherto imported. By the middle 1930s most Latin Americans who thought about these matters were convinced of their nation's need to build a more or less wide range of factory industries.

Meanwhile, important political winds were blowing through Latin America. At the time of the independence movement in the early nineteenth century, its leaders had been much influenced by the ideas of the French Revolution. However, during the rest of the century the net effect of these ideas was seen largely in a long struggle between Church and State and in attempts to establish free-trade concepts in the nations' international economic relations. The masses of the people were relatively little influenced by either of these matters.

THE IMPACT OF NEW IDEAS

By the early years of the twentieth century the situation was changing. The changes brought about by the incipient emergence of national cultures in these countries, as well as the development of small middle classes and wage-earning working groups, created a much wider clientele for the new ideas which were coming from Europe and other areas.

The most important new political force was nationalism. The new middle and working classes were much more conscious of their membership in a distinctive national group than was the old landowning aristocracy which had dominated political life in the nineteenth century and had tended to feel more akin to European elites than to the masses of their own countries. The middle groups were also more conscious of nationality than were the submerged Indian and Negro rural masses, which in many cases were not even aware that their nations existed.

The experiences that many of the countries around the Caribbean had during the early decades of this century with United States interference in their affairs—marked by U.S. military occupation of Haiti, the Dominican Republic, Cuba, Nicaragua, Panama, and open interference in other countries—greatly strengthened nationalistic trends in that region and the rest of Latin America. So did the development within their borders of the large mining, plantation, and transport enterprises owned by foreign firms which often behaved as if they, and not the nation's citizens, were the sovereign power in these countries.

Other ideas and events also had profound influence on the political thinking of the Latin Americans. The Bolshevik Revolution in Russia undoubtedly aroused the interest and sympathy of many Latin American intellectuals and some workers. Although the Communist movement as such has never been very strong in Latin America, there is little doubt that the revolutionary transformation in the Russian society and the example which the U.S.S.R. has presented of how a nation can industrialize and develop its economy with great rapidity have made a profound impression on the thinking of many Latin Americans.

The New Deal in the United States and the Labour Government experience in Great Britain following World War II, with their lessons that a deep movement of social change can be brought about by peaceful means, also un-doubtedly made a profound impression on Latin American thinking. Finally, the struggle for independence and eco-nomic development by the colonial areas of Asia and Africa has aroused wide sympathy and has increased the determination of the Latin Americans to seek their own independent role in world affairs.

THE IMPACT OF THE MEXICAN REVOLUTION

There is little doubt that Latin Americans today regard themselves as a part of the world-wide movement of the "underdeveloped" countries for a place in world affairs. However, Latin America is not merely a follower in this movement for the emergence of hitherto submerged parts of the human family. It has long been a leader in this proc-ess. The Mexican Revolution was the first of the twentieth-century movements for vast social, economic, and political change. Starting in October 1910, it antedated the Rus-sian Revolution by more than seven years. It even preceded the fall of the Chinese monarchy, which launched that vast Asian country on its process of cataclysmic change, cul-minating in the Communist victory in 1949.

The Mexican Revolution has led the world in many ways. Its agrarian reform has been closely studied by lead-ers of similar movements in a score of countries. Its encouragement of the labor movement working in close collaboration with a revolutionary regime has been the model in many other nations. Its incorporation of a great deal of social and labor legislation in the national constitution has been followed not only by the Soviet Union but by a host of Latin American as well as Asian and African nations. Its devotion to rapid economic development has become characteristic of all of the emerging nations of the world. Its use of the State as a catalyst and director of the process of economic growth has been followed in most non-Communist underdeveloped countries.

The Mexican Revolution has been markedly pragmatic. It has never developed a philosopher or political thinker who was capable of giving written expression to its doctrine or dogma: the Mexican Revolution has no Lenin or Trotsky of its own, nor, needless to say, a Montesquieu or Voltaire. Its program is clear from its acts, and its leading spokesmen have been loyal to the accomplishments and aspirations of the Revolution or they have ceased being its spokesmen.

However, in other Latin American countries there have appeared leading thinkers, political philosophers, and politicians. Some of these men have had personal contact with the Mexican Revolution, and have evolved a philosophy and a program not only for what has transpired in Mexico, but for what is occurring throughout the whole Latin American area.

THE IDEAS OF HAYA DE LA TORRE

The dean of modern Latin American political thinkers is the Peruvian leader, Víctor Raúl Haya de la Torre. In the 1920s he spent some years as an exile in Mexico and his thinking was much influenced by that country's revolution. During the 1920s and 1930s he evolved a political philosophy which has been taken over and adapted to local conditions by numerous political leaders and thinkers in many of the Latin American countries.

Basically, Haya de la Torre argues that the economic and political ideas worked out in recent centuries in Europe are not appropriate to Latin America, which has different ethnic roots, a different history, and very different economic and social conditions. He and his followers argue that industrialism and economic development were imported into Latin America as a by-product of the industrial countries' search for raw materials and foodstuffs.

According to the Haya school, the whole orientation of economic and social policy in Latin America must be changed so that the future development of these countries will be carried on for their own benefit and not for that of the countries already industrialized. However, this will not be possible until the semifeudal large landholding systems and other inheritances of the colonial past have been thrown off. These writers therefore urge the formation of political parties which will represent a coalition of all those interested in dismantling the traditional society and hastening economic, social, and political development. The principal groups to enter these parties are to be the urban industrial workers, the peasants, the new middle class, and particularly the intellectuals.

Haya and his followers believe that Latin America needs the help of the capital resources and the skills of the more advanced industrial countries. However, they argue that these contributions must come to Latin America under conditions established by the Latin American governments and peoples themselves and under their supervision and direction. Finally, Haya himself has put particular emphasis on the need for the planning of the region's development on a Latin America-wide basis, and preaches the need for the establishment of one great Latin American nation. Most of those who generally follow his ideas regard these last points in Haya's doctrine as aspirations rather than immediately realizable objectives.

THE COMMUNISTS AND JACOBINISM

Haya's indigenous national revolutionary philosophy is one of the principal ideologies battling for the loyalty of the Latin Americans. Since the early days of the Russian Revolution, the Communists have represented another important contender for leadership in the future of the region. Although the Communists have seldom been of major importance in any Latin American nation, they have built parties in every one of the countries of the region, carrying on an unceasing struggle for power and influence. Soviet prestige has risen in recent years as the result of grave errors in United States policy and increasing evidence of Soviet success in building up a powerful industrial system in a very short time. In Castro's Cuba they have come to full power for the first time in any Latin American nation.

Since World War II, a third important trend of political and social thought has emerged in Latin America which is perhaps best labeled Jacobinism. The political movements led by President Vargas in Brazil and President Perón in Argentina were early examples of this current. Fidel Castro and his followers gave unprecedented vigor and popularity to Jacobin ideas during their first months in power, before they turned the basic sinews of power over to the Communists.

In essence the Jacobins accept the belief of the National Revolutionary parties in the need for rapid economic development and for social revolution to destroy institutions which have been responsible for age-old injustices and for hampering national development and self-expression of the nations of the area. However, unlike the National Revolutionaries, the Jacobins do not hold political democracy in very high regard. Indeed, they regard the "formalities" involved in free speech, free press, and free elections rather as roadblocks designed by conservative elements and "foreign imperialists" to hamper the development of revolutionary changes and the achievement of "national economic independence."

The Jacobins as a result are in favor of the destruction of traditional institutions at all costs, and the extreme assertion of national sovereignty, particularly vis-à-vis the United States, regardless of the consequences. Consequently, instead of being rivals of the Communists for the loyalty of the masses of Latin American citizenry, they have become in recent years their close and powerful allies.

All three of these revolutionary ideologies continue to be resisted by conservative and reactionary elements which, though increasingly on the defensive, remain strong. In a handful of countries they have been able virtually to prevent a serious start being made in the process of modernizing their nations. In others they have fought a bitter last-ditch battle against change. These elements are to be found among the old landlord class, the traditionalist politicians, and the military, though by no means all of any of these groups have taken a reactionary or even a conservative position.

The result of this fierce and many-sided ideological struggle is of great importance to the world at large, and of peculiar importance to the United States. It can be expected that in the coming decades the role of the Latin American nations in general world affairs will tend to increase considerably. Most of these countries are already well in advance of most of the African and Asian nations in terms of economic development, and some of them seem likely to extend their relative position during the remaining decades of the twentieth century.

THE FUTURE ROLE OF BRAZIL

Most promising in this regard is Brazil, a nation occupying more than half of the South American continent, with a population approaching seventy-five million, and with truly vast resources of every kind. Its people are vigorous and have caught the vision of their nation's possibilities. Although Brazil still has a long way to go to come abreast of the older industrial nations, its record of diversifying and developing its economy since World War II has been spectacular. Economic development has been accompanied by a cultural awakening which has already put the nation in the forefront of modern architecture, and is bidding fair to gain universal recognition for the country in literature, in the arts, and in music as well.

There is little doubt in the writer's mind that by the end of the twentieth century Brazil will have taken its place as one of the half-dozen major powers in the world, economically, socially, politically, and perhaps even militarily. Jânio Quadros, who served as president for seven months in 1961, was well aware of his country's potentialities. During his short tenure in office he gave evidence that he intended to have Brazil play an independent role in hemispheric and world affairs and make its voice heard in international councils in accord with its emerging importance. The policy objectives laid down by Quadros are shared by his successors, though their method of implementing these objectives has varied somewhat.

Most of the other Latin American countries are not likely to equal the rank which Brazil seems destined to achieve. However, several of them will certainly become secondary nations of considerable importance. Argentina and Mexico already have the potential markets to justify a broadly based industrial society. Colombia, Venezuela, Peru, Chile, Cuba, and perhaps the nascent Central American Union have the economic resources to achieve a similar objective. They are increasingly showing the determination to achieve such a society. The establishment of the Latin American Free-Trade Area in 1961 indicated the intention of most of the countries to work together in this direction.

THE CHANGING NATURE OF
INTER-AMERICAN RELATIONS

Of course, what the Latin American nations are experiencing is also occurring with greater or less intensity in Africa and Asia as well. There is an increasing awareness in Latin America of their kinship in terms of aspirations and problems with the other underdeveloped nations of the world.

All of this means, of course, that the relative position, in terms of power and importance, of the present-day Great Powers will in all likelihood decline during the last decades of the twentieth century. In the Western Hemisphere the absolute preponderance in power, influence, and prestige which the United States has had over its Latin American neighbors is already beginning to disappear. The decline has perhaps been hastened by egregious errors of omission and commission during the years since World War II. It was inevitable, in any case, as the Latin Americans began to develop more diversified and stable economies, and grew increasingly aware of and desirous of asserting their own national identity.

Present and future trends in Latin America are of key importance to the United States. Whether there is developing in these nations a kind of society with which we can be on congenial terms is a question of utmost concern to this country.

Yet in the recent past we have been all too little preoccupied with what our Latin American neighbors were doing or thinking. We have tended to ignore them unless and until some peculiarly pressing crisis which seemed to menace our own national interest occurred in one or another of them. We made big promises of help for their economic growth during the Second World War and then for fifteen years thereafter largely failed to carry out these promises. We saw fit to support any dictator who would proclaim himself the friend of the United States, instead of being concerned with the evolution of a democratic type of society and political life in these countries. We largely failed to understand the deep-seated drives for social revolution in the area and too often tended to regard as a Communist any leader who sought to upset traditional economic and social institutions and to loosen ever so slightly the economic bonds which to him seemed to subordinate his nation to the United States. Only in 1961, with the launching of President Kennedy's Alliance for Progress program, did the United States government begin to change its attitude and policy.

For the United States' own good, and for that of the whole hemisphere, it is of vital importance that the people of the United States begin to understand better what is transpiring in the other American republics. In the pages that follow I will in somewhat general terms sketch the geographical, historical, and sociological background against which the rapid changes of present-day Latin America are taking place. I shall also discuss these changes and their direction, objectives, and impact on Latin America's relations with the rest of the world, particularly the United States.

The Land

Latin America is an area of great physical contrasts. It contains some of the world's highest mountains, though much of the region is only a little above sea level. It has vast temperate plains which are some of the globe's greatest breadbaskets, as well as dense, impenetrable jungles in the valleys of its great tropical rivers. Although some parts of it can hardly be matched anywhere else in the number of people per square mile, most of the great interior of South America is almost completely without human inhabitants.

Latin America is several times larger in area than the United States. During the 1950s its total population passed that of the United States, and it is predicted that by the end of the century it is likely to be double that of this country. Its people are divided into twenty different republics and there are also a number of dependent territories in the Caribbean area, associated in one way or another with Great Britain, the Netherlands, France, and the United States.

The area and latest population figures for the various parts of Latin America are shown in Table I.

TABLE I

Country	Area (Sq. Mi.)	Population*
Argentina	1,078,769	20,256,000
Bolivia	416,040	3,311,000
Brazil	3,288,050	63,101,627
Chile	286,397	7,298,000
Colombia	439,520	13,522,000
Costa Rica	23,421	1,072,000
Cuba	44,206	6,466,000
Dominican Republic	19,323	2,843,415 (1959)
Ecuador	116,270	4,007,000
El Salvador	8,250	2,434,000
Guatemala	42,042	3,546,000
Haiti	10,714	3,424,000
Honduras	43,227	1,838,000
Mexico	760,373	32,348,000
Nicaragua	57,145	1,278,000
Panama	28,576	995,000
Paraguay	157,000	1,677,000
Peru	514,059	10,213,000
Uruguay	72,172	2,679,000 (1957)
Venezuela	352,150	6,320,000

* Population estimates are for 1958 unless otherwise noted.

SOURCE: United Nations and local-government estimates, published in *The World Almanac*, 1960.

PRINCIPAL PHYSICAL FEATURES

There are five physical features of Latin America which are particularly worthy of note. These are the geographical location, the mountains, the great river valleys, the extensive coastal plains, and the islands lying off the mainland coast.

The Geographical Location

Most of Latin America lies within the tropics. Cuba, Haiti, the Dominican Republic, most of the British West Indies, all of Central America, the South American republics of Venezuela, Colombia, Ecuador, Peru, and Bolivia, and the colonial areas of the Guianas all lie between the Tropic of Cancer and the Tropic of Capricorn. The tropical location of Latin America has profoundly effected the nature of its population and the economies and social problems of the various countries.

The Mountains

A chain of mountains forms a kind of backbone for America. Actually, this chain begins in Alaska, passes in several ranges through both Canada and the United States, and continues down the western part of the whole New World, petering out finally in the South Pacific, only a short distance from the Antarctic continent.

These mountains are of varying height in different parts of Latin America. The mile-high plateaus of Mexico, capped as they are by such great volcanic giants as Popocatepetl and Iztaccihuatl, decline into much lower altitudes in most of Central America, to rise again in the mighty Andes, the second highest group of mountains to be found anywhere on the earth. In northern South America the Andes fan out in several separate ranges, with wide plateaus between them and deep valleys in the midst of each. In the southern half of the continent they become narrower, the plateaus disappear, and two ranges, only a few-score miles apart, outline the great Central Valley of Chile, which runs off into the sea at Puerto Montt. The inner range of the Andes continues down the coast to Tierra del Fuego.

In all, the Andes extend for over four thousand miles, with peaks as high as the 23,081 feet of Mount Aconcagua on the Argentine-Chilean frontier. In Ecuador alone there are fifteen peaks which are over 15,000 feet tall. In Bolivia the plateau is in many places 14,000 feet high, with snow-capped mountains towering even higher to the east and west of the plateau.

In the islands of the West Indies, too, there are mountain peaks and even small mountain ranges. Many of the islands are themselves volcanic peaks, most of them extinct. Also, along the east coast of Latin America, in the Guianas and Brazil, there is an escarpment of relatively low mountains or high hills which account for the peculiar fact that most of the rivers of that area rise near the Atlantic coast and run hundreds or thousands of miles inland before finding their way to the sea.

These mountain ranges have largely molded the economies and societies of the nations through which they run. On the high plateaus and above them in the mountains are rich deposits of iron, tin, wolfram, lead, zinc, and a host of other minerals. The plateaus and valleys provide rich agricultural areas; grains, cotton, coffee, and other products grow with more or less luxuriousness in the crevices of the mountain chains. Grazing, too, has been highly adaptable to some of these areas.

Finally, many streams and rivers which run rapidly from the mountains to the sea provide Latin America with a rich potential for hydroelectric power. Although this important resource has as yet been largely undeveloped, some of the countries, including Mexico and Chile, have made an important beginning in trying to harness their reserves of water power.

As a result of the mountain ranges, a number of regions of tropical America have a climate more like that of the temperate zone. There are large plateaus, such as those of Mexico, Guatemala, and Bolivia, where the climate varies from spring-like to exceedingly cold during much of the year. These plateaus, ranging from half a mile to three miles in height, are among the most heavily populated rural areas of Latin America. Other concentrations of population are found in the deep valleys that lie many thousands of feet above sea level throughout the Andean range.

On the east coast of South America the highlands have had somewhat the same effect. This is particularly true in the states of São Paulo and Paraná in Brazil. Although they lie within a geographical area which at sea level has a very hot climate, they are temperate because of their height and, as a consequence, are heavily populated.

However, although the mountainous areas have attracted more or less heavy populations because of their climate, they have nonetheless presented formidable obstacles to modern economic development. This has been so principally because of the difficulties which they create for the construction of transportation systems. Railroads are particularly difficult to build through them, and for many decades rail transport was economically practicable only if there were especially valuable cargoes which the roads could carry. Hence, it was not until the first decade of the twentieth century that Quito and La Paz, the capital cities of Ecuador and Bolivia respectively, were linked by rail with the outside world.

The same difficulties, though in a less serious degree, have hindered the construction of highways. For example, the link in the Pan-American Highway between southern Mexico and northern Guatemala was held up for many years because of the exceedingly difficult and costly job of building it in treacherous mountainous terrain in the Guatemalan sector.

The Amazon

The third outstanding geographic feature of Latin America has been its great river valleys, found principally in South America. With a few exceptions, the rivers of northern Latin America are of small importance as arteries of communication and trade.

South America contains the world's longest river, the Amazon. This river meanders for some 3300 miles from its origins in the Andes within one hundred miles of the Pacific Ocean to its vast mouth opening into the Atlantic. It drains an area of approximately 2,700,000 square miles, including parts of Peru, Colombia, Venezuela, the Guianas, Brazil, and Bolivia. It is navigated by ocean-going vessels for a thousand miles upstream, to the port of Manaus, while commercial navigation continues as high as Iquitos, some 2300 miles from the mouth.

Most of the Amazon Valley proper is covered by dense tropical rain forest. This forest is dominated by huge trees rising seventy-five to eighty feet above the ground, whose intertwining branches are so thick that the ground beneath never receives the full rays of the sun. Beneath these forest giants is a dense vegetation which seems to reach out to engulf all who seek to penetrate it. The paths which have been hewn through the vegetation, and such open spaces as there are, are covered by a thick humus formed by decayed plants, interspersed with rotting tree trunks. This humus is so thick that it tends to mute all sound, and an approaching man or beast is not heard until he is upon an unwary traveler. It is infested with innumerable insects, rodents, and snakes. The traveler soon learns to step up onto a fallen log which lies across his path, and then to take a long step beyond, so as not to tread unwittingly on the serpents, one of whose favorite resting places is the shady side of fallen trees.

Until the late 1950s when Brazil started the construction of its fantastic highways from the new capital of Brasília, to Belém at the delta of the Amazon, and to Acre in the westernmost reaches of the Brazilian part of the valley, little but trails penetrated the vastness of this tropical rain forest. The main means of communication remained the Amazon itself and its many tributaries.

For a long time a controversy has raged concerning the potential wealth of the Amazon Valley. In Brazil particularly, many have argued that this is an area of vast possibilities and have urged the spending of huge quantities of money and effort to develop the resources of the region.

Much has already been spent there, however, and the results, at best, have been disappointing.

The golden age of the Amazon Valley was the first decade of the present century, during which the deep jungles of the region provided the first sizable quantities of natural rubber to meet the needs of the dawning Age of the Automobile. However, by the outbreak of World War I the lead in this field had passed to the Far East, where plantation rubber proved more economical and reliable than the wild product of the Amazon. Never has the rubber industry of the Amazon been able to recapture this lead. Indeed, all efforts to develop plantation cultivation of the crop in this region—including a heavy investment by the Ford Motor Company in the 1930s—have failed. The key to the problem seems to be the lightness of the soil of the region, and the torrential nature of the rainfall. Between them, these two phenomena mean that once the tropical forest cover has been removed from any part of the area, the topsoil is quickly leached away. It is therefore most difficult to grow anything in an orderly way in the area.

However, hope still persists that a way will be found to grow rubber and other valuable crops there. Many also have ebullient hope concerning the mineral wealth which they are sure exists in the region. As yet, although some petroleum has been discovered in the Brazilian Amazon, it is not considered to have commercial possibilities. Some metallic minerals have also been discovered, but only a sizable deposit of magnesium in Brazil's Amapá Territory north of the river, near the border of British Guiana, actually has been opened to exploitation.

The climate of the Amazon region is a grave drawback to its exploitation. The Amazon Valley proper is a region of intense rainfall, of sickening heat, and of deep, dark forests. Only the Indian and part-Indian natives of the area have so far seemed able to resist the rigors of this climate which has repelled both Negro and white settlers from other parts of Brazil.

Whatever the future riches which the Amazon Valley

may provide for the countries sharing it, at present this region is a serious handicap to economic development. The only activities which so far have proved economical have been the gathering of forest products and their processing on a limited scale. The region lies far from the principal centers of population of the continent and costs of transportation are all but prohibitive. As a result, prices in the urban centers of the region are notably higher than in the more thickly populated parts of the continent.

The development of aviation has greatly facilitated the process of penetrating the Amazon. Since World War II, Brazil has established the largest airline network of Latin America, and built airports at key points throughout much of the Amazon region. Although plane transport is expensive, it makes possible for the first time the "opening up" of large areas of the country. The city of Anápolis, in the lower reaches of the Amazon Valley, was largely built with materials flown in and, for two years, until roads penetrated the area, the same was true of Brasília, the new Brazilian capital.

In recent years the Brazilians have tended to adopt a new tack in the eternal quest to conquer the mighty Amazon. While not relenting in their efforts to carry out a frontal attack upon it, they have concentrated even more on moving into the area from the south. People have been coming into the southern parts of the Amazon basin from the neighboring states of Minas Gerais, São Paulo, and Paraná. It is hoped that the great plains of this region can be populated and their largely unknown resources developed; only then can the march of civilization continue up to the Amazon Valley proper.

Other River Systems

Another of the major rivers of South America is the Orinoco. Rising in northern Brazil, it flows for most of its length through Venezuela. It is navigable for 1000 miles but because it flows largely through tropical rain forest and isolated plains regions, it has remained sparsely populated until recent years.

For several centuries the Orinoco was famous for the denseness of its jungle and its one product, angostura bitters (named after its principal town, Angostura). The area played an important role in Venezuela's struggle for independence a century and a half ago. It was there that Simón Bolívar, driven from the centers of population along the coast, found refuge and rebuilt his shattered armies, preparatory to making a last effort to drive out the Spaniards. It is in honor of this bit of history that Angostura has been rechristened Ciudad Bolívar.

The discovery of important mineral resources has promised new life to the area since World War II. First, huge deposits of iron ore were found near Ciudad Bolívar and these are now being exploited by subsidiaries of the United States Steel Company and Bethlehem Steel Company. A heavy-industry complex based on steel is being developed. In addition, impressive waterfalls near the confluence of the Caroní and Orinoco rivers have been harnessed, and an aluminum industry is being developed there. Instead of being a sparsely populated region, hardly more hospitable to human habitation than the Amazon, the Orinoco River promises to become one of the principal centers of both population and economic activity in rapidly expanding Venezuela.

Colombia's Magdalena River has played a quite different role from either the Amazon or the Orinoco. Although much of it passes through tropical forests, it also meanders for about 1000 miles from near the Pacific Ocean to its mouth at Barranquilla on the Caribbean Sea. For centuries it was virtually the life stream of Colombia, with its tributaries constituting the principal means of transportation for the whole country. In recent years railroads and highways have reduced its relative importance, but it is still a key artery of transport for the republic.

Of all of the river systems of South America, that of

the Río de la Plata is probably the most important at the present time. There is actually no river called the "Río de la Plata"; this is the name for the estuary through which the Paraná, Paraguay, and Uruguay rivers empty into the Atlantic Ocean. These rivers form the boundaries between Argentina and Uruguay, Argentina and Paraguay, Argentina and Brazil, and Paraguay and Brazil.

This river system rises in the interior of the continent, and most of the streams of the southern two-thirds of South America which do not flow into the Amazon empty into either the Paraná or the Paraguay. They are the main arteries of commerce for eastern Argentina, Uruguay, and Paraguay, the last depending almost completely on them to get its products to foreign markets. Buenos Aires, Montevideo, the great Argentine grain port of Rosario, and Paraguay's capital, Asunción, are the most important of the many cities which depend on the Río de la Plata system in whole or in part for their economic life.

The Coastal Regions

Along with the highland plateaus and valleys, the coastal plains of mainland Latin America—the fourth notable geographical characteristic of the region—are the principal centers of population. There are narrow plains along both the Atlantic and Pacific shores of South America and the Pacific and Caribbean coasts of Mexico and Central America. In the southern third of South America the flat area widens out dramatically to form the vast pampas of Argentina, Uruguay, and southern Brazil, reaching right up to the foothills of the Andes.

In the Northern Hemisphere population is relatively light along the coasts of Mexico, which are tropical, hot, wet, and inhospitable to the majority of Mexicans, who are used to living in the dry and semitemperate highlands. Efforts to get people to move down from the higher altitudes to the Atlantic and Pacific coasts have not been particularly successful. The main population centers of the

Central American republics, except Guatemala and Costa Rica, are in the Pacific coastal area; the Caribbean coasts of Nicaragua and part of Honduras are all but devoid of people.

In South America the large port cities of Guayaquil (Ecuador), Lima (Peru), and several leading Chilean cities are on the Pacific coast. The coastal regions of this part of the continent share most of these countries' population with the plateaus and valleys of the Andes. On the eastern coast most of the important cities of Brazil, as well as Montevideo, in Uruguay, and most of the Argentine urban centers are also in the coastal area, or a short distance from it. For centuries, the population did not venture up over the Brazilian escarpment into the interior of that country, preferring to stay along the coast.

Most of the railroads of the region are found in the coastal areas; it is no accident that Argentina, most of which is a great plains region, has for many decades had the best railroad system of all Latin America. In recent decades with the coming of the automobile, roads, which are cheaper to build and maintain than railroads, have begun on a major scale the task of penetrating inland from the coasts throughout Latin America.

The most striking feature of the coastal-plain region consists of the pampas, the great flat plains that stretch inland from the Atlantic Ocean to the Andean foothills. They possess some of the world's richest black soil, which is excellent for growing wheat and other grains, and for grazing cattle. Argentina has made use of them during the last century to become one of the world's principal sources of grain and meat. It was into these fertile plains that millions of immigrants from Italy, Spain, and other European countries streamed between 1880 and 1914. Here was laid the basis for the agricultural and grazing wealth of Argentina, Uruguay, and the Brazilian state of Rio Grande do Sul.

The Islands

The last notable geographic feature of Latin America consists of the islands of the Caribbean Sea, or the West Indies. This was the famous Spanish Main of the sixteenth and seventeenth centuries. It consists of the relatively large islands of Cuba, Hispaniola (on which is located Haiti and the Dominican Republic), Puerto Rico, Jamaica, Trinidad, and hundreds of smaller isles and islets.

Most of the islands are hilly or even mountainous with relatively little arable land—Cuba and Barbados being exceptions to this. Some of the deepest points in the ocean bottom to be found any place in the world are in this West Indian area, the islands being the visible parts of a high mountain chain. A few islands are still volcanic, and in May 1902 one of the most spectacular eruptions of modern times occurred in Martinique, when Mount Pelée virtually exploded, completely destroying the town of Saint Pierre and killing all but one of its 28,000 citizens.

The land along the coasts of the Caribbean islands has been very fertile and adaptable to the cultivation of tropical agricultural products. Since the seventeenth century, the islands have been an important source of sugar, and in the seventeenth and eighteenth centuries sugar cultivation made several of these islands rich prizes which were bitterly fought over by the great European powers. Cane-growing also accounted for the transportation of hundreds of thousands of Africans to work on the plantations of the islands; their descendants make up most of the population there today.

Cuba and the republics of Haiti and the Dominican Republic are independent nations today. The island of Puerto Rico is a Free Associated State of the United States. Most of the rest of the islands are under the British flag, the majority of them (all but the Bahamas, the British Virgin Islands, Jamaica and Trinidad) belonging to the semiautonomous Federation of the West Indies. However, Martinique and Guadeloupe are overseas departments of France, and Curaçao, Aruba, Bonaire, and several other tiny islets, form the Netherlands Antilles, an autonomous part of the Dutch Empire.

SUMMARY

The geography of Latin America has had a very important impact on the kind of civilization which has developed there. It has determined the centers of human settlement, which have been found principally in the highland valleys and plateaus and along the coastal plains. It has influenced the racial make-up of the population, with the Indians concentrated in the mountainous areas, the Negroes being found principally in the islands and along the hot coastal plains, and the Europeans—though found throughout the area—settling particularly in the temperate southern part of the region.

The geography has also largely accounted for the political division of the area and its economic backwardness. The mountains and the tropical river valleys have tended in the past to separate different centers of population from one another and, until recently, these same features have seriously hampered communications, trade, and economic growth. Only with the coming of the automobile and the airplane has it been possible to overcome at least in part the handicaps of the natural environment.

The People

Latin America's rapidly growing population of nearly two hundred million is a study in contrasts and comparisons. The people range from the most primitive Stone Age savages to the most highly sophisticated products of modern civilization. Their forebears came from all corners of the earth, and many millions have in their veins the blood of people of more than one continent. They are statistically very young, though tradition is strong among them and large numbers live in ways inherited from their remotest ancestors.

The density of population in Latin America varies markedly from one area to another. There are relatively heavy concentrations of people in the islands of the Caribbean —though here, too, there is great difference from one island to another—as well as in the plateau and valley areas of Mexico, Central America, and the Andes mountain range of South America. There is another ribbon of population along the east coast of the South American continent, running from the "hump" of Brazil, facing West Africa, to several hundred miles south of Buenos Aires, where the temperate zone begins to give way to colder climes.

In contrast to these relatively heavily occupied regions, there are parts of Latin America where the people are spread exceedingly thinly over vast areas. Until recently the whole center half of South America was all but devoid of people, the inhabitants being primitive Indian tribes who live by hunting and fishing and lack virtually all contact with the outside world. Only in the most recent decades have the people from the populated areas—particularly in Brazil—begun to push into the heartland of their continent. Also much of the east coast of Central America, and large stretches of northern and coastal Mexico, are thinly populated.

Geography and history have determined this distribution of the population of the Latin American areas. In many regions the people have sought the more congenial climate of the upland valleys and plateaus rather than the hot and humid tropical or semitropical coastal areas. East of the Andes in South America the forbidding jungles of the Amazon have been until recent years violently hostile to the incursion of civilized men. As a result, it was only in the southerly, more temperate regions that the population tended to expand into the interior. Elsewhere along the Atlantic coast, the great majority of the population remained within a few hundred miles of the ocean.

The only heavily populated lowland tropical areas of Latin America are the Caribbean islands and a few patches along the South and Central American coasts. Here it was the riches to be gained from the cultivation of sugar cane, or the need for trading centers to handle the precious metals and other products being transshipped from the interior to Europe, which served as a sufficiently powerful factor to overcome the initial handicaps of a tropical climate, and resulted in relatively heavy concentrations of people in a number of areas.

THE INDIANS

The same factors have determined the distribution of people of different racial stocks in Latin America. Before the coming of the Europeans in the fifteenth and sixteenth centuries, the indigenous Indian population had been principally concentrated in those parts of the region which enjoyed a more or less temperate climate. Thus the great Indian civilizations were located in the plateaus and valleys of Mexico and Central America and Andean South America. In the regions with a tropical climate the indigenous peoples were sparse in number and primitive in culture.

There were two principal exceptions to this general pattern. Part of one important civilized Indian group, the Mayas, had moved from their original home in the highlands of Guatemala, to the hot, dry peninsula of Yucatán, several hundred miles to the north. Here they had established a flourishing civilization some centuries before the coming of the Europeans. The second exception was in the southern third of the South American continent, where in spite of a temperate climate, the Indians had remained more or less primitive herdsmen with a level of culture not too dissimilar from that of the Great Plains Indians of what was to become the United States.

In the Mexico-Central America area there had existed a number of civilizations during the centuries preceding the discovery of America. At the time of the arrival of the Europeans most of the region was under the hegemony of a more or less loose military confederacy dominated by the Aztecs, redoubtable warriors who had come down from the north some centuries before.

Although their civilization was basically agrarian, the Indians of this region were masters of architecture, fine metalwork, and intricate textile manufacture. The Mayas, at least, had a written as well as a spoken language (which their conquerors and their successors have been unable to decipher to this day), whereas the Aztecs had an intricate form of picture writing which permitted them to record events and ideas.

The agrarian economy of this northern Indian civilization was based on a mixture of communal cultivation and a nascent feudalism. Much of the land was held by relatively small communities and was cultivated in common by the members of these communities. Other areas had been distributed among the military nobility and were cultivated by people whose status was reminiscent of that of the serfs of medieval Europe.

There were a number of important cities in Indian Mexico. Tenochtitlán, which the Spaniards came to call Mexico City, was the largest of these, but others, including the Maya capital of Chichén Itzá, were also of great importance. These urban areas were the centers of handicrafts and of trade. The merchants constituted an important segment of the community. However, it is thought that many of them functioned as agents of the chief or emperor of the Aztec confederacy, disposing of the tribute and taxation in kind which he received from his subjects and allies.

THE INCAS

In the Andean region there was an even more complex civilization. The people there were faced with the grave problem of making it possible for a large population (considerably in excess of the number of people living in the same area in 1940) to exist on a severely limited amount of arable land. This problem resulted in a surprisingly high degree of scientific agriculture and in a unique and fascinating system of social, economic, and political organization.

When the Incas (the name used for both the ethnic group which dominated the region and the rulers of this group) conquered a new area, one of their first acts was to send in agricultural experts to determine how to increase the agricultural output of their new domains. They usually settled some of their own expert agriculturalists as colonists in the newly conquered regions, introducing their methods of cultivation and making important improvements in agricultural techniques.

The Incas sought to use every inch of available land for growing foodstuffs and other products. They built gigantic irrigation systems along the exceedingly dry coastal area of present-day Chile, Peru, and Ecuador, and in some cases water was brought from as far as one hundred miles away. Likewise, they painstakingly constructed systems of terracing on the sides of the rugged Andean mountains, sometimes close to the snowline. In Peru today one can see the remains of these terraces, only a few of which are still in use. Rocks were collected and were placed in successive rows up the mountainside, and fertile soil was brought up by the basketful from the valleys and packed in behind the rock barriers. Thus, rings of fertile soil not more than six to ten feet wide were built, and on these the Indians planted their precious corn, potatoes, and other products.

The form of social organization of the Incas has led some modern writers to refer to it as "socialist" or "communist," though perhaps "communal" would be a better title. The people were organized in small groups known as ayllus, the members of which were theoretically related to one another. By the time of the arrival of the Spaniards the ayllu was becoming a geographical rather than a family concept.

The land was held in the name of the ayllu, not of its individual members. It was divided into three sections, one for the members of the community, one for the Inca, and one for the maintenance of the religious hierarchy. The latter two were cultivated jointly by the members of the ayllu. The products of the religious land were used principally for the support of the priesthood. Those from the Inca's land were used to pay tribute or taxes. Although some of this was actually sent to Cuzco, the capital of the Inca Empire, most of it was put aside in warehouses, which were conveniently located throughout the kingdom. This was used for distribution among the people in years of drought or other natural disaster when crops were short.

The land for the normal sustenance of members of the ayllu was divided among the members of the community. Each head of a family received the amount deemed necessary to support him and his dependents, and the land was redistributed each year to take account of demographic changes which had occurred in the interim. The individuals had the right to use the land, but not to sell, mortgage, or otherwise dispose of it.

The Incas built a remarkable system of roads throughout their empire. These were for the use of the Inca's armed forces and of the messengers who maintained constant contact with all parts of the far-flung empire, which at the time of the arrival of the Spaniards extended from the north of modern Argentina and Chile through Bolivia, Peru, and Ecuador, and into southern Colombia. At convenient distances along these roads were located deposits of foodstuffs and other provisions which would be needed by travelers.

The Indian civilizations of both North and South America lacked a number of things, which proved fatal when they were pitted against the military might of the Europeans. First of all, they did not possess knowledge of the wheel, and hence had no wheeled vehicles of any sort. They lacked any beast of burden which could carry a weight as heavy as a human being. The Incas had only the llama, which could carry light weights and was a useful source of wool and occasionally of meat. The Mexican and Central American Indians lacked even that. The Indians also had not come to know the uses of iron, though they were skilled in the founding and manipulation of other metals, including the precious ones. Finally, neither of the centers of Indian civilization had evolved any military weapon as powerful as the firearm.

IMPACT OF THE CONQUEST ON THE INDIANS

As a result of all of these factors, both of the great areas of indigenous New World civilization were brought under the yoke of the Spaniards with relative ease and by amazingly small numbers of invading warriors. With the Conquest there began an almost 500-year struggle not only for the possessions of the conquered but for their souls and minds as well.

The Spaniards were intent on destroying the Indian civilizations, while being equally determined to make the Indians themselves serve the interests of their conquerors. Many of the missionaries who accompanied the military conquerors were extreme fanatics who looked upon most of the civilized accomplishments of the Indians as works of the devil. They were determined to wipe out the religions of the conquered race, and to destroy all physical objects which might recall the old faith. The military men and rulers were equally single-minded in their desire to break the spirit of the Indians and prevent any attempt by them to reassert their independence. The Indians were thus converted into hewers of wood and drawers of water for a ruling caste thrust upon them by the Conquest.

Two institutions were particularly favored by the Spaniards. One of these was the *encomienda,* or division of Indians and their land among the conquerors; the other was the *mita,* or forced labor rendered by the Indians to the Crown, and ultimately to powerful individual Spanish landowners.

The *encomienda* was an institution transferred from Spain itself. During their seven-hundred-year struggle with the Moslems, the Christian Spaniards had evolved it as a means of securing and pacifying the areas reconquered from the sons of Islam. A feudal knight who conquered a given region from the Moslems was granted by the king of Castile the right to rule over those whom he had conquered. He was entitled to receive tribute from these people, and was responsible in his turn for seeing to it that they were brought within the fold of the Christian religion.

The *encomienda* was transferred almost unaltered to the New World with the first Spanish conquests in the Caribbean, and subsequently to the new viceroyalties of New Spain (Mexico) and Peru. Officers and men of the conquering armies were given larger or smaller numbers of Indian villages and towns with the right to exact tribute from the residents, and the duty to "civilize" and Christianize them. In the beginning the *encomiendas* were granted for a limited number of years, but they were rapidly extended for the lifetime of the original grantees, and were finally made hereditary. Early in the eighteenth century they were converted into simple landholdings, and all pretense of obligation on the part of the landowner disappeared.

Opinions of scholars differ concerning the effects of the *encomienda* on the Indians. Some feel that the Indians' way of life was not basically altered during the colonial period so long as they provided the tribute to the *encomendero* or landholder. Others feel that the *encomienda* and its exploitation by the conqueror contributed greatly to the spiritual demoralization and material impoverishment of the Indians.

Whatever may have been the effect of the *encomienda*, no one disputes the results of the other institution introduced into the New World by the Spaniards, the *mita*. With their avid craving for gold and silver the conquerors demanded large numbers of workers to get these precious metals out of the Andes and the mountains of Mexico. The work was bitterly hard, and often fatal. Although the Indians drafted for this labor were supposed to be forced to work only a short while and were then to be returned to their native villages, these regulations were observed largely in the breach. An Indian condemned to work in the mines usually died there.

The upshot of this situation was that large areas near the mines were depopulated. Either the adult males died in the mines, or the whole population abandoned the region, escaping to more remote areas where it would be harder for the authorities to find them. The *mita* contributed greatly to the almost catastrophic decline in the Indian population during the first century or so of the colonial era in the areas in which they had been most concentrated and most highly civilized.

In spite of the decimation of the Indian population in the areas where his great civilizations once existed, the indigenous American still remains an important component of the population of Latin America. He still constitutes a substantial majority of the inhabitants of Bolivia, Peru, Ecuador, and Guatemala. In addition, a very large percentage of the present populations of Mexico, Chile, Paraguay, and all of the Central American republics except Costa Rica have considerable Indian intermixture in their ancestry. These same strains are present though to a less extensive degree in Argentina, Brazil, Colombia, and Venezuela, and only in the West Indian islands have virtually all evidences of Indian ancestry disappeared.

In those countries in which the Indian still constitutes a majority of the population, he has tenaciously resisted the encroachments of the white man. Although he has lost the struggle for the land (except in Bolivia, where he is getting control of it again as the result of the Revolution of 1952), he has steadfastly held onto his own language, his own mode of dress, his own culture and, behind a thin façade of Catholic Christianity, his own religion. He has learned to distrust the white man almost completely, and has protected himself against him by withdrawing behind a wall of cultural, linguistic, and religious isolation, giving him the reputation among his white neighbors for being "inscrutable." To the degree that he *is* inscrutable, it is due to his own desire to be so.

Only the Mexico-Central American and Andean areas had Indian populations which could survive in any numbers the treatment they received from the conquerors. It is ironic but true that in the areas in which the Indians were still savages, the Spaniards found it impossible to submit them to serfdom or slavery. These Indians either resisted unto death or rapidly died in servitude. Within a few decades the Indian populations of the Caribbean areas taken over by the Spaniards were largely wiped out. Their remnants were absorbed either into the white population or into that of the Africans, the people who were brought to take the place of the Indians as the servile class.

In Brazil a similar process has taken place. There were few if any highly civilized Indians in that country, and many of the primitive indigenous people who first welcomed the Portuguese to their shores soon ran away into the interior to escape their erstwhile friends' attempts to enslave them. However, in the southern region of São Paulo there was wide mixing of the two races, and the hybrid or mestizo stock of that region, the *bandeirantes*, were famous throughout most of the colonial period for their valor and vigor in pushing as pioneers—and as slave raiders—into the interior of the continent. Although virtually all traces of the Indian have disappeared in the present-day Paulista, the mestizo is still the characteristic type to be found in the cities and villages of the Amazon Valley.

THE NEGROES

Since neither the Spaniards nor the Portuguese in their vast majority came to the New World for the purpose of working with their hands, they were faced with the problem of finding a new labor supply in those areas in which the Indians refused to serve in this role. Very early the first bishop of Chiapas (Mexico), Fray Bartolomé de las Casas, whose battles on behalf of the Indian won him the title of Protector of the Indians, advocated the importation of African slaves instead of the enslavement of the indigenous Americans. Although Las Casas lived to regret this suggestion, the movement which he patronized had gained great impetus before his death in the middle of the sixteenth century.

It was the development of the sugar industry in much of the tropical part of Latin America which was the decisive factor in introducing the vast population of African origin which exists in the region. Starting at the end of the sixteenth century and continuing throughout the seventeenth and through the middle of the eighteenth century, the production of sugar cane expanded more or less constantly in the Caribbean area, in northeastern Brazil, and in some other lowland coastal areas of the continent.

Sugar production lent itself to the system of plantation agriculture and this became the characteristic form of cultivation in these areas. It was also used in the growth of tobacco, indigo, and other products which were of secondary importance in the same regions of the hemisphere. The land, already in the hands of descendants of Spanish and Portuguese conquerors (or of those other Europeans, the English, French, and Dutch, who subsequently seized it from its original conquerors), remained a possession of the white man. The work on this land was done by the millions of slaves brought over from the West Coast of Africa.

The tragedy of the slave trade can only be touched upon here. This commerce developed into a highly organized business. European slave merchants located at strong points along the West African coast encouraged and stimulated the coastal tribes to wage war upon their neighbors farther into the interior of Africa, for the sole purpose of getting human chattels to sell to the slavers. Although the full story can never be known, there are some students of the subject who believe that the population of West Africa was literally decimated by this three-hundred-year-long process.

Those who were unfortunate enough to fall into the slavers' hands suffered untold miseries during their transportation across the Atlantic. As many unfortunate human beings were loaded into slave ships as the vessels could possibly hold. The slaves did not have room to stand up, and they were crushed into the hold side by side with one another. The sanitary and health conditions of the slave ships beggar description, and a ship which chanced to pass a slaver could tell what cargo it was carrying by the vessel's unholy stench, which was perceptible from many miles away.

Once in America the slaves were sorted, sold, and dispatched to the plantations where they were to spend the rest of their lives and where their descendants for many generations were also to live. In the Caribbean at least, they were looked upon as little more than valuable possessions. They worked unending hours under the most brutal conditions, and many were unable to survive this kind of life. Some students of the subject have estimated that as many as half of all the Africans who embarked in West Africa died during the voyage or very soon thereafter.

In Brazil conditions were somewhat different from those in the West Indies. The Brazilian plantation was much less nakedly a commercial enterprise, and was more nearly a great patriarchal establishment, ruled over by the plantation owner, who was figuratively father of all of those on his fazenda, and who frequently was literally father of a sizable percentage of them, white and brown. The fazenda was largely self-sufficient, having its own church and medical dispensary, growing its own food, and having its own slave artisans to make whatever tools were used and to build whatever structures were needed.

Untold wealth was produced by the labor of the slave population. The riches of the West Indian sugar planter became proverbial in European capitals. Small islands were looked upon as virtual treasure houses. Symptomatic of this was the discussion which took place during the negotiations in 1763 leading to the Treaty of Paris, ending the Seven Years' War. The British had conquered both Canada and the French islands of Martinique and Guadeloupe during the war, but had agreed to return one or the other to the French. At Paris they hesitated a long time before finally deciding that Canada was more valuable than the two tiny West Indian sugar islands.

The slave trade itself was the source of untold wealth to many European merchants. During most of the first half of the eighteenth century it was largely in the hands of British traders, and there is a good deal of evidence to indicate that the wealth accumulated in slaving by the merchants of Liverpool and Bristol was one of the major sources of capital during the first decades of the Industrial Revolution.

By the middle of the eighteenth century the prosperity of the sugar islands and of the fazendas of northeastern Brazil had begun to decline. Sugar was in excess supply in Europe, and prices began to fall. Furthermore, the markets for slaves were also becoming glutted. Finally, the Methodist Revival in Britain and the spirit of the Enlightenment on the Continent had had as one of their side effects the growth of a strong antislavery movement. The French revolutionary government of 1789 first attempted to end slavery in the French colonies, though effective emancipation came only a couple of generations later; the British government turned against the slave trade and began to treat those who continued in it as pirates. Finally, the British abolished slavery in their possessions in 1837.

In Latin America the institution of slavery persisted through much of the nineteenth century, being abolished in Brazil and Cuba only during the last two decades of the period. Much of the stigma of slavery continued to hover about the Negroes in many of the countries well into the present century. Only in Haiti, where a slave rebellion during the first decade of the nineteenth century had been responsible for the country's independence, was the man of African descent dominant, and even there a premium was generally put on the percentage of European ancestry of which he could boast.

THE DISTRIBUTION OF THE NEGRO POPULATION

Thus, both geography and history have determined the distribution of the Negro populace throughout Latin America. People of African descent form the base of the population in the countries of the Caribbean. Haiti is almost completely Negro or mulatto, as are the islands which are still colonies of Britain, France, and the Netherlands. A large part of the population of Cuba and the Dominican Republic is at least partly of African ancestry and the same is true of the Colombians and Venezuelans.

In Brazil the percentage of Negroes in the population tends to decrease as one moves south from the northeastern "hump" to the Uruguayan frontier. The average Carioca (resident of Rio de Janeiro) is a mulatto. In the southernmost states the proportion of Negroes is relatively small.

The Brazilians, more than the people of most of the other countries with sizable Negro populations, have suffered from an inferiority complex because of that fact. The author remembers numerous conversations during his first visit to Brazil in 1946 in which Brazilians of the most varied backgrounds expressed deep pessimism about the future of their country because of the alleged drawback constituted by the African-descended portion of its population. This attitude was partly the result of acceptance of value judgments of a world still dominated by Europeans and their offspring. It also arose from a feeling that much of the Negro population of Brazil had remained culturally African and had failed to become integrated in the dominant patterns of Brazilian society.

Fortunately, events since World War II have tended largely to overcome this feeling of inferiority based on racial considerations. The emergence of Negro nations and their growing role in world affairs has contributed to this. Even more important have been the accomplishments of the Brazilian people themselves in economic, cultural, and other fields since 1945.

In addition to the countries in which the Negroes constitute a large part of the population, there is a smaller proportion of people of African descent in most of the other Latin American nations. Significant groups of Negroes live in the tropical coastal areas of the Central American nations, as well as in the same regions of Ecuador and Peru. Even in the southernmost countries of Chile, Argentina, and Uruguay, Negroes are not completely a strange phenomenon.

THE WHITE POPULATION

All of the countries of Latin America except Haiti have significant white populations. However, only three nations are really predominantly of more or less pure European origin: Argentina and Uruguay in South America, and Costa Rica in Central America. In the case of the last of these, most of the Indians were obliterated, pushed out, and their remnants early absorbed into the invaders' ranks; and since few precious minerals were found there, most of the Spaniards who came arrived for the purpose of settling down as small farmers.

Uruguay and Argentina were settled relatively late by the Europeans. The indigenous inhabitants were itinerant and primitive and were largely exterminated or were driven into isolated areas. Mass immigration from Europe came only after independence, in the nineteenth and early twentieth centuries. Its volume was so overwhelming that the sizable mixed Indian and African populace which existed at the end of the colonial period was largely absorbed and lost its own identity in the immigrant stream. Nevertheless, there are undoubtedly more people with some Indian or African ancestry among the present-day Argentine and Uruguayan populations than official statistics indicate.

The tides of European immigration to the Latin American countries varied in time and intensity from one nation to another. Throughout the colonial period there was a small but steady stream of people from the Iberian Peninsula, but the "mother countries" generally tried to prevent citizens of other European powers from going to their American colonies. Only in rare instances did any appreciable number of Europeans from outside of the Iberian Peninsula settle in the Spanish and Portuguese colonies.

With the attainment of independence non-Spanish and non-Portuguese migrants began to arrive in appreciable numbers. During the first half century of separate national existence sizable numbers of Germans settled in southern Chile and in the three southernmost provinces of Brazil. During the last years of the nineteenth century and the first decades of the present one much larger numbers came from the Latin countries of Europe as well as from Eastern and Central Europe. Between the two world wars immigration fell off to small proportions. Since the Second World War the number of newcomers has increased once more, with Argentina, Brazil, and Venezuela receiving the bulk of new settlers.

The great majority of post-independence immigrants entered Argentina, Uruguay, Brazil, and Cuba. Only in those countries did these newcomers change the basic ethnic pattern of the nations to which they came. Elsewhere, although immigrants have made important contributions in terms of ideas, cultural influences, and skills, they have come in relatively small numbers and comparatively few at a time.

The Latin Americans of European descent came from the most diverse sections of the Old World. Of course, the basic element in the white population of the eighteen Spanish-speaking countries is Spanish, while the core of the people of European descent in Brazil is Portuguese. However, in Argentina and Uruguay there are almost as many people of Italian origin as those with roots in Spain; and in parts of Brazil, notably São Paulo, the Italian-Brazilians are as numerous as those of Portuguese background. Smaller numbers of people of Italian descent are found in several of the other Latin American nations, with Venezuela receiving a particularly significant number since World War II.

People of German origin are found in a number of countries, and are of particular significance in Brazil, Chile,

Argentina, and Guatemala. Anglo-Brazilians, Anglo-Argentines, and Anglo-Chileans are a small but important group in their respective countries, and there are also significant Slavic elements in these three nations.

Many of the Latin American countries have been melting pots for the people from Europe. There is wide intermixture among the white people of different national backgrounds. One thinks of such names as Oscar Schnake Vergara (German and Spanish) of Chile, Juscelino Kubitschek de Oliveira (Czech and Portuguese) of Brazil, and Vicente Lombardo Toledano (Italian and Spanish) of Mexico, as examples of people of mixed national backgrounds who have played important roles in their respective nations during recent decades.

THE ASIATICS

The final element in the racial amalgam of Latin America is that which comes from Asia. The largest concentration of Asiatics is the several hundred thousand Japanese in southern Brazil, particularly in the state of São Paulo. Most Japanese immigration into Brazil took place in the first two decades of the twentieth century, and a large proportion of the present-day Japanese-Brazilians were born in the New World. There are other scattered Japanese colonies in Peru, Chile, Bolivia, and Paraguay.

There has been a dramatic change among the Japanese-Brazilians since World War II. Until the end of that conflict they tended to remain strictly isolated, having little to do with other Brazilians except in business dealings. They stayed in the rural areas of the state of São Paulo, where they were expert truck farmers. They participated scarcely at all in Brazilian civic life, and there was virtually no intermarriage by Japanese-Brazilians with other citizens. Their political loyalties remained largely attached to Japan.

However, since World War II the Japanese-Brazilians have changed greatly. Large numbers of younger Japanese-Brazilians have moved into the cities, and have entered a wide spectrum of occupations, including factory work and the professions. They have entered politics, and Japanese-Brazilians sit in the state legislature of São Paulo and in the federal congress. The loyalty of the vast majority of the Japanese-Brazilians to Brazil is now beyond question.

The Chinese also constitute a significant group of Asiatic origin in Latin America. Important colonies of Chinese settled in Peru, Cuba, and Panama in the early decades of the present century. In Peru they have been largely absorbed into the population of the Lima-Callao area and have widely intermarried with Peruvians of other backgrounds. Many of the Chinese were expelled from Panama during World War II. Havana still has a sizable Chinatown.

With the fall of mainland China to the Communists, a new stream of Chinese immigration has come to Latin America. Consisting of anti-Communist refugees, it is small in numbers, but has brought resources in education, skill, and capital which are making a minor but significant contribution to the development of several of the Latin American nations.

Another stream of immigration of considerable significance which has come from Asia has been that of the Arabs. Most of these people have come from the Levant, notably from Palestine, and from the beginning they have played an important role in Latin American affairs. Most of them came as small merchants, and they have been an important element in the establishment of manufacturing enterprises, particularly in the textile field. In recent decades they have begun to play an important role in political affairs as well. At least one person of Arab descent, Gabriel Turbay of Colombia, has been a candidate for president; another, Juan Lechín, was elected vice-president of Bolivia in 1960.

One other immigrant stream from Asia has not been of

particular importance in the independent republics of the hemisphere, but it has been significant in the still dependent areas of the Caribbean. This is the group of people coming from the Indian subcontinent. In the early years of this century many thousands of Indians were brought to Trinidad and British Guiana to work as indentured servants in the sugar fields. Their descendants now constitute the largest single element in the population of those two colonies.

THE MIXED BLOODS

The process of racial mixture has developed at a different pace in each country, but it is significant in all of the Latin American nations. The mixing of the races began in the first years of the Conquest, in the sixteenth century. The conquerors brought few women with them. Even those who had Spanish or Portuguese wives and children back in Europe tended to establish other families with Indian women in the New World. Many of the oldest aristocratic families of the Latin American countries owe their origins to such unions. Although later arrivals brought their Spanish consorts with them, the process of blood mixture of Spanish and Portuguese with the Indians went inexorably on through the next three centuries or more.

With the importation of large numbers of Africans to serve as slaves, the intermixture of European and Negro also began. Seldom were there formalized marriages between members of these two groups, but many a planter or other white man took a Negro concubine. Sometimes the offspring of such unions were kept as slaves by their fathers, but in other cases they were freed, educated, and endowed with a certain amount of this world's goods by their paternal parents.

The mestizos (Indian-white mixtures) and mulattoes have played an important role in molding contemporary Latin America. In the traditional society these groups had no fixed place. They were frequently not accepted in the ruling white groups, but they felt themselves superior to the pure Indians and Negroes. They did not have the tribal or similar loyalties of their mothers' peoples, nor did they have the sentimental and cultural association with Europe which characterized their fathers. It was among this group that nationalism found many of its most ardent adherents, and the Mexican Revolution and other movements for social change found particularly strong support among them.

The people of mixed ancestry are today becoming an increasingly large part of the population. They are the dominant group in Mexico, in terms of power and wealth, and perhaps make up a majority of the population. They are certainly the majority in the Central American nations of El Salvador, Honduras, and Nicaragua. They are the average type in Venezuela, where the white-Negro mixture predominates. People with European plus African or Indian blood probably constitute the majority in Brazil, Cuba, and the Dominican Republic, while the average Chilean has both European and Indian ancestors. In other countries the mestizos and mulattoes are relatively fewer in number and of less importance.

RACE RELATIONS IN LATIN AMERICA

Of course, in any discussion of race mixture and relations among the races in Latin America one must keep in mind the fact that "race" has a somewhat different concept in that area than it does in the United States. Although there is a direct correlation between degree of European ancestry and economic and social prestige and power, the lines between the whites, mixed groups, and indigenous peoples are less clear and precise in Latin America than in the United States.

There is a much wider field of choice open to the individual to decide to which racial group he wishes to belong than is the case in the United States. Whereas in this country anyone with one African ancestor is considered to be a Negro, in Latin America a person who is fair-skinned and does not have markedly Negro features, but who may have some of the physical attributes of the Negro, may be regarded as white, if he has the education and financial standing which would qualify him to be a member of the latter group.

Frequently, in the predominantly Indian countries, the difference between an Indian and a mestizo is a matter of cultural and sociological factors rather than of ethnic considerations. A full-blooded Indian may, by moving from the countryside into the city, learning to speak Spanish well, dressing in European-type clothes, and going to Mass regularly, move from the Indian group to the mestizo category. Not infrequently he will adopt the disparaging attitudes toward the Indians which characterize many mestizos.

It is frequently claimed by Latin Americans and by some North American observers of the Latin American scene that racial prejudice doesn't exist in the twenty republics to the south. However, this is far from the case. A well-known Peruvian writer of partly Chinese descent, Eugenio Chang-Rodríguez, comments thus on this problem:

> Is it true that in . . . Latin America there is no racial prejudice? We believe that it exists. That it is not so sharp as in South Africa or in the United States, or that it is inferior to what is felt in Europe is true, but racial prejudice also exists in Dark America. Perhaps it is necessary to be a Negro, an Indian, or an Asiatic to measure the degree of this cruel reality, which many whites and mestizos do not notice. In the diffusion of the false belief which could be called the White Legend, many factors have served to blind the vision of even discerning scholars. The propagators of the White Legend are not lying, because they do not assert the opposite of what they see; what happens is that they report on what they see, without realizing

that some of it is misleading and false. Excessive optimism has consolidated the legend and made it universal.[1]

It is easy to observe that wealth and power in the Latin American countries still tend to be concentrated in the hands of people who are white or near white. It is also true that the lowest elements on the social and economic ladder tend to be largely African or Indian in background. Of course, in large part this is an inheritance of the colonial past, of the semiservile position in which the Indian was kept for so long, and the slavery of the Negro. It has taken a long time in Latin America, as in the United States, for sizable elements from these submerged groups to raise their economic, educational, social, and political status.

There are perhaps two basic differences in the way in which this problem is viewed and acted upon in Latin America and in the United States. First of all, it is easier for a person of African or Indian or Asiatic background who in some way acquires wealth and education to gain admittance to the upper classes in Latin America than in the United States. In the second place, the Latin Americans tend to regard the melding of the races rather than their eternal separation as the ideal of their societies, regardless of the way they may act in practice.

Dr. Chang-Rodríguez has commented (in the article already cited) on the first of these two points. He says:

. . . The fact is that in the land of Lincoln racial prejudice is stronger than the admiration of money. In Latin America, on the other hand, in spite of the Ariel thesis of Rodo, respect and consideration for money and culture is stronger than racial prejudice. Furthermore, money and culture raises the social category of their possessor and consequently the rich and cultured Indian or Negro comes to merge with

[1] "Perú País Adolescente," in *Hispania,* September 1960.

and get lost in the ethnic group and social class in power, acquiring its virtues and its vices. The complex social stratification with its catalogue of vices, outstanding of which is class discrimination, has complicated matters and has made what is also racial prejudice seem to be only social prejudice.

There is no doubt that there is a great deal less nonsense in Latin America than in the United States about "racial purity" and its supposed virtues. In some of the countries, such as Brazil and Mexico, the abstract ideal held by most citizens, insofar as race questions are concerned, is the merging of all of the distinctive ethnic backgrounds into a new human stock peculiar to that particular nation.

This by no means implies that good white families will not have grave reservations about their children marrying young people of distinctly different racial backgrounds, or that such people will even feel particularly comfortable in the company of a group predominantly of another racial stock. However, it does mean that racial prejudices become much more a matter of the attitudes of the individual than the mores of the group. It also means that there are few legal barriers to the "mixing" of the races.

Friction among the races is of much greater importance in some Latin American countries than in others. It is perhaps most acute in the predominantly Indian countries of Guatemala, Ecuador, Peru, and Bolivia. The Mexican Revolution has had the effect of greatly mitigating the problem in that country. It is of sufficient importance in Brazil and Cuba to have brought forth organizations whose mission it is to defend the rights and seek the advancement of the Negroes. In Haiti the long-continuing conflict between the mulattoes and the people of full-blooded African descent is always just below the surface, as it is in the dependent territories of the Caribbean.

CONTRASTS IN LEVELS OF CIVILIZATION

One final aspect of the people of Latin America is worthy of note. This is the startling contrast to be found in their ways of life. Almost every stage of the development of human civilization can be found in the twenty republics of the area. Although industrialization, the spread of education, and other factors are now creating greater uniformity, it will be many years before the Latin Americans of even a single nation will have the degree of similarity among themselves which today characterizes the people of the United States. Many generations will have passed before this occurs throughout Latin America as a whole— if it ever does.

There are parts of the basin of the Amazon where primitive Stone Age tribes are still living in the conditions prevalent at the dawn of the human race. They are rudimentary hunters with few, if any, handicrafts and no agriculture. Some of them are so completely isolated that no man from the outside has ever lived among them and come out to tell about it.

These most primitive Latin Americans are few in number, though they still inhabit a vast expanse of territory. Much more numerous are those Indian Latin Americans who live with the crafts, agricultural techniques, and forms of social organization which their ancestors used before the Europeans even knew that America existed. Such tribal communities live in the more isolated regions of the highlands of South and Central America. Somewhat akin to them are the Negro peasants of Haiti, who live much as did their African ancestors before their age-old pattern of life was disrupted by the trader in human flesh.

On yet another plane are the people who still live under conditions roughly equivalent to those of medieval European serfdom. These folk work their masters' land, render him personal labor service, and depend upon him almost entirely for whatever rudimentary "social services" and money income they may receive. Peru, Ecuador, and Guatemala still have millions of Indians living in this manner. People of African origin live in not too dissimilar conditions in parts of Brazil where what was once the slave plantation has not yet completely disappeared.

Other millions live as small peasants, growing their own food but also producing at least some goods to be sold on the market. In some of the countries in which coffee is most widely grown, particularly Colombia and Costa Rica, these people are of considerable importance. In southern Brazil, too, the small farmer is a factor of some significance.

Then there are the agricultural workers who are employed on great farms or plantations producing crops for export to the outside world. These include the workers on the coffee, cotton, and sugar plantations of Brazil and El Salvador, the coffee groves of Guatemala, the banana plantations in half a dozen different countries, and the workers on the great haciendas and ranches of southern South America. These people live under a wide range of conditions, varying from the semiservile situation of the coffee workers of El Salvador and Guatemala, through the laborers on the supermodern banana plantations of Central America, to the relatively fortunate position of many of the Argentine agricultural workers, protected as they have been since Perón's day by minimum wages, social security, and trade-unionism.

THE CITIES

Finally, there are the people who live in the fast-developing cities. Table II shows the relatively large numbers of people living in the cities of Latin America in comparison with the total populations of these countries.

Even in the cities there are vast contrasts. The city of Port-au-Prince appears almost a caricature of the sleepy

TABLE II

POPULATION OF PRINCIPAL LATIN AMERICAN CITIES

	City Population	National Population	Approximate % of Total Population in City
Argentina		20,256,000	
Buenos Aires	3,673,575		20
Rosario	467,937		2.5
Bolivia		3,311,000	
La Paz	321,073		10
Brazil		63,101,627	
São Paulo	3,149,504		5
Rio de Janeiro	2,940,045		5
Recife	703,726		less than 1
Salvador	532,619		" " "
Pôrto Alegre	512,951		" " "
Belo Horizonte	507,852		" " "
Chile		7,298,000	
Santiago	1,546,884		20
Colombia		13,522,000	
Bogotá	903,200		8
Medellín	457,530		4
Cali	396,220		3
Barranquilla	340,430		3
Costa Rica		1,072,000	
San José	99,766		10
(Greater San José) ...	212,085		
Cuba		6,466,000	
Havana	785,455		13
(Greater Havana) ...	1,217,674		
Dominican Republic		2,843,415	
Santo Domingo	181,553		7
Ecuador		4,007,000	
Quito	232,000		7
Guayaquil	290,000		9
El Salvador		2,434,000	
San Salvador	203,796		9

	City Population	National Population	Approximate % of Total Population in City
Guatemala		3,546,000	
Guatemala City	284,276		8
Haiti		3,424,000	
Port-au-Prince	134,117		3
Honduras		1,838,000	
Tegucigalpa	72,385		4
Mexico		32,348,000	
Mexico City	2,554,000		8
Nicaragua		1,278,000	
Managua	109,352		8
Panama		995,000	
Panama City	221,200		23
Paraguay		1,677,000	
Asunción	201,340		12
Peru		10,213,000	
Lima-Callao	1,207,250		12
Uruguay		2,679,000	
Montevideo	845,000		33
Venezuela		6,320,000	
Caracas	700,018		11
(Greater Caracas) ...	971,988		14
Maracaibo	343,390		5

SOURCE: Adapted from *Demographic Yearbook of the United Nations*, 1957, pp. 151–54.

tropical capital. Many scores of smaller cities and towns in a dozen Latin American countries preserve in their architecture, in the manners and mores of their people, and to a degree even in their economic activities much of the atmosphere of the colonial period.

In sharp contrast are a dozen or more great cities of the region, which in many ways are more modern than anything to be found in the United States or Europe. They have grown so rapidly that they are virtually new. But within these towns themselves there are such contrasts as the imposing new public and office buildings and magnificent villas of many of the new rich of Caracas, and the miserable cardboard and corrugated tin hovels in which so much of the population of that city lives.

There is sharp contrast too in the mood and mode of the various cities. Buenos Aires is almost flauntingly European, whereas Santiago, Chile, across the Andes, gives one the feeling that it could only exist in Chile. Rio de Janeiro with its magnificent natural setting and its dark-skinned crowds is distinctly tropical; Brasília, the new capital of Brazil, is the architect's dream, a city of several hundred thousand souls built from nothing during the administration of a single president. São Paulo has an Italian flavor, Mexico is proud of its Indian past and couldn't hide its colonial heritage if it wanted to. Until recently Havana reflected the *joie de vivre* and noisiness of its inhabitants.

SUMMARY

The people of Latin America, like the land in which they live, are a study in contrasts. They come from the most varied ethnical backgrounds and live at contrasting levels of culture and civilization. They are undergoing great change, and the tensions arising from this change are a basic factor in the upheaval and revolutionary atmosphere which is the fundamental fact about Latin America today.

The Economy

Latin America is in the throes of its own Industrial Revolution. It is traditionally an agricultural and mining area, and much of the land is cultivated by antiquated methods and under ancient social relationships. However, the industrial countries' search for raw materials and food, beginning at the end of the nineteenth century, has resulted in the development of a modern agricultural sector and of an up-to-date mining industry, and the countries have become more closely tied to the world economy.

The culmination of this process has been the development of manufacturing during the last few generations. The general economic life of the region is now rapidly broadening, with the growth of service industries, banking, and all the other phases of a modern economy. Moreover, the people's aspirations for rising living standards are expanding even more rapidly than the economy, a fact which is the key to many of the region's problems.

Rapid economic change is now the fundamental fact of the Latin American economy. The speed of this change varies greatly from country to country, but it is general throughout the area. Furthermore, popular desire for change is even more pressing than the change itself. It is intensified by a demographic explosion which gives Latin America the most rapidly increasing population of any region of the globe. This rise in the number of people underscores the need for development and for alterations in the structure of the economies of the Latin American nations.

The evolution of the Latin American economies, and particularly the pressure for rapid industrialization and general economic development, has brought changes in the institutions of the area. Inevitably, the governments have played key roles in promoting the growth of new sectors of the economy. At the same time the economic relations of Latin America with the outside world have been undergoing a fundamental change.

The survey of the various sectors of the Latin American economy in the following pages will show the areas in which the traditional institutions have persisted, and where modernization has had its greatest impact. Agriculture, mining, manufacturing, and distribution have all felt differing effects from the traditional and modern forces at work in the region.

Latin Americans are prone to say that much of their economy is semifeudal and semicolonial. There is more than a little truth in this idea, but it is certainly no longer the whole picture. The economy of Latin America, like most other aspects of life there, is exceedingly varied and highly complex.

SEMIFEUDAL AGRICULTURE

Agriculture is still by all odds the most important form of economic activity in Latin America, whether viewed in terms of volume and value of the products turned out, or of the number of people employed in it. However, there are many different types of agriculture in the region, and it is important to differentiate a few of them. For our purpose, we can distinguish what we shall call semifeudal agriculture, large-scale commercial agriculture, and small-scale farming.

Semifeudal agriculture still exists in the Andean parts of

Peru and Ecuador, and in some of the highland areas of Guatemala. In a somewhat different form it also exists extensively in Brazil, and remnants are found in Chile and other countries.

In this form of agricultural activity the great majority of those who work the land are held in a more or less servile position and possess little if any land of their own. The land is the property of large landowners, and it is generally exploited by very antiquated methods.

The classical case of this type of agriculture is found in the Andean regions of South America. There it is customary for the large landowner to grant small parcels of land to tenants for their own use, so they can grow the foodstuffs necessary for their families, keep a few livestock, and build their miserable houses. In return for the use of this land the tenant must work the part of the estate which is cultivated for the account of the landowner, and in many cases must render personal service to the landlord and his family periodically. This service may be as house servant or in other enterprises owned by the landlord, or in some cases the tenant may be rented out by the landowner to someone else who needs his services.

This system of cultivation of the land is highly unproductive. Usually, only the most primitive types of agricultural implements are used. The landlord has little incentive to introduce modern labor-saving methods of cultivation, since they would only serve to make his tenants superfluous. So long as he can make a good living by the exploitation of the virtually free services of the tenants, he is satisfied.

This type of cultivation is also very retrograde, economically speaking. The tenants have virtually no money income. They get paid no wages for their labor on the landlord's acres, and on their own small plots of land they grow only the requirements of their own very low standards of living. They grow their food, their wives weave their clothing, they make and repair their own humble abodes. Hence, these people do not constitute a market for manufactured goods which may be turned out by their countries' industries.

This type of agriculture is thus a drawback to the economic development of those countries in which it exists. It prevents the expansion of agriculture and it severely limits the possibility of the growth of manufacturing and services. Until this pattern is destroyed by some type of agrarian reform, the whole economy suffers.

LARGE-SCALE COMMERCIAL AGRICULTURE

Another characteristic type of agriculture in Latin America is that which grows products for the world market. This type is prevalent in the Caribbean islands, in most of the Central American countries, and in coastal sections of northern South America, where tropical products are grown. It is also characteristic of Argentina, Uruguay, and southern Brazil, where grains, meat, and wool are the main commodities produced.

This type of agricultural and grazing activity differs fundamentally from the first kind. Unlike semifeudal agriculture, this second type ties the countries in which it exists to the world market rather than isolating them from it. It generates sizable amounts of money income. It involves a large capital investment and increasingly modern methods of cultivation.

Although export agriculture has greatly stimulated economic activity in the Latin American countries, it has also vastly increased the instability of their economies. The foodstuffs and raw materials being produced for sale to the West European nations and the United States tend to change prices rapidly and extremely. These prices depend in part on the state of prosperity of the highly industrialized nations. In spite of long-continued efforts of the Latin American exporting countries to control the prices of these commodities, they have found themselves largely unable to do so, at least for any length of time.

This problem is intensified because most of the Latin American countries produce only a very limited number of these agricultural export products, and the prosperity of their economics depends to an exaggerated degree upon what happens to these few products. Brazil, Colombia, Guatemala, El Salvador, and Costa Rica depend principally on coffee. Cuba, the Dominican Republic, Puerto Rico, and several other West Indian areas depend upon sugar. Honduras and Ecuador are principally banana producers. Uruguay is mainly a wool grower, Argentina depends largely on exports of wheat, corn, and meat.

The instability induced by this dependence on one or two major agricultural exports is particularly resented in Latin America, because the prices of industrial products which these countries have to buy do not change as rapidly or as extremely as do prices of their own exports. Over the last twenty years, indeed, industrial prices have moved more or less steadily upward, regardless of the state of the business cycle.

Another aspect of this type of agriculture which has aroused a good deal of controversy has been the large amounts of foreign capital which have been invested in it. In the West Indian countries the sugar industry has been largely developed by British and United States interests; the United Fruit Company and the Standard Fruit Company have been virtually the only firms of major importance in the banana trade. Where the industry itself has not involved large amounts of foreign investment, the transportation and marketing facilities necessary to get the products to market have depended heavily on foreign entrepreneurs. This has been the case with the coffee industries in the northern part of the area, and the grain and meat trade in Argentina and Uruguay.

The combination of very heavy dependence on markets in the highly industrialized nations and large investments from these nations in Latin American export agriculture and in the service industries supplying it constitutes what many Latin Americans call the "semicolonial" aspect of their economies. They feel, with good reason, that the economic dependence of their countries on the highly industrial nations, and particularly on the United States, tends to limit the Latin Americans' political sovereignty. It is possible for the industrial powers to use economic pressure, or threats of economic pressure, to force political concessions from the Latin American countries. There is enough experience with such pressure in the past to give credence to this belief.

SMALL-SCALE FARMING

A third type of farming is increasing in importance. This is the activity of the small cultivator. There are a few areas of the region in which the small agriculturalist has traditionally been typical. This is true in the state of Santa Catarina in southern Brazil, and in parts of the neighboring states of Paraná and Rio Grande do Sul, where German, Italian, and Japanese farmers settled several generations ago and built up a family-farm type of agriculture. It is true in much of Costa Rica and it was true in some parts of pre-Castro Cuba. Small landholding is still prevalent in those parts of the predominantly Indian countries in which the ancient indigenous agricultural communities have not been completely destroyed.

It is likely that small-scale family farming will increase in importance in the years to come. The most important force working in this direction is agrarian reform, or the division of the large landholdings among smaller-scale agriculturalists. Although in some cases it will be found convenient to maintain large productive units, and therefore there will be a variety of experiments with cooperative, collective, and communal farming, there will also be many instances in which land will be given outright to small farmers by the governments carrying out agrarian reforms.

AGRARIAN REFORM

The first Latin American country to undertake a large-scale redistribution of landholdings was Mexico. Starting soon after the outbreak of the Mexican Revolution in 1910, the Mexican government started a program for breaking up the large feudal estates which had hitherto characterized the nation's agriculture. Although the old landholders were left with modest holdings, many millions of acres were given to small farmers in the following four or five decades. For the most part, this land was granted to rural communities, with individual farmers getting only the right to use the land, not the right to mortgage or sell it. These communities were called *ejidos*. At the present time about half the cultivated land of Mexico is in the hands of *ejidos*.

Starting in 1953, the Bolivian government also undertook a wholesale redistribution of land, particularly in the Andean plateaus and valleys, where most of the people of the country live. The land is for the most part being given outright to the small Indian cultivators. Although the process is moving slowly, most of the country's peasants now have at least a modicum of land which they can call their own.

Starting in 1958, Venezuela also began an agrarian reform. It is the best-planned and most scientific effort of this kind which has yet been made in Latin America, having been drawn up by a commission on which all of the country's principal economic and social interests were represented. By the end of 1961 nearly 3,000,000 acres had been redistributed. Land redistribution is being accompanied by the extension of adequate credit and some technical assistance to the new landowners. It has had very positive effects on agricultural output.

The revolutionary government of Fidel Castro in Cuba

also undertook an agrarian reform. Unlike those in other countries, it placed most of the land expropriated from the large landholders in the hands of the government, through its Instituto Nacional de Reforma Agraria. By the end of 1960 only some twenty thousand small farmers had actually been given plots of land, although the process of expropriation was largely completed by that time. Most of the seized land was organized in collective and state farms based on Soviet models.

The governments of a number of other countries were discussing or making plans for agrarian reform by the end of 1961. These included Colombia, the Brazilian state of São Paulo, Peru, and Chile. In Central America a five-nation survey of land-tenure problems was being conducted at the University of Costa Rica, the object of which was to present a detailed program of land reform to each of the governments of the region.

The Latin American experience with agrarian reform indicates that a lot more is involved in the process than merely the redistribution of land, if it is to be successful. The new farmers must be provided with credit, technical information and assistance, and other help in order to get them established as successful farmers. In one way or another all of the governments which have carried out agrarian reforms have attempted to deal with these aspects of the problem, and they have done so with varying success.

If the area's economy is to grow in a healthy fashion, agrarian reform and agricultural development are essential for almost all of Latin America. Because of the exceedingly rapid increase in the population of the area, there is a constant demand for a larger food supply. Furthermore, the even more rapid increase in the population of the cities means that more and more people are dependent upon foodstuffs which they do not grow themselves, while new industries need mounting quantities of agricultural raw materials. Finally, the export of agricultural products remains a prime source of foreign currency, which is needed to buy capital equipment for development and to meet the mounting demand for consumer goods.

MINING AND PETROLEUM

Most of the mining and petroleum industries fall within the modern sector of the Latin American economy. They share with agriculture the burden of providing the Latin American countries with their export products. Some of the nations are as dependent on mineral products and oil for their exports as others are on agricultural commodities. Thus Bolivia depends almost exclusively on mineral exports, with tin normally providing from 50 to 75 per cent of all the foreign currency the country earns. Venezuela depends on petroleum for as much as 95 per cent of its exports. Chile depends almost exclusively on copper and nitrates.

From colonial times Latin America has had a leading place as an exporter of minerals. Until a few generations ago it was famous principally for the production and export of the precious metals. Peru, Bolivia, and Mexico provided for many centuries most of the gold and silver which entered into world trade. In recent years the export of the baser minerals and petroleum have become of much more importance than the sale of precious metals, though Latin America still produces appreciable quantities of gold and silver.

Minerals and petroleum are also coming to play an increasingly large role in the domestic economies of the Latin American nations. They are essential to the newly developing manufacturing industries, particularly those in the metallurgical field, as well as to construction and other forms of economic activity.

Latin America, taken as a whole, is richly endowed with base metals and oil. Brazil and Venezuela have two of the world's largest known iron-ore deposits, while Chile, Peru, Colombia, Mexico, and Cuba also have appreciable resources of this mineral. Chile is the world's second-largest copper producer and has resources which are likely to last for many generations; Peru, Mexico, Brazil, Cuba, and Argentina are among the other countries which also have sizable amounts of copper. Bolivia is a major world producer of tin, and although its presently exploited mines are being depleted, it is generally supposed that the country has large quantities in reserve. Mexico and Peru are major producers of lead and zinc, while half a dozen other countries probably have exploitable reserves of these. Brazil has ample quantities of many of the rarer minerals such as uranium, molybdenum, titanium, and vanadium. Brazil, the Guianas, Jamaica, and several other areas are richly endowed with bauxite, the raw material from which aluminum is made.

Petroleum is widely distributed throughout Latin America. Venezuela is the world's largest exporter, and its reserves are good for another two or three generations at least. Peru, Ecuador, and Colombia are important factors in the world petroleum trade, while Mexico supplies most of her own needs, as do Bolivia and Argentina. Chile has found oil in the extreme south, in Tierra del Fuego, while the Brazilians have sizable reserves in Baía and believe that they have other sources in the Amazon Valley and elsewhere.

The principal mineral product which is in short supply in Latin America is coal. Only Chile, Peru, and Mexico have really adequate supplies for their own use and predictable future needs. Most other countries are more or less heavy importers of coal, and with the possible exception of Argentina, prospects of future discoveries do not seem too good. However, this handicap is at least partly overcome by the ample resources of oil and of potential hydroelectric power. As yet, the latter has only been developed to an exceedingly modest degree, though Mexico, Chile, and El Salvador have made notable progress in expanding their hydroelectric systems since World War II, while

Venezuela, Peru, Brazil, and several other countries have ambitious plans in this field.

The area's mineral and power resources have been an essential asset in the process of industrialization which is now going forward with more or less intensity in all of the Latin American countries. All of the Latin American nations have been developing manufacturing industries during the last several decades and several of them will take their places within another generation among the world's important industrial nations.

MANUFACTURING

Factory industry is both the symbol and the most important part of the modern sector of the Latin American economy. Although several of the countries' governments showed some interest in developing manufacturing during the nineteenth century, it was really not until the First World War that this branch of activity began to become an important element in the economy of the region as a whole. During World War I the Latin American countries found themselves cut off from their customary sources of manufactured goods in Europe and the United States. As a result, they attempted feverishly to provide some of these things for themselves. The textile and light metallurgical industries in particular received great impetus at this time.

The Great Depression of the 1930s had the same effect. Unable to sell their agricultural and mineral exports in customary quantities and at previous prices, they found themselves without the foreign currency necessary to buy the manufactured goods of Europe and North America. Again they were thrown back on their own resources. At this time most people who thought much about such matters in Latin America became convinced that it was absolutely essential for their countries to develop healthy manufacturing industries, so that they would never again get caught in this way because of developments in the highly industrialized nations over which they had little or no control.

Once again in World War II the Latin Americans found themselves unable to purchase manufactured goods on a large scale from their customary trading partners. At this time the idea gained acceptance that the Latin American countries should not only begin to produce textiles, processed foodstuffs, and other consumer goods, but also heavy industrial products such as iron and steel, machinery and autos, heavy chemicals, and similar things.

As a result of these experiences, every government in Latin America is now committed to a program of economic development, with principal emphasis on manufacturing industries and the transportation, power, and communications facilities to service them. Of course, the nature of this development varies with the resources and the population of the country, but the general commitment to industrialization is all but universal in the area.

There are four countries which have developed furthest in the process of industrialization: Brazil, Mexico, Argentina, and Chile. All of these are now virtually self-sufficient in textiles, processed foodstuffs, pharmaceuticals, and cement. All have steel industries. The first three have auto industries which supply the national market, and are now establishing heavy chemical industries. Brazil and Mexico produce a wide variety of machinery and equipment and these branches of industry are rapidly becoming of major importance in their economies.

In all likelihood Brazil has the brightest industrial future of all the Latin American nations. It has adequate quantities of virtually all the resources, agricultural and mineral, which are needed, except coal. It has a population of around 70,000,000 people, which is potentially sufficient to provide an adequate market for large-scale production. It has an exceedingly energetic and imaginative citizenry which is firmly committed to the process of economic growth and industrialization. Its principal handicaps at the moment are an inadequately developed agriculture, which limits the market for its manufactured goods, and insufficient electric power and transportation facilities. However, there are indications that the agricultural situation is beginning to change and vast and expensive efforts are being made to provide the transportation network and power facilities which are required.

At the other extreme from these relative industrial giants in Latin America are such countries as Haiti and Honduras, where the process of industrialization has only just begun. Most of the other nations of the area lie somewhere in between. Some of these, such as Colombia, Venezuela, Peru, and Cuba, are making extensive efforts to step up the process of industrialization; most of the other nations are lagging somewhat behind.

THE WIDESPREAD DESIRE FOR ECONOMIC DEVELOPMENT

Economic development has become virtually an article of faith in the Latin American countries. There are undoubtedly many factors which explain this fact. One of the most important of these is the instability which we have already noted resulting from the excessive dependence of these nations on a very narrow range of export products.

Another basic motive behind the drive for development is the desire to raise living standards. The Latin Americans have become well aware of the difference in levels of living between the highly industrialized nations and themselves, and they have reached the conclusion that this is due largely to the fact of industrialization. They feel that they can only raise their own standards if they have more diversified economies in which manufacturing plays a key role.

Nationalism has also contributed to this desire for development. The Latin Americans generally feel that if their economies are dependent on one or two foreign countries for the purchase of all their exports, and if they depend upon these exports to purchase virtually all the goods which their people consume, the sovereignty of their governments is severely limited. Hence, they see a diversification of their economies, to make them capable of producing most of the consumer goods they need, as well as those capital goods which are within their capacity to produce, as the basic means of providing "economic independence." Only if they have such economies will they have anything approaching equal bargaining power with the industrial giants of the Old World and North America.

THE LACK OF MARKETS

The process of economic development and industrialization faces many difficulties. One of these is the problem of an adequate market. Most of those nations which have become major industrial countries have had large populations which were capable of buying the goods turned out by their factories. As a result, it has been possible for them to obtain the economies which come from turning out very large quantities of goods.

Most Latin American countries are hampered in this regard. With the exception of Brazil, Argentina, and Mexico their absolute populations are small, these being the only nations with more than 20,000,000 people. In addition to this, the persistence of antiquated economic and social systems in the rural areas of most of the Latin American countries has meant that in most cases only a fraction of the total population is in fact "in the market," that is, receives enough money income to buy an appreciable quantity of manufactured goods (or anything else) during a year.

The agrarian reforms and programs for agricultural development which we have already discussed are in part motivated by a desire to extend the national market of the various countries. Another approach to the problem to which the Latin Americans have been giving increasing attention is the possibility of pooling all their national purchasing power by the formation of common markets, free-trade areas, and similar arrangements.

Latin American economic and political unity has been an ideal since the days when the Liberator, Simón Bolívar, called a hemispheric conference in Panama in 1826. In more recent times this ideal has been given a more concrete expression in plans for economic cooperation and even unity among the Latin American countries than in political ideas.

During the late 1940s and early 1950s Argentine dictator Juan Perón proposed a series of economic agreements with his neighbors which would virtually have formed a single economic unit among them. He failed to achieve this largely because of fears of his "imperialist ambitions" on the part of his neighbors and because of the economic crisis which gripped Argentina in the early 1950s. Also, in 1947 Colombia, Ecuador, Panama, and Venezuela agreed to tentative plans for merging their economies. These plans were disrupted by the Colombian and Venezuelan dictators of the early 1950s for selfish reasons of their own.

Although these plans for economic unity failed, the idea persisted. The Economic Commission for Latin America (ECLA), with its headquarters in Santiago, Chile, composed of a number of brilliant Latin American economists, was particularly insistent on the need for economic unity in the area.

In recent years two concrete results have come from the efforts of the ECLA. One of these has been the proposed economic union among the five republics of Central America: Guatemala, El Salvador, Honduras, Nicaragua, and Costa Rica. These plans call for a common tariff wall around all of these nations, as well as planned economic development, with the establishment of different industries to serve the whole area in different member countries. This program has been ratified by all but Costa Rica, and in 1961 a new Central American Bank was officially established to provide financing for various aspects of the program.

The other move has been the formation of the so-called Latin American Free Trade Area, as a result of the signing of the Treaty of Montevideo late in 1959. This treaty calls for the gradual abolition of tariff barriers among the member nations of the Free Trade Area, and the establishment of new industries to serve the whole area in such a way as to avoid competitive and wasteful activities. The treaty was signed at first by seven countries: Argentina, Uruguay, Brazil, Paraguay, Chile, Peru, and Mexico. Subsequently, Ecuador and Colombia also decided to join the Free Trade Area. It officially came into force just before the end of 1960, and the first round of negotiations on tariff reductions took place a few months later.

RETROGRADE ASPECTS OF LATIN AMERICAN ECONOMIES

In spite of the very considerable progress which has been made in the Latin American countries in recent decades in developing more modern and more diversified economies, there are certain aspects of their economic life which are still behind the general trend and which act as brakes on development. Two of the most important drawbacks are the distribution systems and the tax structures of these nations.

Until recent years the systems of distributing goods to the consumer had changed but little from those existing in the pre-industrial period. The average Latin American merchant followed the policy of keeping very little inventory on hand, and seeking the most rapid turnover, with as large a markup per item sold as the market would bear. The idea of selling a large volume of goods at a small margin of profit per item, which played such a large part in developing mass markets in the highly industrialized countries, was foreign to him.

To a considerable degree this antiquated marketing system has been a bottleneck to the rapid expansion of the Latin American economies. However, in the years since World War II this situation has begun to change. In part this change has been the result of the establishment in many Latin American countries of branches of large United States retailing firms, notably Sears, Roebuck, which have led the way in developing new selling techniques for Latin America. Partly, too, it has been the result of local manufacturers going over the heads of the old merchants and seeking to bring their goods directly to the consumers. Finally, it has been due to the rapid spread during the last decade or so of supermarkets and other similar merchandising enterprises in a number of the Latin American countries. However, the region still has a long way to go before it develops a really efficient marketing system.

The tax structure also reflects the traditional society rather than the new industrial one. Most of the Latin American countries tend to rely principally on customs duties and sales taxes of one kind or another for the bulk of their income. Direct taxes on income and inheritance are generally very light and are frequently not collected in fact from those who have relatively high incomes.

This tax system is a drawback to development in several ways. First, it leaves the large agricultural landlord class virtually untaxed. This class makes little contribution to the economic growth of most of the countries, and because of its tendency to buy foreign goods in preference to national ones and to invest abroad rather than at home, constitutes a drain on the scarce resources of foreign exchange. Taxation of the rural landlord class is almost as necessary a reform as redistribution of the land, insofar as the facilitation of economic development is concerned.

The heavy reliance on taxes on consumers is also a

potential drawback to development in another way. Since these taxes bear down heavily on those elements in the community which tend to spend most of what they earn— the principal purchasers of nationally-manufactured goods —they may well tend to restrict the markets for these goods. If the poorer classes had to pay less taxes, they would in all probability buy more nationally-made goods.

The Alliance for Progress program of President John Kennedy, which was adopted at the Punta del Este Conference in August 1961 as a joint program of the nations of the hemisphere, has given a much needed impetus to the development of more equitable tax systems in the Latin American countries. At the Punta del Este Conference it was agreed that in order for a nation to be eligible to participate in the aid which the Alliance will provide for economic development, it must take steps to develop a tax system which will in a general way be based on the ability to pay. By the end of 1961 Mexico, El Salvador, and one or two other countries had already modified their tax structures in conformity with this program.

DIFFICULTIES IN RAISING CAPITAL
FOR DEVELOPMENT

The inequitable tax systems of Latin America have intensified one of the most important difficulties which these countries face in their attempts to achieve rapid economic development. That is, the accumulation of capital. Unfortunately, many of those elements in Latin American society which receive sufficiently large incomes to permit them to save (and then to invest their savings in economic development) do not save. Rather, they tend to spend virtually all of their income, and even to transfer some of it abroad for safety. Since these same groups have been largely able to evade taxation, it has been very difficult to force them to contribute to economic development against their will.

There are three main groups which in the traditional

Latin American society received more than average incomes. These were the landowners, the merchants, and the high government officials. None of them has had any marked proclivity to invest in the modern sectors of the economy.

The landowners have owed much of their social status to their ability to live in relative magnificence, and this has required them to spend virtually their whole income. Furthermore, they have enjoyed the services of very cheap labor, and hence have had little to gain from modernizing their own agricultural activities through the introduction of machinery and new techniques, which would serve largely to make their workers superfluous. Finally, they have had a high degree of suspicion of the new industrial sectors of the economy, and have not wished to become connected with them.

The merchants have been somewhat more willing to invest in the modern part of the economy, but still have been generally reluctant to do so. Accustomed as they are to getting a rapid profit on a small number of goods sold, they are suspicious of such enterprises as factories, which require several years before they are in a position to render a profit.

Finally, the instability of governments in Latin America has generated a tendency among highly paid government officials to put their funds in something "safe," something which would be relatively difficult for a hostile regime to confiscate. They have contributed very heavily to the peculiar situation which exists in Latin America, whereby this area, which is in dire need of capital, is in fact shipping sizable amounts of it abroad, to foreign bank accounts or for investment in foreign land or securities.

INFLATION

As a result of these circumstances, the governments of Latin America have tended to rely on a peculiar type of forced savings, inflation, as a means of building up the funds necessary for investment in economic development. Unable to collect sufficient taxes to meet the growing demands imposed upon them by economic-development needs, these governments have tended to run large deficits. They have borrowed funds from their central banks to cover these deficits, and thus they have poured a much greater amount into the national economies through their expenditures than they have taken out as taxes. As a result, there has been an increased amount of income seeking to purchase a relatively stable quantity of goods, and the upshot of this has been an increase in the prices of the goods. Once the process of inflation has got under way, it has tended to grow upon itself.

The effect of this inflation has been to force urban workers to pay the major part of the real costs of economic development. Although the output of these workers has grown dramatically as a result of their transfer from relatively unproductive agriculture to highly productive manufacturing, they have received only a small part of the return from this increase in output. Although their money wages have gone up over the years, the prices of the goods and services they have had to buy have gone up at least as fast. Hence, the real income of the workers increases little, if at all, once they have become established in the industrial sector of the society.

Some groups, notably the industrialists and merchants, have profited from inflation. Their incomes have been larger than they would probably have been otherwise. The industrialists, at least, have tended to plow back the larger part of their profits into expansion of their enterprises. The governments, too, have had much larger resources available for their economic-development projects than would have been the case if they had had to rely solely on tax resources. Thus, on balance, inflation has probably stimulated economic growth, at least when price rises have not become excessive.

Virtually every Latin American country has been characterized since World War II by more or less serious inflation. Thus, for more than a decade, Brazilians came to consider a 20 per cent annual price rise as "normal," and in 1959 the rate of increase jumped to over 60 per cent. In Bolivia in the early 1950s the rise in prices was considerably greater than anything the Brazilians have undergone, and in Argentina in 1958 inflation was 100 per cent in one year.

THE ROLE OF GOVERNMENTS IN ECONOMIC DEVELOPMENT

The shortage of available capital resources in the private sectors of the Latin American economies is a major reason for the fact that the governments of the area have participated very extensively in the process of industrialization and general economic development. They have done so for reasons of necessity rather than because of any ideological bias. For many large-scale investments, such as power and light facilities, steel plants, and railroad systems, there are no private enterprises within the Latin American countries which are capable of raising sufficient funds. For reasons which we shall discuss later, the governments and people of Latin America do not want to leave these projects to foreign investors.

An additional factor which impels Latin American governments into the field of economic development is that many projects require the acquisition of loans from international lending institutions. These loans provide the foreign exchange which is necessary to buy capital equipment for development projects. But the international lending institutions feel more confidence in the Latin American governments than they do in private businesses in the area. As a result, the governments find it easier to raise the necessary foreign currency than do the private interests.

Latin American governments participate in economic development in a variety of ways. Of course, the ministries of public works, agriculture, and the like contribute sizable funds to building transportation facilities and to extending technical assistance and other help to agriculture, and so on. In addition, however, most Latin American governments have established one or more special lending institutions which either invest directly in important aspects of economic development or lend to private interests in the field. These may be called agricultural or industrial banks, or development corporations. The Latin American nations have been pioneers in experimenting with these institutions, and their example has been followed by underdeveloped nations on other continents.

The classical case of this kind of institution is the Chilean Development Corporation. This enterprise, set up in 1939, has not only established many new industries, such as the large Pacific Steel Company, but also has made extensive loans and direct investments in private manufacturing firms. It has likewise invested heavily in government-owned hydroelectric and petroleum firms which have made an essential contribution toward providing Chile with adequate fuel and power resources.

One reason there is need for such government firms has been the relatively inadequate banking systems of most of the Latin American countries. Although all of the countries have one or more private banks—some of them foreign owned—these institutions are generally concerned principally with making short-term loans to commercial enterprises especially in connection with export and import activities. They have had little interest in, and inadequate resources for, investing in long-term development projects, whether in the field of public utilities or of manufacturing. Hence, there has been a need for the government to establish lending institutions which could make this kind of investment.

It is important to emphasize that in most cases participation in the process of economic development has not been motivated by ideological considerations. It is not because they are socialistically inclined that these governments have undertaken extensive development projects, but rather because they felt that only through their participation could rapid growth be achieved.

THE PROBLEM OF FOREIGN INVESTMENT

In theory at least, one possible alternative to government investment in a wide variety of economic-development projects in Latin America might be private investors from the already highly industrialized nations.

During the last century foreign investors played a large role in the expansion of the Latin American economies. The railroads, most of the early public utilities, and the "factory farms" growing sugar and bananas were established by foreign firms or individuals. Most of the principal mining enterprises were also opened up by foreign capital. Banks, commercial houses, and many factories were likewise the result of foreign investment.

There is little doubt that these firms from outside of Latin America have over the years given a big fillip to the area's economic development. However, they present many handicaps from the point of view of the Latin Americans. They have tended to concern themselves principally with exploiting those parts of the Latin American economy which could serve the needs of the highly industrialized nations—mines, plantation agriculture, and the transport and power serving them—rather than being oriented toward developing rounded economies in the Latin American countries.

Furthermore, in the past the foreign firms have not infrequently paid low wages and maintained poor working conditions, though by and large this is not generally true today. They have frequently meddled in local politics, and have been the excuse for countries outside the area (notably the United States) to meddle in the Latin American nations' internal affairs. Sometimes these foreign firms are so large and powerful as to overshadow the Latin American governments—particularly in Central America. Often they have received special privileges not open to nationals and firms of the Latin American nations themselves, privileges which were not resented at the time they were given half a century ago, but which have become galling as the spirit of nationalism has grown.

Finally, there has developed in Latin America a widespread feeling that the basic elements of these nations' economies should be in the hands of their own citizens or governments. As a result, there is general reluctance to permit foreign ownership of public utilities, railroads, steel industries, and in some countries, petroleum fields. Some politicians go further than this and oppose all private foreign investment within their frontiers, a policy which the Castro regime has put into execution in Cuba by expropriating virtually all foreign enterprises.

However, most Latin Americans concerned with this problem feel that the area needs and should welcome some private investment, though they argue that foreign firms should invest under conditions established by the Latin Americans. They should not receive any specially preferred status, they should go into those fields in which the Latin Americans feel that they would be most useful, and they should try to become national in terms of management and even ownership as soon as is practicable.

FOREIGN AID

There are many Latin Americans who prefer borrowing from intergovernmental lending agencies to accepting private foreign investments. They feel that such loans compromise their countries' sovereignty less than do direct investments by foreign firms, which make these firms owners of large amounts of property within their national borders. Also, loans run for a specified period of time, and when they are paid off the Latin American countries' obligations to foreigners are ended—in contrast to the case of foreign direct investments, which go on for an indefinite period of time.

There is no doubt that there is a role for both private foreign investment and the international lending agencies to play in aiding the economic development of Latin America. With regard to the latter, there are fields in which the Latin Americans no longer welcome private foreign investment, and there are also sizable areas to which foreign private firms are not attracted—road construction, irrigation, low-cost housing, school construction—and for which the governments need large amounts of foreign currency. They turn for help in these fields to the Export-Import Bank and Development Loan Fund of the United States, the International Bank for Reconstruction and Development (and its subsidiaries) of the United Nations, and the Inter-American Development Bank of the Organization of American States.

The Latin American countries have also welcomed some help in the form of outright grants which do not have to be paid back, especially in the field of technical assistance. Most of them undoubtedly want more of this kind of help, both in the form of technical assistance and in terms of capital equipment as well. Generally, they greeted with enthusiasm President Kennedy's Alliance for Progress program for help in building up the "skeleton" of their economies, including transport, housing, and education.

The United States has already extended some considerable loan aid to the Latin American nations. Between 1946 and 1958 this amounted to about $2.2 billion. However, most Latin Americans feel that this total is small, when compared with the $17 billion granted to Western Europe under the Marshall Plan.

The Alliance for Progress program of the Kennedy administration, as it was finally worked out at Punta del Este in 1961, was comparable to the Marshall Plan. It promised a minimum of some $20 billion in help to those countries which would undertake to plan their economic expansion and which would carry out or were already carrying out fundamental reforms in the fields of land distribution and taxes. Most of these funds were to come from U.S. government sources and they were to be used not only for projects in industry, transportation, and agriculture, but also in the "social-capital" fields of education, housing, and public health.

The new program was stated by President Kennedy and other top officials of the United States government in terms of a hemisphere-wide effort to deal with problems which were of equal importance to the United States and to the Latin American countries, the raising of standards of living, and the establishment of a firm basis for political democracy in Latin America. The Alliance for Progress was to be carried out through the Inter-American Development Bank under the supervision of the Inter-American Economic and Social Council, and it thus took on a multinational instead of merely binational aspect. Finally, the countries of Western Europe were to be encouraged to contribute to the Alliance as much as possible.

THE RATE OF ECONOMIC DEVELOPMENT

If the Alliance for Progress proves successful, Latin American economic development should proceed at a much more rapid pace in the remainder of the 1960s than it has done in the recent past. Its progress has been quite erratic in the years since 1945.

Immediately after World War II the Latin American economy underwent a rapid expansion. Between 1945 and 1955 the gross national product increase *per capita* was approximately 2.7 per cent, a rate higher than that of any other underdeveloped area in the non-Communist part of the world.[1] The total gross national product of the Latin

---

[1] U. S. Senate Committee on Foreign Relations: *United States and Latin American Policies Affecting Their Economic Relations*, January 1960, p. 15.

American countries experienced a cumulative gain of 38 per cent during the same period. All aspects of the economy grew rapidly: manufacturing increased 45 per cent, transportation and communications 56 per cent, and agriculture 27 per cent. Mexico, Venezuela, Colombia, Brazil, and most of the Central American countries rose more rapidly than the average; while Argentina, Bolivia, Chile, Paraguay, and Uruguay were at the other end of the scale, advancing relatively slowly.

During the 1945–55 period most of the increase in the Latin American economies was made possible by rapid increases in prices of their export products. Their total rose in value at an average rate per year of 5.4 per cent, though volume rose only 2.3 per cent per year. Total proceeds from Latin American exports increased from $4 billion to $8.7 billion between 1945 and 1955.[2]

After 1955 the rate of growth of the Latin American economy slowed down drastically. Between 1956 and 1960 the per capita rate of increase of the total economy was just about 1 per cent. During this same period the value of Latin American exports dropped 10 per cent, giving some indication of the importance which exports have on the total economy of the area.[3] Most experts agree that Latin American exports will increase in value only very slowly during the 1960s. This means that loans and grants from outside sources are likely to have a key role in determining the rapidity with which the economies of the region will expand.

The slowing down of Latin America's rate of development has fostered the growth of a widespread feeling of frustration in much of the area. This frustration is one of the roots of the crisis in inter-American relations which characterizes the beginning of the 1960s.

[2] United Nations, Department of Economic and Social Affairs: *The Latin American Common Market,* 1959, p. 53.

[3] Louis O. Delwart: *The Future of Latin American Exports to the United States,* National Planning Association, 1960.

Labor Problems

As a consequence of the growth of modern mining and plantation agriculture, the development of railroads and other new means of transportation and communication, and above all the establishment of a manufacturing industry, there has come into existence a large wage- and salary-earning class, concentrated mainly in the urban areas. The problems of the relations between these workers and their employers and supervisors have become of first-rate importance. Many aspects of labor problems in Latin America are markedly different from those in the United States. The Latin Americans share with many of the countries of Asia and Africa the difficulties in labor relations which arise from the transformation of their economies into those of a modern industrial society.

DEVELOPING A MODERN LABOR FORCE

These problems are of many kinds. In the first place, rapid economic growth and industrialization have required the formation of an adequate labor force to carry on these new activities. Second, modern industry has brought trade-unionism, collective bargaining, and extensive government intervention in labor-management relations. Finally, these changes have profoundly altered class relationships and have also provided a new dimension in politics, bringing into political activity broad new masses who are more or less well organized in the trade-union movement, which has been a by-product of economic change.

The evolution of an industrial labor force has required the attraction of millions of workers from the exceedingly backward rural areas to the ultramodern cities. However, the techniques of getting the right worker for the right job have not been very highly developed in Latin America as yet. Most industrial workers obtain their jobs by going directly to a factory and seeking work. Employment agencies, whether State-supported or private, are weak and badly organized.[1] Some white-collar workers and a smaller number of industrial workers are recruited by want ads in leading papers in the larger industrial countries of the region, but these are a small minority. Finally, a few unions maintain hiring halls through which employers can obtain more or less well-qualified workers.

The migration of large numbers of untutored agricultural laborers to work in new industries in the urban areas has involved deep-seated cultural clashes. The workers coming from the countryside are unaccustomed to the kind of life they find themselves leading in their new environment. In the rural surroundings in which they have hitherto lived, they have received little or no money income, either growing for themselves virtually all of the goods which they consumed, or receiving most of the things they needed from their employers or landlords.

In the city they find that their money income is exceedingly large when measured in terms of their previous experience. However, they very soon find out that out of this income they have to pay for the food, clothing, and shelter which they formerly did not have to purchase. In addition,

---

[1] An exception to this is Castro's Cuba. It is interesting to note that early in 1960 the Castro regime issued a decree providing that employers could only obtain new workers through the new government employment bureau and workers could only seek new positions through the same office.

they find in the city a large number of new things upon which to spend their money—goods and services with which they were largely or wholly unfamiliar in their rural environment.

As a result, the new industrial workers often find it exceedingly difficult to learn to apportion their income. They frequently find themselves asking their employers for loans or advances on their wages and, in many cases, it takes a generation for them to adapt themselves to their new surroundings in this sense.

In another manner, too, the new industrial workers are unaccustomed to their new environment. Manufacturing plants and other urban enterprises present them with a new type of discipline. In their rural circumstances they may have been much more exploited than in their city occupations and may have existed at a much lower level of living than they do as industrial workers, but they did not have to be on the job eight hours a day for five or five and a half days a week as they are in factories.

This lack of experience with the intensive discipline of the factory system has presented peculiar problems in labor relations. Where large numbers of new industrial workers are employed, the rates of absenteeism and tardiness are exceedingly great. Furthermore, industrial discipline frequently arouses deep-seated discontent on the part of the workers and gives rise to grievances which are rare in the United States and other highly industrialized nations. For instance, the situation frequently arises in which workers demand the dismissal of a foreman or other member of the supervisory force, on grounds that he has "abused" the workers. In some cases perhaps such abuse has in fact taken place; in others it is a matter of fundamental misunderstanding of the meaning and nature of industrial discipline.

Just as these cultural problems present difficulties in labor relations which are virtually unknown in a more advanced industrial nation, so do the limitations of training and experience of the new Latin American industrial workers. Rural Latin America is for the most part exceedingly backward educationally and technologically. Most peasants and agricultural workers are illiterate. Few of them have had any firsthand experience with machinery or the other technological features of modern industrial civilization. As a result, the employers are faced with the serious problem of providing extraordinary amounts of training for these workers. Several national governments have had to establish extensive apprenticeship schools for training young workers who are about to enter industry, as well as to give after-the-job instruction to those who are already employed there.

EMPLOYER PATERNALISM

The newness of the Latin American urban working class leads to another phenomenon which does not exist, at least to the same degree, in the more highly industrialized nations. This is employer paternalism—concern and action on the part of employers for aspects of their workers' personal lives that are not usually their concern in the United States and similar countries.

Another cause of this paternal attitude is the fact that many industrialists, as well as mine and plantation owners, do not have the benefit of services which in the highly industrialized countries are provided by other elements of the community—the State or private entrepreneurs. If public utilities, housing, banking services, education, even stores, are to be supplied at all, they must be provided by the owner of the specific industrial, mining, or agricultural enterprise.

Latin American employers are, for example, frequently called upon to lend money to their workers. Such loans are usually made at times of emergency such as illness or death, or to help the workers finance the acquisition of houses or other property. They are usually paid back by deductions from the workers' future wages. During a year as many as 25 per cent to 30 per cent of all the workers in a large industrial enterprise are likely to receive such loans in plants of some of the more important nations.

Latin American employers also have to provide housing for many of their employees, a service which has proved to be effective in cutting down labor turnover. Sometimes such housing will be given free, in other cases it is rented; in still other instances the employer undertakes to sell houses to his workers. Not infrequently, he endeavors to teach his employees how to live in dwellings which are considerably better than those they have known. This is part of the process of developing a modern industrial working class in these countries.

In many cases the employers also provide educational opportunities for their workers and their workers' children. While this helps tie the workers more closely to their jobs, it also helps to prepare a more capable work force for the employer himself. The employer may provide schools; in other instances he makes scholarships available to already established institutions.

Another important form of employer paternalism is the company store. It is often the complete property of the employer, though sometimes he undertakes to subsidize a workers' cooperative, in which the workers have a voice and a vote. In any case, the company store usually provides goods at cost or below and thus serves as a subsidy to the worker's wage, at the same time helping to teach him how to live within his money income.

Employers also provide extensive medical care for their employees. The social-security systems of most of the countries compel employers to make sizable contributions toward a State medical system available to their workers, but many employers go considerably beyond this and provide additional medical help both for the workers and their families.

Finally, many industrial employers in Latin America

maintain groups of industrial social workers to help with the personal problems of the workers and their families. These people, usually women, help the workers and their wives learn how to live within their incomes, help out with marital difficulties, and function as a kind of home-economics extension agent. Such activities upon the part of employers' representatives would be resented in a more highly industrialized country, but in Latin America they are not regarded as particularly out of the ordinary.

LABOR AND SOCIAL LEGISLATION

The government, too, is markedly paternalistic toward the industrial workers in Latin America. One of the things which surprises people when they first begin to observe Latin American affairs is the fact that most of these countries do have extensive social-security systems. In most cases the principal emphasis of the social-security setup is on the provision of health insurance for urban workers and their families. However, in some countries, such as Brazil, Uruguay, and Argentina, the social-security system also provides old-age insurance for large numbers of workers. The costs of these various kinds of social insurance are usually paid by the workers and the employers, though in some countries the government also makes, or is supposed to make, sizable contributions as well. This cost is very high, in some countries coming to as much as 25 per cent to 30 per cent of the amount of the total wage bill.

Adequate housing is one of the most urgent problems in the rapidly growing cities, and several Latin American governments have undertaken housing programs for low-income and medium-income families—employers, for example, are required by law to build houses for their workers. Government efforts so far, however, have made only a small contribution to the solution of the general problem.

The governments have also shown considerable concern for the working conditions of the urban laborers. There is extensive legislation to force employers to protect machinery so that it will not cause accidents to workers, and to compensate workers who are injured or who acquire certain diseases as a result of their work. Ministries of labor in the various countries have at their disposal groups of inspectors whose job it is to see that employers live up to these demands.

Latin American labor and social legislation has been criticized from a number of angles. There are many observers, for instance, who feel that these laws exist on the books but are not adequately enforced, and therefore have little effective meaning so far as the workers whom they are designed to protect are concerned. The writer, while admitting the inadequate enforcement of this legislation in many instances, feels that it has served to make the working and living conditions of the workers much better than they would otherwise have been. Perhaps the health insurance provided under Latin American social security has been most effective in this regard. It has not only aided many workers who would not have been able to have adequate medical care otherwise, but it has also helped the economic development of these countries by improving the health of the workers and making them more effective on their jobs.

Another serious criticism of Latin American labor and social legislation is on the grounds of its excessive expense. It is argued in Brazil, for instance, that the employer has to spend about two-thirds as much paying contributions to various social-insurance and other funds as he pays out in actual wages to the workers. Those who make this criticism frequently say that it would be much better to give this money directly to the worker to spend as he wishes. However, aside from the fact that there would be no effective guarantee that what is now put aside for social legislation would be given the workers as wages, there is also the fact that many workers do not yet know how to apportion their money income, and few of them, even if they received this extra income, would be able to obtain the benefits which are now available to them because of the social laws.

Another argument concerning Latin American social legislation is more valid, at least in some cases. This is that benefits are often too great to be borne by the relatively weak economies of these countries and that they tend to add a great deal to the cost of the products turned out by the workers who receive the benefits. There are undoubtedly many exaggerated benefits given under Latin American social-security systems, which should be remedied. There is also some question as to whether the cost of this social legislation is not somewhat slowing down Latin American economic growth. However, this consideration is perhaps balanced by the fact that the extensive social laws are helping to avoid some of the worst outrages which accompanied industrialization in a number of the older industrial countries, such as Great Britain and the Soviet Union.

GOVERNMENT CONTROL OVER ORGANIZED LABOR

An important part of Latin American labor legislation is that which governs the functioning of trade-unions and their negotiations with their employers. These matters are closely controlled by the governments of most of the Latin American countries, at least in theory. For more than a quarter of a century, Latin American governments have followed increasingly the dual policy of encouraging the workers to form organizations, and seeking to have those organizations function under strict government control.

The reasons for the interest of the governments in these matters are complex. Many parties and political leaders have undoubtedly felt real sympathy for the situation of the workers and have wanted to help them to help themselves improve it. Others may have been more opportunistic, wishing to win the support of the growing number of urban workers, who have been coming to play an increasingly large part in the political life of these countries. Finally, some politicians have undoubtedly been influenced by the fact that the trend of events throughout the world seems to be leading in the direction of the development of one form or another of trade-union movement.

Governments exercise a wide variety of controls over the organization and functioning of the unions. First of all, in most countries labor organizations need to have the legal recognition of the government in order to function effectively. In order to obtain this recognition they must conform to regulations established by the government in a wide variety of matters, and they run the risk of losing recognition if they do not continue to conform to government dicta.

Most governments specify the jurisdiction which labor organizations may have. For instance, Chilean law provides for virtually only two kinds of unions: one covering the manual workers of a single factory, known as a *sindicato industrial,* and the other consisting of white-collar workers of a single plant, skilled workers of a particular craft, or workers of several small factories each of which is too small to have the required number of workers for a *sindicato industrial.* This second type is known as a *sindicato profesional.* Many countries provide more latitude for the unions than does Chile, allowing the formation of national unions and of legally recognized central labor organizations.

Once a union is legalized, it is subject to extensive controls. The governments generally assert the right to supervise the labor organizations' financial affairs. Unions are generally prohibited from spending their funds on certain things, notably for strike funds to finance conflicts with the employers and for political activities. In addition, the unions in most Latin American countries have to submit their budgets and their accounts of actual expenditures to the Ministry of Labor for approval.

Trade-union elections are also subject to wide government control. They have to be conducted according to certain stated procedures and the governments usually reserve the right to "intervene" in a union which is alleged not to have fulfilled these provisions of the law and to replace the elected officials temporarily with government appointees, whose job it is to organize new elections.

The labor laws of most of the Latin American countries provide for certain standard procedures for collective bargaining between the workers' unions and employers' groups. Several of these nations provide for compulsory government mediation, with the two sides required to appear before conciliation boards a specified number of times. Only after these procedures have been gone through can either a strike or a lockout be legal.

Most countries prohibit strikes by certain kinds of workers. Usually government employees cannot legally strike; a number of countries ban walkouts by public-utility workers; others forbid agricultural workers from striking. A few countries go even further, forbidding legal recognition of unions of government employees or agricultural workers or both.

Although the legal restrictions upon the unions and upon collective bargaining are very strict in most of the Latin American countries, the rigidity of their enforcement varies: frequently the laws controlling the unions are laxly enforced; on other occasions dictatorial regimes have used the legal restrictions virtually to destroy their country's trade-union movements.

Partly as a result of the aid and assistance which they have received from the governments of the area, the trade-unions are larger and have more power than one might normally expect in countries with the relatively limited degree of economic development which characterizes Latin America. Table III shows the estimated membership of the

labor movements of the Latin American countries at the
end of 1960.

TABLE III

TRADE-UNION MEMBERSHIP IN LATIN AMERICA, 1960

Country	Union Membership	Total Population
Argentina	2,500,000	21,000,000
Bolivia	100,000	3,500,000
Brazil	1,000,000	70,000,000
Chile	300,000	7,000,000
Colombia	150,000	14,300,000
Costa Rica	25,000	1,100,000
Cuba	800,000	6,750,000
Dominican Republic	25,000*	3,000,000
Ecuador	75,000	4,300,000
El Salvador	25,000	2,600,000
Guatemala	15,000	3,800,000
Haiti	10,000*	3,464,000
Honduras	25,000	2,000,000
Mexico	1,000,000	35,000,000
Nicaragua	25,000	1,400,000
Panama	15,000	1,000,000
Paraguay	25,000*	1,650,000
Peru	200,000	10,500,000
Uruguay	75,000	2,750,000
Venezuela	250,000	6,000,000

* Really all but nonexistent due to reigning dictatorship.

SOURCE: Official trade-union statistics modified by author's
own evaluation of the situation; general population statistics
from *Collier's Encyclopedia Yearbook, 1961.*

THE HISTORY OF ORGANIZED LABOR

The history of organized labor in Latin America dates
back to the last decades of the nineteenth century. In those
years European immigrants took the lead in organizing

primitive trade-unions in Argentina, Uruguay, Brazil, and Cuba, and the beginnings of trade-unionism also appeared in Mexico and Chile.

From these early years until World War I the leadership of the organized labor movement in Latin America was principally in the hands of anarchists and anarcho-syndicalists. There was a great deal of violence, due in large part to exceedingly bitter opposition of both employers and governments to the first organizing efforts of the workers. General strikes were frequent, and in a number of countries there were cases of large-scale massacres of striking workers.

By the end of the First World War the labor movement had expanded considerably, having profited from the high level of economic activity and the rapid industrialization of the war period. Leadership in the unions had begun to pass from the anarchists to more moderate elements such as the Socialists, and to the Communists.

The attitude of Latin American governments toward the trade-unions had begun to change. The Mexican revolutionary governments of the war period and the 1920s actively encouraged the growth of a labor movement as part of the process of fundamental economic and social change. A similar position was taken by the government of President José Batlle y Ordóñez in Uruguay between 1911 and 1915, and this friendliness toward organized labor became a matter of national policy in that country. In Chile the first statutes providing for legal recognition of unions were passed in 1924.

During the 1930s and the period of the Second World War official authorization of trade-unions became general throughout Latin America, and the labor movement expanded rapidly. The organized workers began to play a very important part in the political life of many of the countries. By the end of World War II the great majority of the organizable workers of Latin America—those in transportation, manufacturing, plantation agriculture, and mining—were in unions.

During the latter half of the 1940s and the first half of the 1950s there was a wave of dictatorial regimes, many of which severely persecuted the labor movement, but when the political trend was reversed after 1955, the labor movement rebuilt its ranks, and was probably more powerful by 1960 than it had ever been before. One exception to this was Cuba, where the installation of the Castro dictatorship not only resulted in the complete regimentation of organized labor by the government, but also the suspension of much of the country's advanced labor legislation.

HEMISPHERIC LABOR GROUPS

From the early years of the organized labor movement in Latin America attempts have been made to bring together the trade-unions of the whole region in a single confederation. Probably the first time this was tried was in 1907, when a conference of anarchist-controlled unions was held in Buenos Aires. No permanent organization seems to have resulted from this meeting.

After World War I the Confederación Regional Obrera Mexicana and the American Federation of Labor sponsored the formation of the Pan-American Federation of Labor, the first successful attempt to establish a hemispheric confederation of workers. It remained active for a decade, but afterward was dormant until it was finally liquidated formally in the early 1940s.

Meanwhile, the Communists and anarchists had both succeeded in establishing Latin American labor confederations. The Confederación Sindical Latino Americana was set up in 1929 to bring together all of the Communist labor organizations of the region. The Asociación Continental Americana de Trabajadores, established in the same year, united the numerous but small anarchist-led groups of Latin America. It still exists, and holds occasional congresses.

In 1938 the Confederación de Trabajadores de México, with the backing of President Lázaro Cárdenas, summoned a congress to meet in Mexico City. It was attended by delegates from most of the important national labor movements of Latin America, and here the Confederación de Trabajadores de America Latina was established. For some years, the CTAL was a united front of labor movements of various political tendencies. However, from 1944 on it was completely dominated by the Communists. In the later 1940s and the 1950s it declined seriously in numbers and influence, all but one of its non-Communist affiliates withdrawing, and it became little more than the general staff of the Communists in the Latin American labor movement.

One of the main causes for the decline of the CTAL was the formation of two successive rivals. Largely through the efforts of the American Federation of Labor and its Latin American representative, Serafino Romualdi, most of the non-Communist national trade-union centers were brought together in January 1948 in the Confederación Inter-Americana de Trabajadores. Three years later, after the formation of the world-wide International Confederation of Free Trade Unions, the CIT was liquidated, its member organizations joining with several which had not belonged to the CIT to form the Organización Regional Inter-Americana de Trabajadores. The ORIT was established as the American regional group of the International Confederation of Free Trade Unions.

Subsequent to the formation of the ORIT, two other Latin American labor confederations were established. The first of these was the Agrupación de Trabajadores Latino Americanos Sindicalizados, set up in 1953 by the unions under the control of the followers of Argentine dictator Juan Perón. The ATLAS became little more than a paper organization after the fall of Perón.

Finally, in 1955 the trade-unions controlled by lay Catholic groups in various parts of the hemisphere were brought together in the Confederación Latino Americana de Sindicalistas Cristianos. This confederation includes not only regularly organized trade-unions, but also Catholic groups functioning within united labor groups. It is the regional organization of the International Federation of Christian Trade Unions.

After the Castro Revolution in Cuba still another attempt to form a Latin American labor confederation was undertaken. At the end of 1959 the Confederación de Trabajadores de Cuba, dominated by the Castro government, issued a call for the formation of a "revolutionary Latin American labor confederation." Although for a while it had the support in this effort from the Confederación de Trabajadores de Venezuela, the CTV withdrew from the attempt after the break between the Democratic Action Party and the Communists in the Venezuelan labor movement late in 1960. Elsewhere, the effort to form a new hemisphere confederation received support principally from the Communist-controlled national labor bodies. By the middle of 1961 it was clear that it had made relatively little headway in mobilizing any significant non-Communist labor group.

CHARACTERISTICS OF THE LATIN AMERICAN LABOR MOVEMENT

Trade-unionism and collective bargaining have certain special characteristics in Latin America which are a reflection of the economic situation of the area and the political conditions under which organized labor has developed there. The trade-unions tend to be financially weak, often lack trained leadership, but are frequently very militant, and are very much influenced by politics. In many countries collective contracts tend to be relatively simple, though in others they are becoming increasingly complicated.

The financial weakness of many of the Latin American labor movements has two basic causes. In the first place, the workers who belong to the unions are for the most part still very badly paid. They cannot afford to contribute very much in dues in many of the countries. Second, Latin American workers are not used to paying dues to their unions or to any other organization. This is one aspect of the problem of learning to live on a money income, but it is also a general cultural characteristic of these countries. In those nations in which the Church does not enjoy the financial support of the government, even it complains of the reluctance of its faithful to pay regularly for its support.

However, this situation is changing. In those countries such as Argentina, Brazil, Chile, Mexico, and Cuba, where the "checkoff," that is, the deduction of union dues from the workers' pay by the employer, who turns them directly over to the union, is general, the labor movement is quite prosperous financially.

In many cases the Latin American labor movements have lacked a sufficiently trained leadership, particularly on a local-union level. In some countries this is a result of the fact that the law limits the number of times a union official can be re-elected, and thus forces continuous turnover in the leadership. In other instances the lack of well-trained leadership is a reflection of the generally poor education and training of the workers.

This situation, too, is changing. Governments have in recent years been relaxing their rules concerning re-election of union officials. At the same time both the trade-union movements and the national governments have become increasingly concerned with the development of a capable union leadership. Most national trade-union centers, and many national and local unions as well, now have labor education programs, the main purpose of which is to train adequate leadership. The Inter-American Regional Organization of Workers (ORIT) has also spent a good deal of time and money in conducting regional labor education seminars. The U.S. government, through its Point Four activities, has also paid some attention to this matter. Finally, several Latin American universities, such as the

University of Chile and the Catholic University of Rio de Janeiro, have entered this field.

Frequently, the Latin American trade-unions are a good deal more "militant" than their brother organizations in the United States and Western Europe. They are much more willing than are the unions in the highly industrialized countries to engage in "solidarity" strikes, partial or general walkouts to support the efforts of a particular union to get a favorable agreement with its employer. Perhaps this is the result of the relative immaturity of the labor movements in some of the countries. It is also undoubtedly due to the much greater feeling of "class consciousness" on the part of the Latin American workers, which is often matched by a similar and equally strong feeling among employers, who sometimes resist labor demands more violently than do their counterparts in North America and Western Europe. Finally, adequate substitutes for militant strike action have so far not evolved in many of the Latin American countries.

POLITICAL NATURE OF LATIN AMERICAN ORGANIZED LABOR

Finally, a high degree of involvement in politics is characteristic of the Latin American labor movements. This involvement arises partly from the financial weakness of many of the unions and their need to look outside their own ranks for financial help. It also arises from the political instability of the area, which makes it necessary for the unions to ally themselves very strongly with a political group that will guarantee the labor movement a minimum of freedom in which to operate and a sympathetic attitude toward their difficulties with the employers.

The political parties, for their part, contribute much to this politicalization of the Latin American labor movements. Many of these parties work very openly within the trade-unions, trying to influence internal union elections, seeking to attract the personal support of leading labor figures. To a very extensive degree, the political parties dominate the trade-unions, rather than the unions being able to make very effective demands on the parties. Not infrequently, labor leaders who are also important in a political party will sacrifice the interests of their unions for those of their parties.

Many kinds of political parties are interested in the trade-unions. The Socialist parties of the area have been working in them since the early years of this century. The Communist parties have also been very active in the labor movement since World War I. In several countries in which the nineteenth-century Liberal parties have adopted a modern program, they have turned their attention to organized labor, as in Colombia and Honduras. The Radical parties of Argentina and Chile have gained some considerable influence among the unions of white-collar workers. The new Christian Democratic parties which have arisen since World War II have had some success in the labor movements of Brazil, Chile, and Venezuela.

Finally, two kinds of indigenous parties have paid particular attention to organized labor. One kind includes the parties of the Jacobin Left, such as Getulio Vargas' Labor Party in Brazil, Juan Domingo Perón's Peronista Party in Argentina, and Fidel Castro's 26th of July Movement in Cuba. The other kind includes the National Revolutionary parties. In Peru the Apristas have dominated the labor movement for a generation, while the Democratic Action Party of Venezuela, the Popular Democratic Party of Puerto Rico, the National Liberation Party of Costa Rica, and the National Revolutionary Movement of Bolivia have controlled organized labor in their respective countries for somewhat shorter periods of time.

The deep involvement of the labor movement in partisan politics has both advantages and disadvantages for the unions. There is no doubt that much of the labor legislation now on the books is due to this, and there is also no doubt that in many crucial labor-management situations the sympathy of a government official of the same party as the union leader has been exceedingly helpful to the union in question.

On the other hand, there are a number of cases of the party to which the principal labor leaders belong falling from power and the union movement falling with it. This has been particularly true when democratic regimes have been overthrown by dictatorships. Also, the labor movement has not infrequently suffered when the interests of a labor leader's union have been deemed by him to be less important than the interest of his party.

However, deep political involvement has probably been inevitable and there are indications that it may be a passing phase in the history of Latin American organized labor. If the area can achieve greater political stability and increased trade-union strength, the day may not be far off when the labor movements will be able to speak to the political parties on a plane of equality rather than of subordination. The unions will be no less interested in political affairs than they now are, but they will be able to think of them much more in terms of their own self-interest, and much less in terms of the interest of one or another political party or government administration.

COLLECTIVE BARGAINING

In most Latin American countries collective bargaining is becoming the rule in transportation, mining, manufacturing, and plantation agriculture. As we have noted, there is a good deal of government intervention in this process, and in Brazil, for instance, government decrees fixing working conditions are still much more prevalent than are collective agreements. Even the latter have to have government approval in order to become valid and binding on all of the parties concerned.

Collective contracts in Latin America frequently concentrate on the problem of wage adjustments and other changes in the worker's money income. In most countries there is little discussion in collective agreements of such problems as seniority systems to regulate promotion and layoffs, controls over hiring and firing, production problems, and the like. One of the basic causes for this has been the extensive inflation throughout much of Latin America since World War II. Preoccupation with keeping the workers' wages abreast of the increases in the cost of living has left little time for attention to nonmonetary problems of seniority, productivity, and so on.

On the workers' side at least, there is relatively little technical preparation for collective bargaining. With some notable exceptions, such as oil-contract negotiations in Venezuela, many labor-management bargaining sessions in Argentina and Mexico, and a few instances in Chile and other countries, a union preparing to go to the bargaining table seldom has the assistance of the economists, industrial engineers, and other technical experts that are commonplace in collective bargaining in the United States and Great Britain, for instance.

Undoubtedly this circumstance contributes to lack of understanding between the parties in Latin American labor relations. Neither side is really very well aware of the bargaining position of the other, and hence many errors of judgment are made, intransigence being expressed where a more flexible attitude might be seen to be justified if each side knew more about the facts of the situation.

The widest diversity in collective agreements is found in the scope of their jurisdiction. There are national industrial accords in the oil industries of Mexico, Venezuela, and many segments of the Argentine economy, but more usual is the plant-wide contract or, at most, an agreement covering only one firm. In Brazil the law requires generally that contracts cover all employers in an industry in a given region, though there are some cases of national ones covering several companies, as in civil aviation.

In cases in which more than one employer is concerned in collective negotiations, there is a wide diversity of type of representative organization. In some cases there will be only the most informal type of consultation among employers. In Chile the author knows of some instances in which a "follow-the-leader" policy is maintained. A major employer first reaches an agreement with the union, after which the rest of the employers accept substantially these same terms after perfunctory negotiation with the union.

Usually, employers' organizations are more formal than this. The labor laws of many of the Latin American countries provide for the legal recognition of employer groups called by the same generic name as the workers' unions, *sindicatos,* which enjoy approximately the same status as the workers' groups. More often than not, the employers do not relish such a State-supervised organization, not liking the State to have anything to say about their groups' elections, finances, or policies. As a result, unless they are forced to do so, employers usually don't make much use of these legalized *sindicatos.* Rather they form "civic associations." These may not have any legal recognition, or may have the same legal status as a club or other organization which becomes incorporated. In any case, they involve very little actual government control over the group's affairs.

As the Latin American countries become more highly industrialized, collective bargaining will become more complicated, as will collective agreements. The trade-unions will continue to play an important role in the economies of these nations, and the nature of their political activity will probably change as the unions achieve greater independence from the political parties. However, it is characteristic of Latin America that, unlike the earlier industrial nations where trade-unions did not develop for several centuries after the beginning of industrialization, both trade-unions and collective bargaining have existed from the beginning of the area's industrial revolution.

Society

The change taking place in Latin America today is as much a social revolution as an economic one. Traditional class and personal relationships are being destroyed, but new ones are not as yet firmly established, with the result that conflicts among individuals, classes, and interest groups are many.

The traditional society of Latin America consisted basically of only two classes. At the top there was the landholding and commercial aristocracy; at the bottom there was the great mass of the rural population, consisting of tenants and agricultural workers. The middle groups in society were very small and had little sense of cohesion or separate identity; many of their members were "poor relations" of members of the upper class.

THE TRADITIONAL RULING GROUP

The small ruling group prided itself on a high degree of European ancestry and on its aristocracy. The latter implied that its members did not engage in any physical labor. The status of this class was determined not only by its ancestry and its wealth, but also by its members' ability to spend all of their relatively large income.

Land was the key to power for the Latin American aristocracy; most of the members of the ruling classes belonged to families which were large landholders. Those who did not belong to the ruling groups but succeeded in gaining prominence and wealth hurried to buy land, thus giving themselves the Latin American equivalent of a patent of nobility.

The concentration of land in the hands of a relatively small number of families had gone far during colonial days. It went even further during the first century of the republics, as the Indian communities in several of the countries were despoiled of their holdings. The aristocracy had not only a monopoly of wealth, but also a monopoly of culture. Its members provided most of the students in the primary and secondary schools as well as in the universities. Its members filled the liberal professions. They were the political leaders, and composed part of the officer class in the armed forces. During the first hundred years of independence the writers, painters, university professors, priests, and other members of the intelligentsia came principally from this class.

The members of the upper class felt much more in common with the wealthy and aristocratic of Europe than they did with their own fellow countrymen. To the degree that their pocketbooks would allow, they visited Europe, becoming almost as famous in Paris and on the Riviera as did the *nouveaux-riches* North American millionaires. They followed the European fashions closely, both in clothes and ideas.

The ruling group also had full control of government, politics, and the administration of justice. The lower classes had little participation in the first two of these, except when they were occasionally called upon to join the armed forces of one side or another in the not infrequent civil wars which the countries of the area suffered during the first century of independence. The lower-class person of Negro or Indian descent had little standing in the courts of law, at least if his opponent was a member of the aristocracy. This fact was of particular importance in the Indian countries, where the courts were often used by the landowners to wrest additional acres from the Indian communities.

Although it was perhaps not an ever-present feeling, there is no doubt that the members of the upper classes lived in fear of an uprising of the lower elements in society. Nothing was more cruelly suppressed than an attempted revolt by the masses in the Indian countries. The Brazilian oligarchy ended the monarchy at least in part because of the temerity of Princess Regent Isabella in signing the decree abolishing slavery in that country.

THE TRADITIONAL MIDDLE
AND LOWER GROUPS

The middle groups in the traditional society of Latin America were small and weak. They included small merchants and landholders; white-collar workers, particularly those in government service; craftsmen, and small industrialists. They were drawn from both the upper and lower classes and felt relatively little identification as a separate group with interests apart from those of the classes from which the individual members had come.

The great mass of the people lived and worked on the land, without owning any of it. They were dependent on those who did own it, working for them with little or no pay, receiving what meager education, medical care, and other services the landlords gave them.

The relationship between the aristocrat and his retainers was patriarchal. He was the "father" of those on his plantation or hacienda, they looked to him for everything they received, and he treated them as children.

The horizons of the masses of the people were very limited. They seldom wandered very many miles from the place where they were born. Their loyalties were to their master, or in the case of some Indian groups, to their communities or their tribes. To many of these people the nation meant little or nothing. A story, perhaps apocryphal, is told of an inquiring foreigner asking an Ecuadorean Indian the name of the president of the republic and receiving the reply: "I don't know. Ask the priest. He knows things like that."

PATRONAGE AND KINSHIP RELATIONSHIPS

Unlike the United States, where virtually every citizen belongs to many organized groups—church organizations, unions, fraternal societies, women's clubs, alumni groups, neighborhood societies, sports associations, political clubs, and scores of other associations—few such groups existed in the traditional patriarchal society of Latin America. Rather, society was held together by a web of informal but powerful links among individuals.

Two types of relationships were of primary importance: those of patronage and those of kinship. There were complex links binding members of the upper and lower classes to one another. The latter sought to gain the patronage of the former for purposes of protection and defense.

One of the most important links was that of *compadre* (literally "co-father"), the relationship arising from baptism. Tenants sought to get their landlords to be godfather to their children, and workers attempted to get the same favor from their employers. The status of godfather created extensive obligations for one who assumed it. Not only could his godchildren turn to him for help and support throughout their lifetimes, but so could all of the members of the godchildren's families. A *compadre* could be asked for money, help in getting a job, protection from governmental authorities, and for almost anything else which the godchild or his family might need.

Even without becoming a *compadre* the employer or landlord was considerably obligated to help his ex-workers or ex-tenants, even when they had moved to other parts of the country. The mere fact of dependency for a longer or shorter period of time created lifetime obligations. Of course, these obligations were reciprocal. The dependent member of the relationship owed loyalty and service to his patron. Sometimes this obligation went to the point of serving in punitive expeditions against neighboring landlords, or service in *ad hoc* armies raised to support the political aspirations or opinions of the landlord.

Equally pervasive were the obligations of kinship. The family was not confined merely to mother, father, and children, but included far-removed aunts, uncles, and cousins. Any member of the family was obliged to aid any other member, once the blood relationship had been established, and each individual in the family had the right to call upon any of his relatives for help if he needed it.

The wide network of relationships established by patronage and kinship meant that the individual was not alone in traditional Latin American society. He had a complicated series of duties and privileges which would seem strange to a contemporary North American, though perhaps not so to his ancestors of a century ago. However, these obligations were very personal, owed by him or to him because of his special position in a family or a patriarchal relationship. He felt little obligation to anyone standing outside of these two relationships. Even charity, which was conducted by the women of the upper classes, was part of the patronage responsibility of members of those classes. One felt little general obligation to the community, or to its members with whom he did not have any ties either by blood or patronage.

RELATIONS BETWEEN THE SEXES

Relationships between the sexes were quite different from those with which most North Americans are familiar today. The women of the upper classes were placed on a figurative pedestal and were jealously guarded, lest their honor be sullied. Unmarried women could not go out of their homes without escorts. Virtually none of them worked for a living. Marriages tended to be arranged in terms of convenience for the family as a whole rather than of the wishes of the two parties most intimately involved.

Among the lower-class groups, however, relations between the sexes tended to be informal insofar as the law was concerned. In countries in which the slave traditions persisted, legal marriage was perhaps the exception rather than the rule. In the Indian countries marriage was sanctified by Indian dignitaries rather than by the Catholic Church or the State. Among people of mestizo or mulatto ancestry legal marriage was probably also considerably less than universal.

However, the women of the lower classes were much more truly their spouses' partners than was the case in the aristocracy. They worked alongside them in the fields and they often contributed significantly to the family coffers as small traders. They did the housework. They had dignities and responsibilities which their better-born sisters probably sometimes envied.

SOCIAL CHANGE

All of these social relationships are in flux in Latin America today. Industrialization has brought about the emergence of important strong middle groups in society. It has also paved the way for the recognition of the lower classes. They are seeking control of the land, rising standards of living, and participation in civic life. Furthermore, the area has been influenced by the ideas of nationalism and democracy which have undermined the moral positions of the old social institutions of the area. However, although the old social patterns are disappearing, it is not yet completely clear what is going to take their place.

THE RISE OF THE MIDDLE GROUPS

The most important change in society during the last few decades has been the evolution of the middle groups. The phrase "middle groups" is preferred to "middle class" by most of those who have studied this problem, because their members generally lack a sense of belonging to a peculiar and recognizable element in society. In no Latin American country has the situation as yet developed as far as in the United States, where the great majority of the population consider themselves part of the middle class.

An important element in the middle group consists of the industrialists, many of whom are immigrants or sons of immigrants. They are the one group in Latin American society which has a "saving instinct," and tends to put its profits back into the business. Although many of its members are well-to-do, their wealth has not automatically given them entree into the upper classes. They are regarded by the old landowning and commercial aristocracy as newcomers, *nouveaux riches*—as "getting their hands dirty," because they are concerned with manufacturing rather than agriculture. Furthermore, the industrialists as a group have economic interests that are in conflict with those of the older aristocracy. They wish to expand the national market for the products of their factories and are likely to favor agrarian reform and other programs designed to provide the agricultural laborers and tenants with money income.

Allied with the industrialists are the merchants engaged in selling their products, as well as the managerial personnel of both industrial and allied commercial enterprises. Together with the industrialists, these groups make up the upper elements of the middle groups.

Another element which forms part of the middle groups consists of the white-collar workers. They regard themselves as being superior to the manual workers because they do not work with their hands, but, like them, they are paid employees. They have a considerable feeling of group solidarity. However, they are now recruited in large part from the lower classes, and have little chance of being accepted as the social equals of even the industrialists, let alone the old aristocrats.

Of major importance within the white-collar group, and virtually constituting a separate element, are the government employees. They have a marked sense of cohesion and are an element strongly committed to economic and social change, which is bringing with it a sizable increase in the government bureaucracy. They constitute a powerful political element in several Latin American countries.

Another new class engendered by the industrialization of the Latin American countries is the urban wage-earning class. The mines, factories, and service facilities of the cities and towns are manned largely by workers drawn from the lower classes. However, they are separated from the agricultural laborers and tenants because they are no longer tied by the same bonds of dependence upon a patriarchal lord. They enjoy to a greater or less degree the benefits of trade-unionism, and have a political power which few groups of agricultural workers or tenants in Latin America can claim.

Some observers regard the urban working class as one of the middle groups. However, the workers have strong interests in conflict with those of other middle elements, particularly their own employers, and although the middle and working-class groups tend to cooperate in struggles against defenders of the old order, they should probably be regarded as two separate elements in contemporary Latin American society.

The middle groups are less influenced by the traditional social customs than either the old aristocracy or the elements of the lower classes. For one thing, they are often of recent foreign ancestry or of mixed racial origin, and do not participate to the same degree as either the aristoc-

racy or the lower classes in the kinship or patronage relationships. Their position in society is an indefinite one,
without the clearly defined obligations and rights which
both upper-class and lower-class Latin Americans have
traditionally possessed. As a result, they are the element
most willing to accept and advocate change in economics
and politics as well as in social relationships.

The middle groups are more "organizationally minded"
than the traditional upper class. It is among them that such
Yankee institutions as the Rotary and Lions are becoming
popular; and it is notable that in Latin America these organizations are much more serious in their outlook and
engage in much less tomfoolery than is the case in the
United States. Also, industrialists, merchants, and other
constituent elements of the middle groups have developed
a complicated network of trade associations and other organizations for the furtherance of their own interests.

THE URBAN WORKERS

The urban wage-earning classes have a closer connection with the traditional pattern of Latin American society
than do the middle groups. The urban workers are usually
recruited from peasants or agricultural laborers who have
recently moved to the cities, and considerations of kinship
remain strong with them. Indeed, it is frequently the case
that a rural worker migrating to the city will take with
him the name and address of some more or less distant
cousin who has moved there before him, and the cousin is
bound to give him room and board until he can get himself
established, as well as to help him find employment.

The new members of the urban working class also seek
to establish in the cities a kind of patronage relationship
that is similar to that in the rural environment from which
they have come. At least in the beginning they tend to
look upon their employers much as they looked upon their
old landlords. They go to them for help with their per-

sonal and family problems, as well as for financial assistance in cases of emergency.

The patronage relationship also has its reflection in contemporary politics in Latin America. In recent years a number of political leaders—notably the late President Getulio Vargas of Brazil, and former President Juan Perón of Argentina—have attempted to picture themselves as a kind of national "patron," giving the workers of the whole nation the same kind of protection and help which they were traditionally accustomed to receiving from their individual employers or landlords. This adaptation of traditional social patterns to the contemporary Latin American scene helps to explain, too, the prevalence of social security and other protective legislation in Latin America. The State has tended to take over from the traditional patron the task of taking care of health needs, emergency financial crises, housing, and retirement of at least the urban manual and white-collar workers.

The longer the worker stays in the cities, however, the weaker becomes the hold of the old social patterns upon him. The son of the man who has migrated to the cities is likely to regard as slightly ridiculous his father's concern for the welfare of distant cousins. At the same time he is likely to regard as positively obnoxious his father's loyalty to his "patron," that is, to his employer. The younger generation of urban workers tends to look for help and protection to new institutions such as the trade-unions and political parties, rather than to the old kinship and patronage institutions.

INCREASE IN SOCIAL MOBILITY

The conflict between traditional social relationships and the forces leading to their destruction has generated a good deal of confusion in Latin American society. It has created social tensions and a feeling among many workers of being "lost" that is potentially very dangerous. We in the

United States are not completely unfamiliar with such a problem, but it is relatively new in Latin America.

These changes have added greatly to social mobility in Latin America. In the traditional society there was little or no chance for a rural tenant or worker to move into the landowning upper classes. Virtually the only institutions through which a person of relatively humble origins could move up in the social hierarchy were the army and the Church. Admission to the officer class and priesthood was open to people coming from the lower class, and it was possible for such a person to rise to the higher ranks of these institutions (particularly the armed forces, the higher-ranking clergy being drawn principally from the aristocracy or from Europe) as a result of hard work, luck, and a certain degree of unscrupulousness. Generals and bishops were more or less automatically members of the upper classes, and the general's children could frequently marry into the old aristocratic families.

This situation has now altered. The social hierarchy is much more complex. Although it is still exceedingly difficult for someone of the lowest ranks of society to rise into the highest levels, it is not so hard for someone to move up one or two ranks in society. An agricultural tenant can become an urban industrial worker; an industrial worker can move into the white-collar class, and so on.

Social changes in Latin America provide at least part of the explanation for the intensity of nationalistic feeling in the area. The horizons of millions of middle- and lower-class citizens have been broadened. They have lost the protection of the traditional patron and the membership in a tight-knit local group. As they have lost their faith in the traditional institutions, members of the middle-class and urban working-class groups have placed their loyalty and hopes for protection in the nation, which has suddenly become the institution in society which seems to them to have most reality. It has offered them a substitute for the protection which they no longer receive from traditional institutions.

SHIFTS IN POWER RELATIONSHIPS

The diversification of the social structure reflects the shift in power within Latin American society. Few Latin American nations are any longer completely dominated by the old aristocracy or its representatives. While in most countries the agricultural landlord is still exceedingly powerful in the rural areas, power in the nations as a whole has generally shifted to the urban areas, and is shared by the middle groups and urban workers. However, this process of shifting power is by no means complete. As we indicate elsewhere in this volume, the power of the rural aristocracy to prevent redistribution of its landholdings and even to avoid all but nominal taxation is a serious handicap to the economic growth of many of the Latin American countries.

The vacuum left by the disappearance of traditional social institutions is reflected on the local level of government. Local administration has traditionally been a tool of the strongest local landowner. There was little popular participation in its decisions or its activities; indeed, it seldom entered the minds of the members of the provincial lower classes that they could participate in the process of government, local or national.

Even though local administration has become more sensitive to the wishes of the majority of the populace, it has not yet taken on the extensive role which it has in most European countries and in the United States. The local officials, instead of seeking to mobilize the energies and imagination of the local populace, have tended, in a traditional manner, to look to the national "patron," the national government, for the resolution of all their problems.

Latin American political leaders are becoming increasingly aware of this problem. Recently, President Rómulo

Betancourt of Venezuela, in addressing the Second National Congress of Municipalities, exhorted his listeners as follows:

> The President is convinced that the problems of the country are so varied and complex, and the Nation has such a vast geographical area and such a dispersed population, that administrative decentralization is essential. This process need not clash with the necessary planning on a national scale. . . . The Four Year Plan which we are carrying out is not incompatible with, but rather coincides with, municipal autonomy and with effective steps toward local self-government.

CHANGES IN STATUS OF WOMEN

The traditional position of women has been going through a fundamental change as part of the general social transformation which Latin America is now experiencing. Hundreds of thousands of women in the middle groups are now working as white-collar workers. Other hundreds of thousands from the lower-class groups have joined their husbands and brothers in tending machines in the area's factory industries. Ever larger numbers of women of all classes are getting a formal education, many of them even going to the university. As a result, women are also becoming an element of some importance in the professions. They first got a foothold in primary- and secondary-school teaching, but are now to be found among the lawyers, doctors, and other liberal professions.

The life of those women who have not gone to work outside of their homes has also been undergoing a change. In increasing numbers they are forming women's clubs and other similar organizations, which are taking a growing role in civic affairs. They have also gone into politics. Only Paraguay does not give them the right to vote—and it is perhaps significant that that right is all but meaningless in Paraguay. Members of the fairer sex are found in increasing numbers in city councils, state or provincial legislatures, national congresses, and even in cabinets. At least one woman, Eva Perón, has aspired to the highest office in the State. They are active in the area's political parties at all levels, sometimes in organizations parallel to those of men, but increasingly within the same party groups.

The relations between the sexes are changing with this alteration of the status of women. They are no longer regarded by the law as their fathers' or husbands' chattels. In virtually all of the countries women can and do hold property in their own name. Their equality with men before the law is becoming generally recognized.

Custom has changed somewhat more slowly than the law. However, since World War II the tradition that an unmarried woman of "quality" may not venture from her father's house without a chaperon has been disappearing in one country after another. Marriage is increasingly a matter to be settled between the young man and young woman involved, rather than by their parents. Divorce is becoming more frequent.

SUMMARY

Thus, Latin American social institutions are changing rapidly and drastically. The traditional institutions of patronage and kinship have been seriously undermined, and new forms of relationship among individuals are developing. However, this process is as yet far from complete, a fact which goes far toward explaining the instability of Latin American society at the present time.

Government

The Latin Americans had little experience with self-government before they achieved their independence from the Old World. There were no local legislatures comparable to those in the thirteen British colonies in North America. Government laws, rules, and regulations came from above, from the courts of Madrid, Lisbon, and Paris, or from the viceroys and other officials appointed by the kings. The top officials of the government hierarchy were generally Europeans, sent to America for the specific purpose of governing the American colonies.

The only approach to self-government which existed during the colonial period was on the municipal level, and even that tradition was a weak one. Occasionally, *cabildos* or town meetings of leading citizens were called to deal with specific problems, and it was these which generally took the lead in the move toward independence. On another plane, numerous Indian communities remained more or less free to run their own affairs.

POLITICAL PHILOSOPHY OF INDEPENDENCE LEADERS

The fathers of Latin American independence were followers of the French, British, and United States philosophers of political democracy. Many of them were inspired by the French Revolution and by writers such as Montesquieu and Rousseau, who were the forerunners of this great convulsion. Others were students of Hobbes, Locke, and other British thinkers and were admirers of the British form of constitutional monarchy. Almost all the principal Latin American independence leaders were acquainted with the ideas of Benjamin Franklin, Thomas Jefferson, and George Washington, and with the U. S. Declaration of Independence and Constitution.

In the light of their own lack of experience with self-government and their acquaintance with European and North American political thinkers, it was perhaps natural that they would turn to French, British, and U.S. models when they came to write constitutions for their new governments. For almost a century, the legal framework of most of the Latin American regimes was copied from one or the other of these models.

Many of the constitutions contained "declarations of the rights of men" more or less copied after the French revolutionary document of that name. Virtually all of them drew the clear distinctions among the three branches of government—executive, legislative, and judicial—advocated by the French philosophers and enshrined in the U. S. Constitution. Some of the Latin American constitutions, notably the Argentine one of 1853 (which is still in force, though it has been drastically modified), even borrow phraseology and form from the U.S. document of 1789.

One of the Latin American countries followed the British model for more than half a century. This was Brazil which, during the Empire that lasted from 1822 until 1889, enjoyed a domestic peace and tranquillity unmatched elsewhere in the area, under a constitutional monarchy much like that of Britain before the Reform of 1832.

Virtually all of the constitutions of Latin America since independence have been democratic in form. However, until recent decades the democratic content of the constitutions tended to remain an aspiration of the people who wrote them rather than a faithful reflection of the way in which government was actually conducted.

CONSTITUTIONAL STABILITY AND INSTABILITY

With a few outstanding exceptions the Latin American countries during their first century or so of independence tended to swing violently from dictatorship to short-lived periods of freedom (sometimes bordering on anarchy), and back to dictatorship again. In virtually all of these nations, politics and government remained the monopoly of a small aristocratic ruling class.

In only a few cases were there long periods of relative stability and firm constitutional government. Chile had the same constitution from 1833 until 1924. Until 1890 the country was governed by a strong president; thereafter, without any change in the constitution, a parliamentary regime was substituted, under which congress repeatedly and almost capriciously overthrew the cabinet of the day.

Another example of governmental stability was Argentina. After the overthrow of the dictatorship of Juan Manuel de Rosas and the writing of the constitution of 1853, the country enjoyed a long period when there were few attempts at armed insurrection against the regime, virtually none of which was successful. The 1853 constitution even served as the vehicle for the transfer of political control of the nation from the rural aristocracy to the middle class in the election of 1916. The "constitutional rhythm" was broken only by the military-conservative revolution of September 6, 1930.

Four other countries had long periods with the same constitution, though in these cases, constitutional stability did not mean governmental stability. Quite the contrary. Uruguay, which had the same constitution from 1830 until 1919; Costa Rica, with the same one from 1871 until 1940; Colombia, with a constitution lasting from 1886 until the present; and Mexico, which had the same basic document from 1857 until 1917, were the scene of frequent turbulence and dictatorships during their long periods of apparent constitutional stability.

Most of the countries were much less lucky with their constitutions. Some changed them with extreme frequency. For instance, Ecuador and Peru have had seventeen constitutions, the Dominican Republic has had twenty-three, Venezuela twenty-four, and Bolivia fourteen. Table IV shows the vagaries of constitutional development in all of the twenty Latin American republics.

TABLE IV

DATES OF LATIN AMERICAN CONSTITUTIONS

Country	Dates (Parentheses indicate amendments)
Argentina ...	1819, 1826, 1851, 1853 (1860, 1866, 1880, 1898), 1949 (1853 constitution restored 1957)
Bolivia	1826, 1831, 1834, 1839 (two), 1843, 1851, 1861, 1880, 1931, 1937, 1938, 1945, 1947 (1961)
Brazil	1824, 1832, 1834, 1891, 1934, 1937, 1946
Chile	1811, 1812, 1814, 1818, 1822, 1823, 1826, 1828, 1833, 1925
Colombia ...	1811 (two), 1819, 1821, 1830, 1831, 1843, 1853, 1858, 1863, 1886
Costa Rica ..	1825, 1839, 1844, 1847, 1848, 1859, 1869, 1871, 1949
Cuba	1901 (1928, 1934, 1935), 1940 (suspended 1959)
Dominican Republic ..	1821, 1844, 1858, 1866, 1868, 1872, 1874, 1875, 1877, 1878, 1879, 1880, 1881, 1887, 1896, 1907, 1908, 1924, 1927, 1934, 1942, 1947 (various amendments), 1962
Ecuador	1812, 1821, 1839, 1843, 1845, 1851, 1852, 1861, 1869, 1878, 1884, 1897, 1906, 1929, 1945, 1946

Country	*Dates* (Parentheses indicate amendments)
El Salvador ..	1824, 1841, 1864, 1871, 1872, 1880, 1883, 1886, 1939, 1950, 1962
Guatemala ..	1824, 1851, 1879, 1945, 1954
Haiti	1807, 1811, 1820, 1843, 1849, 1859, 1860, 1867, 1874, 1879, 1889, 1918, 1929, 1932, 1935, 1939, 1944, 1946
Honduras ...	1825, 1839, 1848, 1865, 1873, 1880, 1894, 1904, 1908, 1924, 1936, 1957
Mexico	1814, 1824, 1835, 1841, 1843 (1844), 1857, 1917
Nicaragua ..	1825, 1838, 1848, 1854, 1858, 1893, 1898, 1905, 1911, 1913, 1939, 1951
Panama	1904, 1940, 1946
Paraguay ...	1813, 1844, 1870, 1940
Peru	1823, 1826, 1827, 1834, 1839, 1855, 1860, 1867, 1879, 1880, 1920, 1933
Uruguay	1830, 1919, 1934 (1942, 1952)
Venezuela ...	1811, 1819, 1821, 1830, 1857, 1858, 1864, 1874, 1881, 1891, 1893, 1901, 1904, 1909, 1914, 1922, 1925, 1928, 1929, 1931, 1936, 1947, 1953, 1961

SOURCE: Adapted from William Pierson and Federico Gil: *Governments of Latin America* (New York: McGraw-Hill, 1957), p. 161.

In recent years, the Latin American countries have been less prone to copy foreign models for their constitutions. They have adopted documents more appropriate to the realities of their own situation and have even introduced some innovations which have actually been copied in other parts of the world, particularly in the other economically underdeveloped nations. There is a great deal of variety in the constitutions and governments of the twenty Latin American countries, but certain generalizations can be made about them.

One general characteristic of the form of government in Latin America is that it is democratic, at least on paper.

Though most of the constitutions contain provisions which make it possible for a president to negate the democratic structure if he wants to do so, no constitution in Latin America today is avowedly dictatorial. Basically, this is a tribute to the aspirations of the Latin American people.

CENTRALISM VS. FEDERAL SYSTEM

Latin American governments are generally centralized. It has not always been so. One of the important struggles of the nineteenth century in a number of countries centered around the issue of whether or not these nations should have a federal form of regime. The vast size of these countries, their relatively small populations, and the difficulties of transportation from one part to another caused by towering mountains, tropical jungles, and vast river systems fostered a feeling of separatism in sections of these republics. As a result, federalism had a great attraction.

Even today two of the republics are officially known as the United States of Brazil and the United States of Mexico. Until a decade ago a third was officially labeled the United States of Venezuela, but in 1952 was rechristened Republic of Venezuela. A modified form of federalism persists today only in these three nations and Argentina and Colombia.

The improvement of transportation and communications facilities, the growth of a spirit of popular nationalism, and the failure of provincial governmental units to develop sufficient financial resources for their own needs, have strengthened the tendency toward a unitary form of government. Today, in most of the Latin American nations, the states or provinces are mere administrative subdivisions of the central government. Their top administrative officials are appointed by the president of the republic and they have no separate legislatures or judiciary systems. Their budgets are provided by the central government; the provinces have little or no taxing power.

Even in those countries which still formally possess the federal system of government, the importance of the central administration is overwhelming. The national governments have appropriated for themselves all of the most lucrative tax sources, leaving the provinces or states with an inadequate financial basis for maintaining real political autonomy. The states or provinces are constantly turning to the central government for additional funds. For instance, during 1960 the federal government of Venezuela provided in special grants to the states over $60,000,000, in addition to the regular federal budget which in any case supplied most of the revenues for the states.

The federal governments have also tended increasingly to absorb administrative functions as well as financial resources. Thus, in Mexico during the last few decades the all-important questions of labor and agrarian-reform policies have been transferred from the states to the central administration. The principal functions of the states are in the fields of education, public health, and local public works. Even in these areas of government the federal administrations share jurisdiction and their activities generally overshadow those of the state regimes.

In all of the federal systems, too, the central government has the power to dissolve the administrations of the provinces or states. In the cases of Venezuela and Colombia, the governors of the states are named by the president of the republic in the first place. In Argentina, Brazil, and Mexico, where the governors are elected, the federal administration can remove the governors, dissolve the legislatures, and appoint "interventors" to run the states until new elections can be called. Although the constitutions would seem to limit the right of the central government to act in this way, the tradition, particularly in Argentina and Mexico, has been for them to "intervene" in the states with considerable frequency.

THE POWERS OF STATE AND MUNICIPAL GOVERNMENTS

The powers of the states remain strongest in Brazil, Argentina, and Mexico. There have been no "interventions" in the states by the federal government in Brazil since the re-establishment of constitutional government (after the Vargas dictatorship) in 1946; and since that time several of the state administrations—particularly in São Paulo, Minas Gerais, and Rio Grande do Sul—have shown a considerable degree of autonomy and initiative, particularly in the field of economic development and agrarian policy.

In Argentina provincial autonomy became almost meaningless under Perón. Subsequent to the restoration of a constitutional regime in 1958, an attempt was made to re-establish provincial autonomy. However, in the middle of 1962 most of the provinces were "intervened," were being run by people appointed by the federal regime.

In Mexico the states are notoriously weak from a financial point of view. However, within their financial limitations the states have been largely left alone in recent decades. Only infrequently has the federal regime stepped in to oust a state administration. The states have done some worthwhile work in local public works and educational programs.

Along with weak state and provincial governments have gone weak municipal regimes in most of the Latin American countries. This has been the result partly of the fact that the tradition of virile and independent municipal government was destroyed in early modern Spain and therefore was never transplanted to the Spanish colonies in the New World—in sharp contrast to the situation in England and its colonies. In part, too, it is due to the fact that the municipalities, like the states and provinces, have never been given adequate revenues to conduct their affairs.

An added factor has been the excessively large role played by the national capital among the cities of most Latin American countries. Usually the capital city has been the only really important municipality in the country. Even when there were other relatively large urban centers, it has been true that it was the capital city which was most likely to make and unmake national governments. As a result, the national regimes have had a particular interest in keeping as much control as possible over the municipal government of the capital.

The upshot of this has been that in many cases the chief executives of capital cities have not been elected, but rather appointed by the national administration. In some instances, as at various times in Buenos Aires, the capital has not even been able to elect a municipal council. Most of the public works, educational activities, and other elements of civic administration have been undertaken by the national government, conscious as it was of the importance in foreign eyes of what went on in the seat of government.

STRONG PRESIDENTS

Another general characteristic of the governments of Latin America is that they have strong presidents. Although at one time or another several of the countries have experimented with the parliamentary form of government, in which the cabinet is chosen from and responsible to parliament or congress, no nation in the area really has such a system today and only a few keep even a semblance of it. In Chile, while it is still possible for congress to oust a member of the cabinet, this is very difficult and is seldom done. In Cuba the 1940 constitution provided for a prime minister who presumably had at least some responsibility to parliament; but until 1959 he was really chosen by the president and stayed in office at the pleasure of the president. (Of course, the revolutionary regime of Fidel Castro has raised the prime ministership to the post of major responsibility and authority and at the same time has abolished the congress.)

The powers of the Latin American presidents are very extensive. They are elected separately from, and are independent of, the congress in all Latin American countries. They appoint all top civilian and military officials, and although in some cases the approval of one or both houses of congress is required, such approval is rarely withheld.

The president is chief of the armed forces in all cases except Guatemala, where the military head is elected annually by congress. Although the military usually has a wide degree of autonomy, it is also true that so long as a president retains the loyalty of the army, navy, and air force, he has a virtual monopoly of force at his command. Most countries have a national police force of greater or less strength, also at the command of the president.

The president often has wide financial powers as well. If congress does not approve the annual budget in time, he is constitutionally authorized to get around this problem in a variety of ways. Most frequently, he is allowed to continue the previous year's budget in force, going to congress for any specific supplemental appropriations he may desire. As a result of this arrangement, Cuba went without an official, congressionally approved budget for almost two decades, in the 1930s and 1940s.

In most countries, too, the president has, under normal circumstances, wide powers to legislate by decree. Professors Pierson and Gil comment as follows on these presidential powers:[1]

> . . . Generally speaking, a considerable part of the laws is enacted in Latin America by presidential decree rather than by the normal legislative process. There is a difference in both theory and practice among the countries as to legislation by presidential decree, how-

[1] William W. Pierson and Federico G. Gil: *Governments of Latin America* (New York: McGraw-Hill, 1957), pp. 210–11.

ever similar the results may be. . . . Thus some constitutions have given formal recognition to the decree laws; practice and custom have in some countries given a sanction to them not only for emergencies and for *de facto* governments, but for such decrees in times of peace; likewise, some courts by upholding or by invalidating them have definitely recognized them as possible sources of law.

Even if there is a requirement of subsequent approval by the legislative branch, the executive in the countries affected has become a sharer in legislative power. When this restriction is not in effect, the legislative capacity of the executive is indisputable, and the president becomes the principal lawmaker.

SUSPENSION OF CONSTITUTIONAL GUARANTEES

The powers of the president to govern by decree apply to normal times. Even more extensive are the powers granted the chief executive by all Latin American constitutions to suspend parts of the constitution in case of national emergencies of one kind or another. This power is one of the strongest weapons in the hands of an ambitious president, although in some of the countries it is circumscribed by elaborate precautions, designed to prevent its abuse. In some instances "constitutional guarantees" can only be suspended by a vote of congress, in others any decrees or orders issued by the president during the suspension of guarantees must be approved within a given period of time by the congress or they cease to be valid. In some cases the suspension of guarantees can only be for a strictly limited amount of time.

The exact additional powers that the president receives by suspension of parts of the constitution vary from country to country, depending upon the individual constitution. However, he is generally empowered to suspend or abridge the individual freedoms, such as those of free press, assembly, and speech. The president is frequently given the authority to arrest people without warrants and to suspend the right of habeas corpus. Sometimes he receives even more extensive powers.

There is no doubt that these powers are frequently abused in Latin America. They are sometimes used to throttle opponents guilty of little more than becoming influential. They are sometimes maintained in effect for exaggeratedly long periods of time. For instance, Argentina lived under a limited suspension of guarantees during all but a few weeks of the period between December 1941 and May 1958.

On the other hand, it may be admitted that on some occasions, when the opposition to a legitimately constituted democratic regime has refused to confine its activities to normal democratic channels, the suspension of guarantees has actually served to strengthen the position of democracy. Thus, the constitutional regime of President Rómulo Betancourt of Venezuela suspended guarantees for short periods of time on several occasions, when faced with attempted military coups on the one hand, and well-organized street riots by Communist-inclined elements on the other.

In addition to powers granted to the chief executive by the constitutions of Latin America, the presidents frequently have further power coming to them from sources not dealt with in the constitutions. Frequently they are the leaders of dominant political parties. This is notably true in countries which are undergoing fundamental revolutions, such as Mexico, Bolivia since 1952, and Venezuela since 1959. It has also been true in a number of other countries.

The most outstanding example of extragovernmental powers of the president is Mexico. The Partido Revolucionario Institucional under one name or another has been the government party since 1928. The president's position as head of the party is almost as important in terms of power as his post as head of the government.

DE FACTO GOVERNMENTS

Peculiar problems are presented by de facto governments in Latin America. Political instability in the area has frequently led to a situation in which a constituted regime is overthrown by force and some kind of provisional government takes its place. Obviously, the coming to power of such a de facto regime is itself an unconstitutional act, and hence the constitutional restraints on it are dubious.

This problem presents one of the paradoxes of the governmental system of Latin America. Very frequently, in spite of their own unconstitutional manner of achieving power, many de facto regimes attempt to keep their actions within the bounds of the constitution, and most of them cite the constitution more or less frequently in defense of their actions.

De facto regimes almost always concentrate both executive and legislative powers in their own hands. They usually dissolve the legislature and govern by decree until the re-establishment of constitutional government. Sometimes the constitution makes some provision for such a situation by insisting that once an elected congress is re-established, it must approve all the decree laws issued by the provisional government or they cease to be valid. Such is the case in Argentina.

ATTEMPTS TO LIMIT PRESIDENTIAL POWER

The problem of too great concentration of power in the hands of the president has preoccupied political thinkers and democratic political leaders of Latin America since the days of independence. Many solutions to the problem have been offered. A parliamentary system, in which parliament or congress and not the president is supreme, was one of these. However, as we have seen, it has not worked out in practice, and has been largely abandoned.

Another approach to the problem has been the plural presidency, which has been experimented with in Uruguay. José Batlle y Ordóñez, who was twice president of that republic (1903–7 and 1911–15), proposed during his second period in office that his country experiment with this system, which he had seen successfully applied in Switzerland.

Batlle's proposal was that a nine-man executive council be established to replace the president. Two-thirds of its members were to be chosen from the majority party, one-third from the largest opposition group, and the titular position of head of the state should rotate among the six majority members, each man serving a year.

Batlle fought hard for his proposal, and was only half successful. In 1919 a new constitution provided for the executive council, but maintained the president as well. The various functions of government were divided between council and president, with the key powers being retained by the latter. This system worked reasonably well for a decade and a half, but was a victim of the Great Depression, being abolished in a *coup d'état* by President Gabriel Terra in 1933.

In 1946 Batlle's proposal was revived, this time more or less in its original form. A constitutional amendment approved that year provided for it, and it began operating fully at the end of 1950. For the first eight years, the majority of the council was composed of members of Batlle's own party, the Partido Colorado, but in 1958 control passed to the opposition Partido Nacional. In spite of agitation by some Nacionalistas for the abolition of the plural executive, no move in this direction had been taken by 1961.

THE ROLE OF THE LEGISLATURE

Another characteristic of Latin American government is the relative weakness of the legislative branch, a situation that is virtually a corollary of the strong executive. In some nations the preponderant position of the president is written into the constitution. He is empowered to introduce legislation. He is sometimes permitted to declare certain bills "emergency" measures, thus forcing congress to consider them immediately, and in most cases virtually assuring their passage. Of course, in dictatorial regimes congress possesses no independence whatsoever.

Only in a few countries does the legislature traditionally have great influence. The Chilean president traditionally must negotiate with his congress, instead of being able to dictate to it. The Brazilian congress since 1946 has been notoriously slow in passing legislation a majority of its members didn't like, regardless of the point of view of the president. The Uruguayan congress also has marked independence, though party discipline tends to be strong, so the executive always has a core of strong support in both houses.

In most other countries of the area the president ordinarily holds the whip hand over congress. Usually the constitution provides for only relatively short sessions of congress each year, and allows the president to govern by decree when congress is not in session. Furthermore, most members of congress largely owe their positions to the president, even in regimes which cannot properly be called dictatorships. This is notoriously true in Mexico. In such a situation the congressmen do not tend to bite the hand that sees to it that they are fed.

Even when the president doesn't tend to hand-pick members of congress, there are cases, such as the situation in Venezuela after the re-establishment of constitutional government in February 1959, in which congress consists of well-disciplined party factions. In such a situation, where the president's party has control of congress, he will seldom be seriously challenged by the senators and deputies, although more or less serious amendments may sometimes be made in legislation proposed by the president.

Of course, in all but the dictatorial countries, the congress does serve one very useful purpose. It is a forum of discussion and debate. Even though the legislative body of a Latin American country may not basically alter a proposal of the president, in the process of passing the executive's proposals, members will have a chance to criticize the measures proposed, as well as the general policies of the government.

THE STATUS OF THE COURTS

Latin American courts are even weaker than the legislative branches of government. They seldom dare to challenge arbitrary actions of Latin American governments, and when they do so, the presidents frequently resort to "court packing," or other measures, to bring them into line. Even some of the highest courts of the Latin American countries are not above intimidation or the taint of corruption.

There are notable exceptions: Argentine courts before Perón and those of Cuba before Castro were noted for their honesty and their occasional flashes of courage in the face of arbitrary acts of the executive part of the government. The Chilean courts have a high reputation inside and outside of their country, as do those of Uruguay, and in both cases they constitute an important part of the government. The same or similar things could be said about the judiciary in a few of the other nations.

CONSTITUTIONAL INNOVATIONS

In some ways the Latin American countries have experimented with innovations in government and public administration. We have already noted the Uruguayan experience with the plural presidency. There have been other instances. In a few of the countries there has been experimentation with a fourth branch of government, in addition to the customary executive, legislative, and judiciary. Colombia, for instance, has for decades had a council of state, the main purpose of which is to be a watchdog of the constitution. Other countries have experimented with an accounting tribunal (*tribunal de cuentas*), as a check on the general (and particularly the financial) behavior of members of the other branches of government.

However, the most important Latin American governmental innovation has been the writing of extensive social and labor legislation into the constitution. This was first done by the members of the Mexican convention which wrote the constitution of 1917. They included in that document long articles outlining the principles of agrarian reform and instructing future regular congresses to pass legislation along these lines. They also included a similar article outlining in detail what was to be included in a labor code, which congress was also instructed to enact.

The pioneering nature of the Mexican constitution of 1917 can be understood when one remembers the situation which prevailed in some of the world's major countries at that time. The Mexican constitution was signed a month before the March Revolution in Russia, which overthrew the tsar. At that time the United States had very little labor legislation, virtually none of it on the federal level, and enacted a social-security system only two decades later. Even Great Britain did not yet have a full social-security system.

Most of the other Latin American countries have followed Mexico's lead. Virtually all new constitutions written during the last two or three decades have included a long catalogue of social and labor legislation as a key section. So have a number of the new countries of Africa and Asia in writing their first constitutions. Even the new constitutions of some of the older countries—such as postwar France—have also followed this pattern. All of this is not to indicate that many of these countries have necessarily been aware that they were following the example of Mexico and other Latin American nations—but merely to show that they have been doing so.

Another innovation which has been experimented with in several of the Latin American countries has been the inclusion in congress of representatives selected on the basis of the functional group with which they are associated rather than from a geographical constituency. The Brazilian constitution of 1934 included such functional representatives of workers, employers, and other elements in the chamber of deputies. All the Ecuadorean constitutions since the middle 1930s have included senators representing workers, employers, journalists, and other specific groups. In Argentina under Perón two provinces adopted constitutions which provided that half of their single-house legislatures should consist of such functional representatives.

ELECTORAL PROCEDURES

The Latin Americans have also experimented with a number of innovations in electoral procedures. In most of these countries one votes for a party list rather than for individual candidates. In several nations devices have been worked out to give the franchise to illiterates. Perhaps the case of Venezuela is typical in this regard. There, each party is given a color and the voter is harangued to support the "whites" (Democratic Action Party), the "greens" (Christian Socials), the "browns" (Democratic Republican Union), or the "reds" (Communists).

Uruguay and Chile have had particularly notable electoral laws. In the former, where there are two traditional parties, the Colorados and the Blancos, the law permits the organization of an unlimited number of legally recognized factions within these two parties. At election time each faction can run its own candidates, but when the votes are counted, those cast for all of the rival Colorado and Blanco tickets are first calculated. If the various Colorado rivals receive more votes than do all of the Blanco contenders, the Colorados are declared to have been victorious. However, which candidate actually wins depends on which of the Colorado nominees has the largest number of votes. Thus, if there are enough Colorado candidates, one of them can win an election with fewer votes than the leading Blanco nominee. (Of course, the same situation may favor the Blancos as well as the Colorados.)

In Chile, where there are a score of legal parties, the electoral law permits coalitions among them. Thus, in most elections there will only be half a dozen lists of candidates for any particular office. The law provides that each list will elect the number of candidates in proportion to its percentage of the total votes cast for the office involved.

To determine which specific candidates are elected, the votes cast for all those on each list are counted, and each coalition receives the number of posts justified by its proportion of the total vote. Those nominees at the head of each list are declared elected. This sometimes creates peculiar situations in which the first man on a coalition list may be elected though he got only a few hundred votes, while a nominee far down on the list may receive thousands of votes but fails of election because of his position on the ticket.

DICTATORSHIP

Up to now we have been speaking of what might be called the formal structure of government in the Latin American countries. For instance, in our discussions of the relative strength of the executive, legislative, and judicial powers we were in fact discussing the circumstances as provided by the written constitutions and under circumstances in which dictatorship does not exist.

However, there also exists an informal government typified by the prevalence of dictatorship in a number of these countries, regardless of what the constitutions may say.

All of the Latin American republics have suffered from

dictatorship sometime during the twentieth century. Some of the countries have had dictatorial regimes during virtually all of this period, in others such tyrannies have been the exception. Since World War I, alternating waves of dictatorship and democracy have tended to sweep over much of the Latin American area.

Dictatorship in Latin America has many causes. Certainly one of these has been, historically, the vast social and economic gaps which have existed between the upper and lower classes and the fears of the upper groups of popular revolt. As the social hierarchy becomes more complex, this root of dictatorship is being destroyed. Another factor has undoubtedly been the marked influence of the military in Latin American political affairs, which we discuss elsewhere in this book. So has the great importance which personalism had in politics for the first century or more of Latin American independence, and the consequent weakness of political parties in terms of ideology and organization. Finally, the tradition of dictatorship is itself a strong factor leading to its continuation.

Dictatorships have been brought about and maintained through various devices. In some cases dictatorial regimes make ample use and abuse of constitutional provisions for government by presidential decree, or by the frequent suspension of constitutional guarantees. However, in many cases the dictators are able to rule by more subtle, and perhaps also more insidious, measures. By maintaining an all-seeing secret police system, a cowed and subservient congress and judiciary, and strong and loyal armed forces, they are able to govern absolutely but without ostensible violations of constitutional process.

THE TRUJILLO REGIME

Perhaps the prototype of modern dictatorships in Latin America, and certainly the most all-encompassing and effective example in recent times, has been that of the late

Generalissimo Rafael Leonidas Trujillo in the Dominican Republic. The generalissimo showed himself a genius for maintaining an absolutist tyranny behind the façade of a democratic constitution.

The various constitutions of the Dominican Republic, under which Trujillo ruled the country from 1930 until his death in 1961, provided all of the standard civil liberties—the rights to speech, press, assembly, organization, etc. Although they contained the classical presidential power to suspend constitutional guarantees, the dictator seldom found it necessary to make use of these powers. The "constitutional rhythm" seemed to go on largely undisturbed.

However, behind this façade there existed a total and brutal dictatorship. Its keys were the intense activity of the dictator, who was personally acquainted with virtually everyone of any importance among his country's two and a half million citizens; a series of secret police institutions spying constantly on the general populace and on one another and reporting directly to Trujillo; and a constant game of "musical chairs" by which Trujillo never allowed any civil or military official to stay in the same post long enough to build up a personal following which might in any way menace the dictator.

A unique constitutional device was used during most of the Trujillo dictatorship to assure the generalissimo's complete control over all officeholders, and particularly over members of the legislature. The constitution provided that when any member of congress vacated his seat, his replacement would be chosen by the house to which he belonged from a list submitted by the head of the party to which the late member belonged. Since during most of the dictatorship there only existed one legal party, of which Generalissimo Trujillo was the head, in fact he named all replacements. He reinforced his power, furthermore, by demanding of each officeholder, whether elected or appointed, an undated resignation before taking office. Trujillo then could send in resignations of whatever officeholders he wished to remove. Not infrequently, members of congress, judges, and ministers first knew of their resignations by reading about them in the newspapers.

All of this was supplemented by a process of degradation and humiliation of all people of any importance in the country, a process designed constantly to remind these people of who was the real boss of the nation. Thus, if one did not engage in the most extravagant praise of the dictator when making a public speech, regardless of the subject of the discourse and the irrelevance of Trujillo to this subject, one was in grave danger of losing one's job or of being jailed or even worse. Furthermore, through letters to the editors of the two daily newspapers of the capital, written by Trujillo or under his orders, virtually every high official of the regime was accused at one time or another of the foulest and most heinous crimes imaginable, and was forced to reply to these charges in the most abject manner.

Trujillo's dictatorship was more absolute and lasted longer than most in Latin America. However, it merely refined the techniques which have been widely used by dictatorial regimes throughout Latin America. In these regimes the formal provisions of the constitution have meant very little.

THE FUTURE OF DICTATORSHIP

The future of dictatorship in Latin America is difficult to predict. There are certainly countries which have developed a tradition of orderly change of government and of wide freedom and civil liberties. There are important forces working to undermine the classical form of personalist and military dictatorship, such as the changes coming about inside the armed forces, the broadening economic base, the more complicated social structure, greater popular participation in politics, and the growth of forms of government more adapted to Latin American realities.

However, although the traditional kind of dictatorship

may be on the decline, a new menace of tyranny has become more important in recent years. This is the "popular" dictatorship, first epitomized by that of Juan Perón in Argentina, and after 1959 dramatized by Fidel Castro in Cuba. This arises from the growing frustration of large segments of Latin American public opinion at the slowness of economic growth and social change in the years following World War II. It is particularly serious because it tends to undermine the popular aspirations for democracy which have characterized Latin America since independence, regardless of what kind of regime may actually have been in power in any given country at any given time.

SUMMARY

Generally, Latin American forms of government are still in the process of evolution. In recent decades these countries have tended to turn away from foreign models and to try to develop governmental institutions which grow out of their own circumstances and reflect their own characters. This development is an integral part of the great transformation through which all aspects of Latin American society have been passing.

Politics

To most North Americans, the politics of the Latin American republics are exceedingly confusing. There appears to be little rhyme or reason to the seemingly endless series of coups and countercoups. Little is known about the political parties of the region, and what is known only serves to confuse one further.

This view of the political life of Latin America is seriously distorted. Although it is true that the *coup d'état* is still used with too great frequency as a method of changing governments, this is only a part of the picture. What most North Americans don't realize is the fact that several of the republics have a record of political stability which would equal that of the great majority of the nations of the world, even most of those of Europe. Furthermore, there exist in Latin America serious political parties, with well-defined philosophies and programs. These parties are coming to play an increasingly important role in Latin American politics.

One reason for the confusion of the average United States observer of Latin American political affairs is the fact that Latin American parties tend to use names with which we are not familiar and which in some cases seem either peculiar or dangerous. There are parties which call themselves "revolutionary" or "renovationist," or "traditionalist," or "red" or "white," or which use words in their names which are almost untranslatable, as does the Partido Aprista Peruano (Peruvian Aprista Party).[1]

Of course, these names do have meaning for the Latin Americans who use them. They refer to a particular type of revolution or a well-known set of traditions, or use the names of colors which have a long history of association with a particular set of political ideas in the particular country in which they are used.

Another element of confusion is the fact that not infrequently the names used by the Latin American political parties have little connection with what those names would seem to imply. Thus, one is surprised to learn that the Social Democratic Party of Brazil is one of the most conservative parties of that country, or that the Liberal Party of Chile is probably *the* most conservative party there. Or there occurs a seemingly incongruous juxtaposition of words in the title of a party, such as those used by the Institutional Revolutionary Party (Partido Revolucionario Institucional) of Mexico.

However, perhaps North Americans would be less confused if they would consider for a moment the titles which have clung to their own parties. To the average foreigner, it remains a mystery what the connection of the names "Republican" and "Democratic" is to the principles (if any) for which these two venerable institutions stand.

There is more order and reason in the titles and philosophies of the Latin American parties than appears at first sight. In the pages that follow we shall try to outline the major groupings into which these parties fall, and mention some of the principal organizations which belong to each of these groupings.

Most of the political parties of Latin America can be divided into three principal categories. First of all, there are those which are merely organized around a particular po-

[1] This name is derived from the initials of the Alianza Popular Revolucionaria Americana (APRA), the first name which the party bore.

litical leader to foster his own political ambitions or to support his regime once he is in power, which we may call the "personalist" type of party. Second, there are the traditional parties which come down from the nineteenth century. Third, there are what we may label the "modern" parties, those which are of relatively recent origin and which have arisen from the events and problems of the twentieth century. The last two categories themselves can be divided into various subgroupings.

PERSONALIST PARTIES

It is perhaps the personalist party with which the average North American is best acquainted. This kind of group is organized without any particular philosophy or program except that of furthering the interests of a particular political leader. It may be organized while that leader is on his way to power, or once he holds the control of the State in his hands. In the nature of the case, such a party is transitory and is likely to disappear along with the man around whom it is organized.

The functions of such a party are limited. It does not usually have local groups which discuss issues and make their opinion known to the higher echelons. Its membership is largely composed of those dependent upon the leader for patronage or those who hope to get such patronage if he is successful. The rank and file has little to say about the policies, programs, or activities of the party, since all decisions are made at the top, in the last analysis by the man around whom it has been organized.

There are not many such organizations of any importance still functioning in Latin America. Perhaps the most notorious has been the so-called Partido Dominicano, the vehicle of the dictatorship of the late Generalissimo Rafael Trujillo in the Dominican Republic. Of some importance, too, is the Movimiento Popular Pradista, organized in 1956 for the election of Manuel Prado as president of Peru, and which has been the principal government party during his term of office. There is also the party which has supported the fortunes of President José María Velasco Ibarra, four times president of Ecuador.

These personalist groupings are becoming less and less important. The major reason for this is that political parties increasingly tend to be organized around ideas and philosophies, or as the expression of some particular interest group in the specific Latin American country. Although individual leaders may play a key role in establishing this more doctrinal type of party, the party itself can go on without the leader, and party activities consist of a great deal more than merely supporting one particular person.

THE TRADITIONAL PARTIES

The traditional parties of Latin America arose out of the great struggles which took place during the first century of independence. Basically, these struggles were two: the relationship between Church and State, and the question of federalism versus a centralized form of government. The traditional parties also sometimes took opposing points of view on matters of their countries' international economic policies.

In most Latin American countries two types of parties grew up in the nineteenth century, although in different countries they may have taken different names. These were the Conservatives and the Liberals.

The Conservatives generally were the supporters of the traditional rights and privileges of the Church in Latin American society. They supported its close association with the State, and tended to protect its property rights and its control over civic functions such as the registration of births, marriages, and the administration of cemeteries. They supported the Church's dominant role in education. The Conservatives also usually stood for a highly centralized form of government and were violently opposed to federalism, which would have devolved some considerable powers to the states or provinces. They usually were more hostile than their opponents to the ideas of free trade and the introduction of foreign capital into their countries.

Their major opponents were the Liberals. These people were to a greater or less degree inspired by the ideas of the French Revolution in religious matters and of Manchesterian free-trade liberalism in things economic. Frequently, too, they were for the granting of a greater degree of autonomy to the provinces.

The greatest battles of these two parties were fought over the Church-State issue, which was the overshadowing political problem of the nineteenth century. The Liberals sought to push the Church out of the educational field, and to transfer to the State the control of most civic affairs. In the last resort they sought separation of Church and State. *Coups d'état*, revolutions, and civil wars were generated by these issues. In most of the countries the Liberals emerged more or less victorious, although in many they did not achieve their ultimate objective of complete separation of Church and State.

In all of these struggles the great mass of the people did not participate, except when they were conscripted to fight on one side or another. It is not impossible that if the people had been consulted, the victory would not have gone to the Liberals. In any case, both Liberal and Conservative parties were largely made up of and were controlled by the members of the landowning and commercial aristocracy. The agricultural laborers and tenants and such urban workers as there were had little or nothing to say about these parties.

Today, the Conservative and Liberal parties persist in some of the Latin American countries. In some nations the two-party habit became ingrained and the old parties continued to be influential as a result. In Nicaragua, Honduras, Argentina, Paraguay, and Uruguay the traditions surrounding them have had enough popular support that it has been possible for the Conservative parties to remain more or less vigorous, though the issues which gave rise to these parties have long since ceased to be of major significance. In Ecuador and Chile, where the landholders remain exceedingly strong, the Conservative parties, too, are powerful.

THE LIBERALS

Liberal parties, too, survive in a number of countries. In some cases, as in Chile, they have become exceedingly conservative. In one instance, Nicaragua, the Liberal Party has been the tool of the long-lived dictatorship of the Somoza clan. In other cases, such as Colombia, Honduras, and Uruguay, the Liberal parties have moved with the times, and have sponsored the establishment of social-security legislation, labor laws, economic development, and (in Colombia) agrarian reform. It is in these latter countries that the future of the Liberal parties looks brightest.

The Uruguayan Liberals are worthy of particular mention. The party there is known as the Partido Colorado, and in the period before the First World War it came under the leadership of an extraordinary man, José Batlle y Ordóñez. Under his leadership the Colorados pioneered in sponsoring a program of social-security and labor legislation, nationalization of public ultilities and some other basic industries, and the stimulation of economic development, and particularly of manufacturing.

By advocating the establishment of a nine-man executive council in place of the single president, Batlle also took the lead in trying to curb the Latin American propensity toward an overly strong executive and even dictatorship. This system was finally fully adopted on Partido Colorado initiative, a generation after Batlle's death, as we have noted in a previous chapter. Whatever the fate of the executive-council scheme, Batlle's efforts firmly set Uruguay upon the path of progressive democracy.

Batlle's program split his own party. The majority, following his leadership, formed the Partido Colorado Batllista, which was the ruling party of the country until its defeat in 1958 by the Conservative or Nationalist Party. However, even the Nationalists have not sought to overturn the basic accomplishments of the Batllistas.

In the latter years of the nineteenth century Left Wing Liberals in Chile formed the so-called Radical Party, and in neighboring Argentina a similar group called the Unión Cívica Radical made its appearance at the same time. These parties were basically similar to the Liberals on most issues, though a bit more to the Left, and made a special appeal to the growing middle class. In Chile the Radicals became the principal spokesmen for the white-collar workers and small urban artisans, while in Argentina they appealed to the same elements, and also won the loyalty of a large part of the new class of industrialists and the urban wage earners. In both countries the schoolteachers became closely identified with the Radical Party.

A similar Radical Party developed in Ecuador in the early years of the twentieth century. However, it merged with the still-strong Liberals several decades later and the Ecuadorean Liberal Party took the name Partido Liberal-Radical.

THE MODERN PARTIES

What we have labeled the "modern" parties have been of more recent vintage than the traditional groups. They have been organized around modern issues such as agrarian reform, labor legislation and other social problems, economic development, representation of the middle and working classes, and nationalism. Some of these parties have been organized on European models, such as the Socialists and Christian Democrats. Others have been purely indigenous parties, growing completely out of local circumstances, such as the National Revolutionaries and the

Jacobin Leftists. Most of these parties have been democratic, though the Jacobin Leftists are disillusioned with democracy, and the totalitarian parties—the Fascists and Communists—are frankly opposed to political democracy.

THE SOCIALISTS

The first Socialist parties of Latin America developed in the two decades before the First World War. In Argentina, where the party was established in 1896, as well as in Uruguay and Cuba, where it was born somewhat later, the main impetus for the Socialists came from European immigrants. However, the Chilean Socialist Labor Party, established in 1913, was purely native in its origins.

The fortunes of the Socialist parties have varied greatly from time to time. At one time or another there have been such parties in more than a dozen Latin American countries. At the present time the only Socialist parties of major importance are that of Chile, which, with the help of the Communists and several smaller groups, almost elected its candidate for president in 1958; and that of Ecuador, where it is the third largest party. The Argentine Socialist Party is small but has great prestige. However, it split into two bitterly opposed groups, the Partido Socialista Argentino and the Partido Socialista Democrático, in 1958, and in 1961 the former split once again. Relatively small Socialist parties also exist at the present time in Uruguay, Brazil, Peru, Colombia, Venezuela, and Panama.

Most of the Socialist parties of Latin America have suffered in recent decades from an inferiority complex toward the Communists. They have tended to feel that they had to be "more to the Left" than the Communists, and frequently have been willing to form alliances with them. These alliances have tended to have a debilitating effect upon the Socialists, and have also led several of them into what we have called the Jacobin Left—a kind of Titoism with a disdain for political democracy not to be found in

the historical tradition of most of the Socialist parties of
other parts of the world.

THE CHRISTIAN DEMOCRATS

The other major group of Latin American parties formed
on the model of European counterparts is the Christian
Democrats. Most of the Christian Democratic parties have
been established since World War II, though two of them,
the Unión Cívica of Uruguay and the Falange Nacional of
Chile, are of much older vintage.

The most important Christian Democratic parties are
those of Chile and Venezuela. In 1958 the Falange Nacional of Chile merged with a number of smaller parties
to form the Partido Democrático Cristiano. It has become
the third largest political group in Chile, a country with a
large number of parties. Its leadership is of particularly
high intellectual quality, and it has had a considerable degree of success in penetrating the country's labor movement.

The Venezuelan Christian Democratic Party, known as
the Partido Social Cristiano Copey, was established in
1946. Its influence is considerable in the westernmost states
of the republic and among students, though its trade-union
following is relatively limited. It entered the coalition government of President Rómulo Betancourt early in 1959,
and has played a leading role in carrying out that government's extensive social-reform and economic-development
programs. It is the third largest party in the country.

Christian Democratic parties also exist in Uruguay, Argentina, Peru, Bolivia, Ecuador, Paraguay, Cuba, and
Brazil. The last of these supported the election of Jânio
Quadros as president of Brazil in 1960, and played a role
in his government.

The Latin American Christian Democratic parties are
politically on the moderate Left. They base their philosophy on the papal encyclicals Rerum novarum and Quad-

ragesimo anno, and have had the support of considerable numbers of progressive-minded Catholic laymen and some clergymen as well. They have sought to gain influence not only among the normally Catholic middle class, but also among the working class, many of whose members have largely left the Catholic fold.

Although the Christian Democrats have frequently cooperated with other elements of the Democratic Left in Latin America, they have differed from them in having a specifically religious basis for their philosophy and program. Also in some cases they have sought to obtain certain advantages, particularly in the field of education, for the Church. These efforts have sometimes engendered disagreements with other Democratic Left groups.

THE NATIONAL REVOLUTIONARY PARTIES

Probably the single most important group of political parties in Latin America today is what we have called the National Revolutionary parties, organizations with an ideology which has grown out of the national experience of the Latin American countries, without any particular inspiration from outside the area. They have stressed the need for finding Latin American solutions for Latin American problems. The programs of these parties differ somewhat from country to country, since the nature of each nation's problems is somewhat different. However, they recognize a kinship among themselves and have frequently cooperated with one another. In August 1960 they held the First Congress of Popular Parties in Lima, Peru, where the bonds linking them with one another were considerably strengthened. They maintain (jointly with the Liberal parties of Honduras and Colombia) a training school in Costa Rica, known as the Institute for Political Studies, to which secondary leaders are sent for training in political theory and ideology, organizational techniques, public speaking, and other subjects.

All of these parties favor social revolution in the broadest sense. They support agrarian reform, the breaking up of large unproductive estates and their distribution among landless peasants. They advocate extensive labor legislation and social security for the protection of the urban workers, and encourage the organization of these workers into unions. In those countries in which there exist oppressed racial groups, they seek the emancipation of these.

In the second place, the National Revolutionary parties are nationalist, seeking to establish more firmly the independence of their countries. In particular, they work to end the excessive dependence of their nations on trade in a small number of products and with a narrow range of countries. They also seek to establish conditions for the entry of foreign investors into their country's economies which will protect these nations' national sovereignty.

Third, these parties advocate their countries' economic development. They seek this not only to strengthen their nations' independence, but also as a means of raising the standards of living of their people, and of stimulating the forces leading toward social transformation. They believe in the government's taking a positive role of encouraging and engaging in the process of economic growth. They have no ideological opposition to State intervention in the economy, but on the contrary favor a mixed private-enterprise and State-run economic system.

Fourth, the National Revolutionary parties are secular in philosophy. They do not base their political program on any particular religious credo and they believe in a wide degree of separation of Church and State. In recent years they have become less anticlerical than they were a few decades ago and they have shown a willingness and ability to work with Christian Democratic elements in several countries.

Finally, these parties are democratic. They believe in the choosing of governments by the electoral process and the preservation of the rights of political minorities. This means that they support the traditional freedoms of speech, press, assembly, and belief.

National Revolutionary parties are found in a number of countries. They include the Democratic Action, National Liberation, Aprista, and Popular Democratic parties, the largest political groups in Venezuela, Costa Rica, Peru, and Puerto Rico respectively. The National Revolutionary Movement (MNR), which has presided over the government of Bolivia since that country's revolution of April 9, 1952, is also a member of this group, as is the Febrerista Party of Paraguay. The latter is one of that country's three principal parties. The Auténtico and Ortodoxo parties of Cuba, which were their country's largest parties until the Castro Revolution, could also be placed in this category.

In recent years several of these parties have borne the responsibility of government. This has been true in Venezuela, Bolivia, Puerto Rico, and Costa Rica. In Peru the Aprista Party seems very likely at this writing to come to power as a result of the election of 1962.

The National Revolutionary parties in office have been seeking to put their programs into effect. Their success in doing so is likely to determine the future of democracy in Latin America for many decades to come. If they succeed in demonstrating that it is possible to achieve the widely held ambitions of social change, economic development, and strengthening of national sovereignty through the democratic process, this will deprive totalitarian elements of much of their appeal. On the other hand, if the National Revolutionary parties fail, there seems to exist virtually no likely alternative except the totalitarian-minded groups.

This is of great importance to the United States, as well as to Latin America. The National Revolutionary parties have been generally sympathetic to the position of the United States in the Cold War. Totalitarian groups, on the other hand, have favored and sought the support of the Soviet Union and its allies. Thus, a defeat for the National

Revolutionaries will be a defeat for the United States, while a victory for the totalitarians will vastly strengthen the position of the Communist powers in the New World.

THE JACOBIN LEFT

Some of the most bitter opponents of the National Revolutionaries and other parties of the Democratic Left are what we may call the Jacobin Left. These are political parties and groups which have many of the attributes of the Jacobins of the French Revolution. They favor social revolution at whatever cost, and they are excessively nationalistic to the point of xenophobia.

The Jacobin Left has lost faith in political democracy. They have come to feel that the checks and balances of the democratic process, and its "nose counting," are both stratagems for postponing revolutionary action and for benefiting the defenders of the status quo. They do not believe in civil rights except for themselves and their friends. All other groups are, to their way of thinking, "counter-revolutionaries," and are not entitled to civic freedoms.

The antidemocratic bias of the Jacobin parties is of great significance, historically, in Latin America. Hitherto, virtually all popular political movements in the area have been at least formally committed to political democracy. Even the dictators have felt it necessary to make a pretence of using democratic forms for their regimes. It is serious indeed that a political movement appealing to the great masses of the people of Latin America can do so with more or less success on the basis of a fundamental attack on the democratic process.

The elements of the Jacobin Left also take a very different position on world affairs from Latin American democratic groups. They quite frankly favor the cause of the Soviet Union in the world struggle, and in most cases they are perfectly willing to work locally with the Communists in their respective countries.

The Jacobin Left is not a new element in Latin American politics. In the late 1940s and early 1950s the then president of Argentina, General Juan Domingo Perón, took a Jacobin Left position and sought to build up a movement throughout the hemisphere. Although he had considerable initial success, he was handicapped by fears of some of his neighbors concerning Argentine expansive ambitions, by his own status as a general, by the weakness of his country's economic situation, and by his failure to rally much support from outside the hemisphere.

A decade later a more flamboyant and popular leader appeared in the Jacobin Left in the person of Fidel Castro. He did not suffer from the fears which Perón had aroused in his neighbors, and he succeeded in obtaining strong moral, political, and economic backing from the Soviet Union, its European satellites, and Communist China.

Castro's revolution aroused widespread enthusiasm and support throughout Latin America. Even after its totalitarian direction became obvious, he was able to rally many of the elements which had become disillusioned with political democracy and the apparent slowness of economic development and social change in the various Latin American countries. He was vastly more successful than Perón had been in rallying behind himself the hitherto scattered elements of the Jacobin Left. However, he lost much of his appeal when, in the third year of his revolution, he proclaimed himself a Communist, and in effect turned power over to the Cuban Communist Party.

There are few parties in Latin America which can be classed as belonging to the Jacobin Left. However, there are elements in many of the Democratic Left groups which sympathize with the Jacobins, and there is considerable unorganized support for this point of view.

The oldest organized Jacobin group consists of the Peronistas, who, in spite of their leader's downfall some years before, remained in the early 1960s a potent force in Argentine political life. The 26th of July Movement of

Fidel Castro was the strongest of the Jacobin elements, being in charge of its country's government. The Party of April and May, which appeared on the political scene of El Salvador after the overthrow of President José Lemus late in 1960, was another important party of the Jacobin Left.

In Venezuela two parties fall into this general category. One of these was established in April 1959, when the Left Wing of the Democratic Action Party was expelled from that group, and formed the rival Movement of the Revolutionary Left (MIR). The other is the Republican Democratic Union (URD), a party with a fifteen-year history, which became the strongest advocate in Venezuela of the Castro position after Fidel's accession to power.

Finally, a number of Latin American Socialist parties have become part of the Jacobin Left. Those of Chile, Brazil, Ecuador, Uruguay, and one faction of the Argentine party unequivocally took their place in this camp after 1959. They had been moving in this direction during the 1950s and threw their support strongly behind Castro even after the dictatorial nature of his regime became quite clear.

A number of the National Revolutionary parties have had trouble with Jacobin elements in their own Left Wings. Both the Democratic Action Party of Venezuela and the Peruvian Apristas found it necessary during 1960 to expel such groups from their midst. The National Liberation Party of Costa Rica also had some trouble with similar elements, though no disciplinary action was taken.

THE COMMUNISTS

The Jacobin Left has generally tended to form alliances with the Communists. There are Communist parties in every Latin American country. A few of these, such as the Communist parties of Argentina, Chile, and Uruguay, antedate the First World War and were founded as Socialist parties, which went over to the Communist International after its establishment in 1919. Others, such as the parties in Haiti and the Dominican Republic, were formed as late as the middle 1940s.

The Communist parties of Latin America share the aims of their counterparts in virtually every other part of the globe. They are first dedicated to doing whatever they can to serve the Soviet Union. Second, they seek to establish a dictatorship of their own party in the particular country in which they are operating. The second objective will be readily sacrificed to the former, as has been indicated a number of times.

The Communists direct their appeal particularly to the urban industrial workers and to the intellectuals. They frequently picture themselves as the only "real" workers party, and are particularly active in seeking influence in the organized-labor movement. Recognizing the particular importance which the intellectuals have in Latin American political affairs, as well as the social conscience and often belligerent nationalism of this group, the Communists have devoted special attention to winning influence in cultural, artistic, and professional circles, with rather more lasting success there than they have had among the workers.

In recent years the Communists have begun to devote an increasing amount of their attention to the agricultural workers and peasants. Perhaps this is partly due to the example of the successful use of the peasants by the Chinese Communists on their road to power. However, it is due even more to the fact that the rural workers have begun to play an increasing role in the affairs of the Latin American countries, and have numerous grievances which the Communists can seek to exploit. Communist influence in the countryside is of some importance in Brazil, Chile, Guatemala, Peru, Colombia, Ecuador, and Cuba.

Three appeals of the Communists have been particularly effective during recent decades in Latin America. One of these is their attempt to picture themselves as the most efficient and faithful purveyors of revolutionary change. This was one of the principal arguments used by the Communists in Guatemala during the early 1950s, and was accepted by many non-Communist political leaders associated with the Arbenz government, in which Communist influence was very great.

Their second appeal has been to the example of the Soviet Union—and to a lesser degree, to Communist China —as a country which has been able to industrialize and develop its economy very rapidly. They have also increasingly argued that only the Soviet Union will be able to help the development of the Latin American countries "with no strings attached." Naturally, they have not stressed the terrible human cost of development in the Communist countries, or the political infiltration which the Soviet Union has used in those nations to which it has extended economic aid and technical assistance.

Finally, they have stressed violent expressions of nationalism, particularly directed against the United States. They have blamed all of the evils and shortcomings present in Latin America on the United States and have constantly urged the need for these countries "to free themselves from Yankee imperialism." The growing frustration in Latin America at the slowness of the area's economic growth and the bitterness aroused by the United States support of Latin American dictators during the 1940s and 1950s have created fertile ground for the Communists' arguments and propaganda.

The Communists have suffered under two major handicaps. First has been the fact that, in spite of their protestations of ardent Latin American nationalism, they have frequently been suspected by the Latin Americans of being little more than agents of the Soviet Union. This was particularly the case in the years immediately following the Second World War. In addition, there has been widespread suspicion of the dictatorial intentions of the Communists, which has alienated many who might otherwise have been attracted to them.

The advent of the Jacobin Left, and particularly its rapid increase in popularity after Castro's victory in Cuba, gave the Communists a new opportunity. It makes it possible for them to collaborate closely with a group which does not blatantly boast of its "loyalty to the Soviet Union," but nonetheless is very willing to work with both the Soviet Union and the local Latin American Communists. Thus, for the first time since World War II, the Communists are able to acquire "protective coloration" from a political movement with deep roots in the Latin American scene.

OTHER TOTALITARIANS

The Communists have not been the only totalitarians to appear in recent years. Their own dissident group, the Trotskyites, has been active in a number of countries. For a short time in the early 1950s they were an element of considerable importance in Bolivia, as a result of their close association with Juan Lechín, the mineworkers' union leader, who was and is a major power in the Nationalist Revolutionary Movement (MNR). Elsewhere they have never become a party of consequence, though they have some influence in intellectual circles in Argentina, and have organizations in seven or eight countries.

During the 1930s and early 1940s the Fascists, too, were a significant element in Latin American politics. Parties which were quite frankly inspired by European fascism were important in Chile and Brazil, while other political groups in Peru, Uruguay, Argentina, and Mexico were on friendly relations with the German Nazis, Italian Fascists, and Spanish Falangistas. At the present time the only party of fascist origins which is of considerable importance is the Falange Socialista Boliviana, until 1960 the major opposition party in Bolivia.

SUMMARY

Politics in Latin America is no longer merely a game played among individual leaders bidding for support of the small aristocracy and the armed forces. Although personalism still plays an important role in Latin American politics, as it does in that of other countries, it is no longer the dominant factor. There now exists a wide range of political parties, representing competing ideologies, political philosophies, and interest groups. A schematic arrangement of the major parties in the twenty Latin American republics and Puerto Rico is presented in Table V.

TABLE V

LATIN AMERICAN POLITICAL PARTIES

	Argentina	Bolivia	Brazil	Chile	Colombia
Personalist	—	—	—	—	—
Conservative	Democrático Nacional	Unión Republicano Socialista	Partido Social Democrático	Partido Conservador Unido	Partido Conservador
Liberal	—	Partido Liberal	União Democrática Nacional	Partido Liberal	Partido Liberal
Radical	Unión Cívica Radical Intransigente Unión Cívica Radical Del Pueblo	—	—	Partido Radical	

Christian Democrat	Cristian Democrático	Social Democrático Cristiano Social	Cristiano Democrático	Cristiano Democrático	—
Socialist	Partido Socialista Argentino Partido Socialista Democrático	—	Partido Socialista Brasileiro	Partido Socialista	Partido Socialista Popular
National Revolutionary	—	Movimiento Nacionalista Revolucionario Movimiento Nacionalista Revolucionario Auténtico	—	—	—
Jacobin Left	Partido Peronista	—	Partido Trabalhista Brasileiro Part of Socialist Party	—	—

	Argentina	Bolivia	Brazil	Chile	Colombia
Communist	Partido Comunista	Partido Comunista	Partido Comunista	Partido Comunista	Partido Comunista
Fascist	—	Falange Socialista Boliviana	Partido Representação Popular Partido Nacista (dissolved 1941)	—	—

	Costa Rica	Cuba	Dominican Republic	Ecuador	El Salvador
Personalist	—	—	Partido Dominicano	—	—
Conservative	Partido Democrática			Partido Conservador	

Liberal	—	Partido Liberal	—	Partido Liberal-Radical	—
Radical	—	—	—	—	—
Christian Democrat	—	Movimiento Cristiano Democrático	—	Partido Social Cristiano	—
Socialist	—	—	—	Partido Socialista	—
National Revolutionary	Partido Liberación Nacional	Auténtico Triple A	Partido Revolucionario Dominicano Vanguardia Revolucionaria Dominicana	—	—
Jacobin Left	—	26 de Julio	—	Partido de Abril y Mayo	—

	Costa Rica	Cuba	Dominican Republic	Ecuador	El Salvador	Guatemala	Haiti	Honduras	Mexico	Nicaragua
Communist	Vanguardia Popular	Partido Socialista Popular (succeeded in 1961 by Organizaciones Revolutionarias Integradas)	Partido Socialista Popular	Partido Comunista	—					
Fascist	—	—	—	—	—					
Personalist						Movimiento Democrático Nacional	—	—	—	—
Conservative						—	—	Partido Nacional	Partido Acción Nacional	Partido Conservador

Liberal	Partido Liberal	—	Partido Liberal	—	Partido Liberal
Radical	—	—	—	—	—
Christian Democrat	Partido Cristiano Democrático	Partido Social Cristiano	—	—	—
Socialist	—	—	—	—	—
National Revolutionary	Partido Revolucionario	Movement Ouvrier Paysan	—	Partido Revolucionario Institucional	—
Jacobin Left	Partido Revolucionario Auténtico	—	—	—	—
Communist	Partido del Trabajo Guatemalteco	Parti Socialiste Populaire	Partido Comunista	Partido Comunista	Partido Comunista
Fascist	—	—	—	—	—

	Panama	Paraguay	Peru	Puerto Rico	Uruguay	Venezuela
Personalist	—	—	Movimiento Pradista Democrático	—	—	—
Conservative	—	Partido Colorado	—	Partido Estadista	Partido Nacional (Blanco)	—
Liberal	—	Partido Liberal	—	—	Colorado Batllista	—
Radical	—	—	—	—	—	—
Christian Democrat	—	Movimiento Democrático Cristiano	Cristiano Democrático	—	Unión Cívica	Copey Social Cristiano
Socialist	—	—	Partido Socialista	—	Partido Socialista	—
National Revolutionary	—	Partido Febrerista	Partido Aprista	Partido Democrático Popular	—	Acción Democrática

Jacobin Left	—	—	Partido Acción Popular (Belaunde)	—	—	Part of Socialist Party	Unión Republicana Democrática Movimiento Revolucionario de Izquierda
Communist	Partido del Pueblo	Partido Comunista	Partido Comunista	Partido Comunista	Partido Comunista	—	—
Fascist	—	—	—	—	—	—	Movimiento de Izquierda Revolucionaria

The Military

Most people of the United States have a caricature-like
impression of the armies of Latin America. They think of
Latin American military officers strutting around in brilliant
and bemedalled uniforms and spending most of their time
in overthrowing their nations' governments. Although there
is a certain degree of truth in such a picture, it is grossly
exaggerated and presents only one side of the case. In
fact, the role of the armies, navies, and air forces in contemporary Latin America is complicated and rapidly
changing.

THE ORIGINS OF MILITARY INTERVENTION
IN POLITICS

The armies of Latin America were born during the
struggle for independence a century and a half ago. They
were raised from the local civilian population, sometimes
from among volunteers who were eager to fight for the
national cause, or frequently from among peasants and
city folk who were drafted into the service of the struggle
for independence whatever their personal convictions may
have been.

Many of the leaders of the armies which won national
sovereignty for the Latin American countries were men
who had served in the Spanish forces before the outbreak

of the struggle, such as José de San Martín of Argentina and Simón Bolívar of Venezuela. A few were renegades who had first fought with the Spaniards against the colonials and then switched sides near the end of the struggle, such as Agustín de Iturbide of Mexico.

The achievement of independence left the Latin American armies in an exceedingly crucial position. In many of the new countries the struggle had been a long and devastating one and the new States were faced with a seriously undermined economy, inadequate finance, and widespread chaos. With the removal of the authority of the Spanish Crown only three centers of great power and prestige remained: the Church, the landed aristocracy, and the new armies.

The civilian population had had little experience with self-government during the colonial period, and neither Spain nor Spanish America had had a tradition of civilian domination over the military. Quite the contrary, throughout the Spanish Empire the military man had enjoyed a unique and privileged position.

The leaders of the new armies reflected this Spanish tradition. There appeared few George Washingtons, who despite the greatest provocation from the civilian revolutionary authorities, refused the temptation to substitute his will for that of the people's elected representatives. The cases were frequent in Latin America in which exasperated or ambitious military leaders dissolved the civilian government and asserted the authority of the military over the civilians.

Thus the right of the army to have the last word in politics was already strongly asserted during the wars for independence. This right was greatly strengthened during the first century of independence. During this period the role of the military was a many-sided one. Of course, they stood as guardians of national sovereignty and not infrequently engaged in wars with neighboring states and even with powers from outside of Latin America, including both the United States (in the case of Mexico in 1846–48) and several European nations.

However, the military leaders also served as the principal defense of most of the economic and social institutions which had been inherited from colonial days. Many of the military leaders of the independence struggle were inspired by the ideals of the American and French revolutions, and many of the members of the lowest classes in Latin American society had been recruited into the revolutionary armies as common soldiers.

Nevertheless, the revolutionary military leaders were no more anxious than the large landowners and merchants to see the movement for independence followed by uprisings of the Indian and Negro masses. Thus the generals stood as bulwarks against such social revolution, which even in the first half of the nineteenth century was an oft-recurring nightmare to the members of the ruling classes.

On the other hand, in the great struggle which dominated nineteenth-century politics in Latin America the military leaders were often on the side of change. This was the fight over the economic, civil, and political privileges of the Church. The great military *caudillos* of this period generally sided with the Liberals, who wanted to destroy the position of the Church, and it was largely thanks to these military chieftains that victory largely went to the Liberals.

As a result of the army's varying role in the national life of the Latin American countries, the right of the military to interfere in civilian political affairs became a tradition. As a matter of course, civilian politicians who were disgruntled with the regime in power would turn to friends in the armed forces for help in overthrowing that regime. Military leaders who were themselves ambitious or who were in disagreement with the policies being followed by the constituted government, moved against that government with increasing frequency. Once this became the traditional way of doing things, it was exceedingly difficult to change. Indeed, this tradition of military intervention became the strongest reason for the continuance of such intervention.

An important contributing factor to the leading role of the military in politics was the fact that the armed forces constituted one of the few elements of social mobility in nineteenth-century Latin American society. It was possible for a boy of humble origins to enter the armed forces and by means of periodic promotion, good luck, and *coups d'état* to rise to high rank. As a top-level military officer, such a man automatically moved into the ruling group, and was in a position to make his fortune as well. In some countries it was for long a standing joke that the presidency of the republic was the highest rank in the military hierarchy.

During this period the *caudillo* or popular military hero became a familiar figure in Latin America. He generally was a man with a charismatic personality, who won the admiration and the loyalty of a large enough segment of the population to make himself an important force in his country's political life. Having ridden to power on this wide popular support, he established his own personal dictatorship, benevolent or not so benevolent. Some of the *caudillos* stayed in power a long time, such as Porfirio Díaz, who dominated Mexico from 1876 until 1910; or Juan Vicente Gómez, who ruled Venezuela from 1909 until 1935. The success of others was less long-lived.

MILITARISM IN THE TWENTIETH CENTURY

The nineteenth-century tradition of military domination of politics seemed to be on the decline during approximately the first third of the present century. Army *coups d'état,* or *golpes de estado,* as they are known in Latin America, became less prevalent, and the armed forces of many of the countries seemed to be more interested in becoming technically good soldiers than in running the government.

With the advent of the Great Depression, however, this trend was reversed, and between 1930 and 1955 the area was once again plagued with military tyrannies. Argentina, which had not seen a successful military uprising for nearly seventy-five years, saw the army overthrow the legally elected president on September 6, 1930, and from then until the present the army has dominated the government directly or indirectly. Even Chile and Uruguay, where civilian government seemed firmly established, were the scenes of short-lived military regimes in the early 1930s, while most of the other countries of the region suffered the same fate.

The victory of the Allies in World War II paved the way for the democratization of a number of Latin American countries, including Brazil, Peru, Cuba, and Venezuela. However, the year 1948 saw a reversal of this trend once again, and by the beginning of 1955 ten of the twenty Latin American republics were governed by military tyrants, and an eleventh was ruled by a civilian dictator supported by the army. In two other countries, Chile and Panama, military men were president thanks to popular and democratic elections.

The downfall of General Juan Domingo Perón as president of Argentina, in September 1955, set in motion yet another wave of revolt against military dictators in Latin America. Generals Odría in Peru, Rojas Pinilla in Colombia, Magloire in Haiti, Pérez Jiménez in Venezuela, and Batista in Cuba fell during the next three and a half years. So did civilian dictator Julio Lozano in Honduras.

The downfall of these dictators was of particular importance because it was accompanied by a series of apparently sincere statements by leading military figures throughout the hemisphere to the effect that it was time for the leaders of the armed forces to retire from political activity and "return to the barracks." General Pedro Aramburu, who served as provisional president during most of the interim regime after the fall of Perón, made a particularly moving speech to the army just before his retirement from his high office in May 1958. He said that most of the ills from which the country had suffered since 1930 were the responsibility of the armed forces, which had made and unmade governments at will, and he urged the retirement of the soldiers from politics.

In Colombia, as well, the military men who overthrew General Rojas Pinilla and paved the way for the return to civilian democratic government, likewise pledged themselves to end once and for all the process which General Rojas Pinilla had started of governing "in the name of the armed forces." In neighboring Venezuela the military men who took over from General Pérez Jiménez early in 1958, a year later honored their pledge to return the government to civilian hands. Thereafter, the principal military leaders asserted over and over again that the duty of the armed forces was to defend the constitutional government selected by the votes of the people.

Whether the political situation of the 1960s will permit the military men to honor their pledges of abstaining from using their concentrated force to change governments remains to be seen. Long-smoldering, deep-seated revolutionary movements have begun to burst forth and completely to change the political life of the region, a development in which the military almost certainly will be called upon to play a role.

CHANGES IN THE NATURE OF THE MILITARY

A contributing factor to the possible retirement of the military from politics is the increasingly technical nature of warfare, and hence of armed forces. In Latin America as elsewhere this trend has led to more intensive and professional training of the military.

As a matter of fact, foreign missions have been training some of the Latin American armies and navies for more than half a century. More than fifty years ago German missions were sent to Argentina, Bolivia, Chile, and some other Latin American countries. French missions went to Peru and several other nations. At the same time the British navy was called upon to dispatch missions to train several Latin American maritime forces.

Since World War II the training missions of European powers have been superseded by similar groups from the United States. In 1960 there were thirty-eight service missions from the United States training Latin American armies, navies, and air forces. Not only have U.S. missions been stationed in various Latin American countries, but an increasingly large number of Latin American army, navy, and air-force officers have been sent to the United States for advanced training.

In addition to training by foreigners, the younger officers of the Latin American armies have benefited from better and more careful education in preparation for their military careers. Early in this century military training schools were established in most of the Latin American countries, usually under the name of Polytechnic Institutes. Some of the larger armed forces have also established Superior War Colleges for advanced training for higher-ranking commissioned officers.

One effect of the increased technical qualifications of many of the officers of Latin American armed forces has been a growing rivalry between the graduates of the Polytechnic Institutes and their older-fashioned, less-qualified fellow officers. A number of the *coups d'état* since World War II have been carried out by these better-trained officers, desirous of pushing into retirement their higher ranking but less qualified superiors.

The higher degree of education and technical skill developing in the Latin American armies has led to the growth of a higher degree of *esprit de corps* among their officers. They have tended to develop a pride in their profession which older Latin American military men lacked. This has led to two contradictory tendencies. On the one hand, it has led the officers to seek to become increasingly proficient in their purely professional duties. At the same time it has instilled in them a certain depreciating attitude toward civilians, who are often less educated and less well trained in the technics of modern civilization. It thus has tended to reinforce the old conviction among Latin American military men that they have a "right" to step in in moments of political crisis to "save the nation."

The need for more complicated military equipment, as well as the patriotism inherent in members of the armed forces, has led many of the Latin American officers to become strong supporters of economic development and of economic nationalism. They have felt the need for encouraging metallurgical and other industries which would provide at least some base for the production of military equipment within their nations' borders. At the same time they have become convinced that public utilities, petroleum industries, steel plants, and other strategic establishments should be in the hands of the national government and not in those of foreigners.

Another aspect of the increasingly mechanized nature of modern warfare and military establishments has been the development of serious interservice rivalries among the armies, air forces, and navies of a number of the Latin American nations. Until recent years it was only the army which consumed the military portion of the budget, and which was able to throw its weight around in political affairs. The navies were small and tended to be apolitical. Air forces only began to become really important in World War II.

This has now changed. Navies and air forces have both greatly increased in importance. There is now often bitter competition among the three armed services to share the financial pie. The navies and air forces have also begun to play a role in politics. The navies of Argentina, Colombia, Venezuela, and Cuba played an important role in the fights against the Perón, Rojas Pinilla, Pérez Jiménez, and Batista dictatorships. In the first three of these, naval officers had a major voice in the provisional governments organized after the ousting of the dictators. The air forces also played a significant part in these events in Argentina, Colombia, and Venezuela, and in the last case the air force revolted in a body three weeks before the ouster of the Pérez Jiménez regime.

Perhaps one result of the increasingly professional nature of the Latin American armed forces will be that they will concentrate more on their strictly military duties and will have less to do with political affairs. Strong sentiment for this undoubtedly exists particularly among the academically trained officers. Such a result would be more likely if means are found of using the military more effectively in the process of developing the economies of their respective countries. In such efforts the skills of many of the officers as trained engineers, aviators, and technicians could be provided with a field in which they could find full employment. At least one country, Bolivia, has sought completely to reorganize its armed forces along these lines.

CHANGES IN THE POSITION OF THE MILITARY IN SOCIETY

Several other long-run factors are tending to reduce the influence of the military in political affairs. For one thing, the economy of the Latin American countries is becoming a good deal more complex, with the result that the social structures of these nations are much more intricate and fluid than they were a few generations ago. The armed forces are no longer the principal means of social mobility. It is now possible for people of relatively humble origins to move up the scale through business enterprise, trade-union activity, or politics.

Furthermore, the progress of economic and social

change in Latin America is abolishing the classical role of the armed forces as defender of the semifeudal society inherited from colonial days. Only in a few nations is the army still acting as a last-ditch defender of the economic and social status quo. In some cases it is even taking the side of quite revolutionary changes.

New civilian institutions have developed which counteract the political influence of the military. The development of political parties which have a consistent ideology and program and which are not merely organized around a single political figure has reduced the importance of the classical *caudillo*. The leaders of these political parties are much more aware of the dangers inherent in constant military interference in political life than were their counterparts of nineteenth- and early twentieth-century Latin America.

The trade-unions are another institution which tends to undermine the position of the military as the ultimate decision-maker in politics and government. As they grow in strength, the ability of the unions to paralyze completely their respective countries' economic activity by general strike increases. That this weapon can be very effective as a government's defense against attempted military coups, or as a means to overthrow governments, has been demonstrated several times in the years since World War II.

THE IMPACT OF CASTRO ON THE LATIN AMERICAN MILITARY

Since 1959 an entirely new factor—the advent of the Castro regime in Cuba—has influenced the role of the Latin American military men in politics. Not only did the armed civilians of Castro defeat one of Latin America's larger and better-armed military forces, but once in power Castro challenged the whole institutional structure of the Latin American armies. By putting guns in the hands of disciplined groups of his civilian followers, and cutting down the size of his official rebel army to a minimum, Castro virtually silenced the army's voice in civic affairs. His rapid drift toward alignment with the Communists inside and outside of Cuba also shocked Latin American officers.

These events have had several effects. First, they turned the attention of officers of other countries of the area toward the need for training their forces in the techniques of guerilla warfare. In the second place, they tended to convince the military leaders of a number of the countries of the need for supporting democratically elected but radical governments, which could come to grips with the problems which were creating fertile soil for *Fidelismo*. These officers became convinced that the real alternative to such radical democratic regimes (which would at very least not try to destroy the army as an institution) was no longer a "good old-fashioned" military dictatorship, but rather a *Fidelista*-type regime.

PRESENT POSITION OF THE MILITARY

However, whatever the tendencies toward a reduction of the active political role of the armed forces in Latin America may be, the military still possesses in the early 1960s an exceedingly important position in the life of most of these countries. This position is reflected in the excessive share of the national budgets which goes to support the soldiers, sailors, and aviators.

In most of the Latin American countries the military receive 20 per cent or more of all of the funds expended by the respective governments in a given year. Typical are the cases of Argentina, where in the 1940s and 1950s the armed forces appropriation constituted from 25 per cent to 50 per cent of the total budget; Chile, where it has been about 50 per cent; Peru, which spends about 25 per cent of its total funds on the military; and Venezuela, where the percentage during the Pérez Jiménez dictatorship was as high as 50 per cent. At the other end of the scale were Mexico, where military expenditures in the late 1950s amounted to only about 12 per cent; and Costa Rica, which abolished its armed forces in 1948.

The excessive nature of these expenditures becomes obvious when one considers the functions which are in fact performed by the Latin American armed forces. The Latin American military are exceedingly antiquated by the standards of modern warfare. None of them is really equipped to fight even the World War II type of conflict, let alone engage in the warfare of the atomic age. Nor will the resources of any of the Latin American countries or all of them together permit them to attempt to keep up with the kind of arms race being engaged in by the world's major powers, even if such an attempt were in any sense desirable.

None of the armed forces of Latin America could defend their countries for more than a few hours from an attack by one of the major military powers of the globe. The fact may be unpalatable to many of the Latin Americans, but their real defense from attack from outside the hemisphere is the strength of the United States, and against that strength itself the Latin Americans are militarily helpless.

Furthermore, the role of the Latin American armed forces as defenses against one another is minimal. The Inter-American System developed in and around the Organization of American States during the second quarter of the twentieth century has provided the most efficient system of settling international disputes that has probably ever been evolved. Certainly there has been little need to maintain jet-equipped air forces, tank regiments, and aircraft carriers for the purpose of defending one Latin American country against another.

After the early 1950s a serious challenge to this Inter-American System arose as a result of the activities of the dictatorships of Rafael Trujillo in the Dominican Republic and Fidel Castro in Cuba. The former attempted on several occasions to overthrow governments and to arrange the assassination of heads of state in Costa Rica, Venezuela, and other countries. The latter has sought to export his peculiar type of revolution, through invasion, the infiltration of arms and men, and other means, to several of the other Latin American countries.

This situation was made more serious by the fact that the armed forces of the Dominican Republic and Cuba are among the largest of the Latin American region. Both of these regimes were probably getting help in their efforts from elements outside of the Western Hemisphere. Certainly, their activities represented the most serious challenge to the smooth operation of the inter-American peace machinery which had appeared in more than a quarter of a century. The disappearance of the Trujillo dictatorship somewhat mitigated the problem, but the Castro regime still represents a major impediment to the Inter-American System.

However, another factor which is decreasing the need for armed forces to defend one Latin American country from its neighbors is the growing feeling of solidarity among the nations of the area. In Central and South America there are important efforts afoot to merge the economies of large blocs of countries with a view ultimately to forming a single Latin American nation, at least in an economic sense. There is growing sentiment in the area for eventual political union as well.

THE ARMS RACE AND DISARMAMENT POSSIBILITIES

The classical role of military forces as defenders of national sovereignty has for some time had little more than symbolic significance in most of Latin America. But this has not prevented highly costly arms races among the countries of the region, races which are more matters of national prestige than of national defense, though they are nonetheless expensive because of that. Typical of this kind of thing is the fact that when Brazil purchased an antiquated aircraft carrier in the middle 1950s, the Argentine navy was not content until its government purchased a similar bauble a few years later.

Whether meaning to or not, the United States undoubtedly contributed to these arms races during the post-World War II period. Most of the new armament received by the Latin American countries in this period was purchased or was received as a gift from the United States. Almost any such grant or sale to one country created a demand for similar beneficence to one or more neighbors. By the late 1950s there was some indication that the U.S. armed forces had become convinced of the futility of such competitive arming in the other American republics, and were trying to convince the Latin Americans to accept aid in terms of technical training and equipment for engineering corps and other military units which could make a positive contribution to the economic development of the area.

Several proposals have been put forward to deal with the problem of competitive armament. In 1959 President Jorge Alessandri of Chile suggested the calling of a Latin American conference to discuss the limitation of armaments and the reduction of those presently maintained by these countries. The suggestion was warmly supported by President Manuel Prado of Peru.

Another kind of suggestion was made in 1960 by a Spanish-Mexican writer, Victor Alba. He proposed that the Latin American nations pool their armed forces, establishing an area-wide army, navy, and air force which could undertake on a serious basis the problem of providing really adequate defense of the region against outside attack. However, he recognized the impossibility of such a program being effective until the industrial base of the Latin American nations has been sufficiently broadened to provide them with the possibility of producing within their borders the military hardware necessary for regional defense. The problem of adequate military defense, he insisted, could not be dealt with apart from the question of economic development and social transformation of the whole area.

Unless the nations of the region decide seriously to undertake some kind of joint defense effort, the role of the Latin American military forces is really reduced to that of glorified police forces. For this purpose most of the armies of the area are clearly excessive. This is particularly true when one considers that many of the countries maintain national militarized police forces—*carabineros*—in addition to their armies, navies, and air forces. Certainly, if it is to be frankly recognized that the principal job of the armed forces is to be the defense of the constituted government and the maintenance of public order, large-scale reduction in present military forces is clearly indicated.

The second real role of the Latin American armed forces, as we have already indicated, has been that of a kind of Praetorian Guard, making and unmaking presidents at will. Few people concerned with the fate of democratic and progressive civilian government in the hemisphere wish to see this role continued indefinitely.

SUMMARY

The Latin American armies, navies, and air forces have played a role in the affairs of their countries which seems strange to North Americans. Their importance to national defense has been less than to internal politics. The future functions of these armed forces seems to depend on many factors outside the purely military sphere, such as the economic development of the Latin American countries, the tendency toward unity among them, and the methods by which the great social transformation now under way in the area is carried out.

The Educational System

An educated and technically trained population is one of the basic necessities of a complex modern society, and it is the task of a nation's educational system to develop such a population. The traditional schools of Latin America have been unequal to this task and expansion and reform of the educational facilities is one of the most pressing endeavors being undertaken by the Latin Americans today.

Traditionally, the educational institutions of Latin America have had as their fundamental task the training of young people of the very small ruling oligarchies. The whole educational system from the primary grades on up was pointed toward preparing graduates to enter one of the three professions favored by members of this small elite group: law, medicine, or civil engineering. There was little interest in providing mass education or in developing institutions which might fit a workman's son to be a better citizen and a more skilled worker.

As a result of this bias of the traditional educational system, the emphasis of the schools was heavily classical. The students were introduced to the great philosophers, the leading political thinkers of ancient, medieval, and early modern times, and the literature of their own and several foreign languages. However, there was little interest in the physical sciences, or in economics, sociology, or psychology. Such things as home economics, agricultural science, or apprenticeship training were almost totally ignored.

THE EARLY HISTORY OF EDUCATION

The first schools in the area were established by the Catholic Church. Within a few decades of the beginning of the Conquest, universities were organized in a number of the Spanish colonies, and lower schools were established to provide potential students for the centers of higher learning, the universities of Santo Domingo, Mexico, and Lima being among the world's oldest. Favored sons of the colonial elite were also sent to Spain and Portugal for further training.

Throughout the colonial period education remained principally the task of the clergy and it continued to be heavily religious and classical in its orientation. Then during the first two or three generations of independence the Church lost control of most of the great national universities of Latin America, as well as of the lower schools. The State generally assumed the educational task, and in a number of countries it was legally given a monopoly in this field, with the Church being specifically forbidden to maintain educational institutions other than seminaries. However, this change did not alter the basic nature of the educational system as a training ground for the aristocracy.

THE FORM AND ADMINISTRATION OF THE EDUCATIONAL SYSTEM

During the nineteenth century Ministries of Education were established in virtually all of the Latin American countries, and in most cases, a highly centralized school system evolved. Although in those countries in which the federal system of government was adopted the different units of the federation were given some of the task of educating their citizens, in all of the countries the national government had priority in the field.

Generally, French and Iberian models were adopted for the schools, which in every case were established on three levels. In most countries primary education begins at six or seven years of age and runs for six years. These primary schools are followed by *liceos* or *gimnasios,* which are secondary schools of six years' duration. A student emerging from these institutions receives what is known as a *bachillerato* or bachelor's degree.

Higher education consists of the university, where the European model has also generally been followed. A beginning student enters a particular faculty of the university, depending upon which profession he intends to follow. There is nothing comparable to the colleges of the United States, where the student receives a general liberal-arts training. From the beginning he is pointing toward a career in medicine, law, engineering, or some other profession.

Generally, too, there are differences in the preparation of members of the teaching profession in the Latin American and United States educational systems. Training schools for primary schools, which are generally known as *escuelas normales,* are on a secondary-school level in Latin America, instead of being institutions of higher learning as in the United States. However, the schools training secondary-school teachers are of university or near-university status.

There is little special training for members of the university faculties. Normally, the professors are recruited from among the leading lights in the particular profession for which a faculty is training future members. Until very recently there were very few universities in Latin America which had full-time university professors.

THE INADEQUACY OF THE SCHOOL SYSTEMS

The public school systems of Latin America are generally free. In theory any student who is mentally capable of doing so may go from the first grade of primary school through the university without having to pay anything for his education in terms of tuition or fees. Indeed, in most of the countries at least primary education is not only free but also compulsory, according to the law.

However, in spite of these apparent advantages the Latin American educational systems have generally in practice fallen far short of what they are supposed to be in theory. School buildings and teachers are inadequate, budgets of the Ministries of Education are too small, and the educational systems as a whole do not offer what their potential students need.

Illiteracy remains a major problem. The percentage of people who cannot read or write varies from 14 per cent in Argentina to 89 per cent in Haiti. Table VI shows the amount of illiteracy in the twenty different republics.

THE HANDICAPS OF ILLITERACY

It is hard for a reader in the United States to conceive of the difficulties which illiteracy presents for the development of a modern industrial society. We hardly are aware of the vast use which we make of our reading knowledge, not only in our jobs, but in our everyday living. We read instructions, we read signs telling us how to do things or what to do or what not to do. We keep ourselves more or less informed about what is going on in our community, nation, and world through the newspapers. We take unto ourselves some of the knowledge which our forefathers have stored up over countless generations by reading books.

TABLE VI

ILLITERACY IN LATIN AMERICA

Country	Year	Per cent of Illiteracy* of Population Age 15 or Over
Argentina	1947	14
Bolivia	1950	68
Brazil	1950	51
Chile	1952	20
Colombia	1951	38
Costa Rica	1950	21
Cuba	1953	22
Dominican Republic	1950	57
Ecuador	1950	44
El Salvador	1950	61
Guatemala	1950	71
Haiti	1950	89
Honduras	1950	65
Mexico	1950	43
Nicaragua	1950	62
Panama	1950	30
Paraguay	1950	34
Peru	—	—
Uruguay	—	—
Venezuela	1950	48

* The criterion for illiteracy is inability to read and write.

SOURCE: Adapted from the United Nations' *Demographic Yearbook 1957*, p. 13.

But perhaps the lack of literacy is most critical in the economic field. In a modern factory there are innumerable occasions when it is convenient to give information, directions, or instructions by writing. It is helpful in teaching a worker how to use his machine, in instructing him where he may and may not smoke, in telling him, via a bulletin board, what is going on in the plant. In the field of labor relations it is important to be able to write down grievances which workers may have, to be as specific as possible so that if necessary those higher up on the hierarchy of both management and labor can deal adequately with the problems raised. If the worker involved cannot read what it is he is supposed to be complaining about, he is to a certain degree helpless to understand what is being done about it.

On the other hand, one should not overestimate the handicaps of illiteracy. Among many of those in Latin America who do not know how to read and write there exists a wealth of folk knowledge, passed on down through the generations by word of mouth. In industry manual dexterity and mechanical skill may in large part overcome the lack of ability to read. In politics several countries have found it possible to bring the masses of the people to the ballot box before they have learned to read, identifying candidates and parties on the ballot by means of color or symbols instead of words. In general, visual and aural means of communication, such as motion pictures, television, and radio, have been at least some compensation for lack of the three R's.

ANTI-ILLITERACY CAMPAIGNS

Nonetheless, the Latin American countries have become increasingly aware of the drawbacks to their national development presented by illiteracy. They have been making extensive efforts to teach their people to read and write.

Of course, the fundamental instrument for overcoming illiteracy, or at least preventing its growth, is the basic primary school. Virtually all of the countries have realized the need for increasing the quantity of their elementary schools, and of augmenting facilities for training teachers for these institutions.

One of the most outstanding jobs of any of the Latin American governments in recent years has been that of Venezuela since the beginning of 1958. At that time there were approximately 700,000 children in the country's primary schools, and almost half of the nation's school-age children were not going to classes. Almost no peasants' children were registered. By the beginning of the 1961–62 school year the number of primary-school students had risen to over 1,300,000 and for the first time in the country's history there were classrooms and teachers available for every child of first-grade age, except in the most remote parts of the nation.

Fidel Castro's government in Cuba has also made spectacular progress in extending the country's primary schools, though the task was not as great there as in Venezuela. Other Latin American countries have made less drastic efforts in this direction.

However, the development of the primary schools will serve mainly to prevent the growth of illiteracy, rather than to overcome the problem of adults who have already grown up without learning to read or write. For this purpose, extensive adult-education programs are necessary.

In this field, too, Venezuela and Cuba have made greater progress in recent years than most of the other nations of the area. The Venezuelans have used existing school buildings, as well as factories and the homes of workers and peasants, and have depended heavily on volunteers, including school children, as teachers. The Castro regime has gone so far as to close down all secondary schools and send the students out to rural areas to teach the illiterate peasants.

There is a good deal of controversy throughout Latin America concerning the efficacy of spending large amounts of relatively scarce resources on teaching adults their three R's. Many feel these resources would be better used to intensify the work of training the new generations, and express doubt concerning the likelihood that many of the adult students would retain their newly gained knowledge to read and write.

REASONS FOR CHANGES IN
TRADITIONAL SCHOOL SYSTEMS

The efforts to provide sufficient school buildings and teachers to make compulsory primary education a reality, and the drive against adult illiteracy are only two aspects of the changes which are now at work in the educational systems of Latin America. These changes involve not only the quantity but also the quality of schooling in the area.

Three things have shaken fundamentally the traditional educational pattern in Latin America. First has been industrialization, which has created the need for an increasingly large working class with at least the knowledge to read and write and elementary concepts of mathematics, mechanical arts, and physical science. The second has been the political revolution which has accompanied industrialism, resulting in ever more pressing demands by elements outside of the old oligarchy for access to education. The third has been the impact of educational ideas coming from outside of Latin America, and particularly from the United States.

In the field of ideas two North Americans have had a particular impact on Latin American education: Horace Mann and John Dewey. In the latter half of the nineteenth century Horace Mann had many firm supporters in Latin America. Most notable among these was Domingo Faustino Sarmiento, the Argentine schoolmaster, philosopher, and president of the republic, who became the real father of the Argentine public school system and propagated Mann's ideas far beyond his own nation's frontiers. In the present century John Dewey has been widely read and discussed and his influence on educational thinking and policy has been great. This is true in part because of the greatly increased contacts between Latin American educators and their North American counterparts, who have themselves been so profoundly affected by Dewey.

THE NATURE OF EDUCATIONAL CHANGES

As a result of all of these influences, several currents of change are notable in the Latin American educational system in recent decades. One has been the drive which we have already noted to provide enough primary and secondary schools to give a good general education to the great mass of the populace, while at the same time giving the brighter youngsters a foundation for pursuing higher studies if they so desire. The second has been the incorporation of new subject matter—physical and social sciences—in the general school curriculum, and restriction of the emphasis on the classics. The third has been the tendency to establish vocational schools which put special emphasis on training young people to be skilled, semiskilled, or white-collar workers in the new industries which are burgeoning throughout the area. Some countries, such as Mexico and Venezuela, have given special attention to training young farmers.

The Latin American university has also been undergoing fundamental changes during the last few decades, changes which tend to bring it more in line with the needs of those it serves. Some of the universities in the region are very old, several of the most important ones having been established during the sixteenth century. They were originally set up by Churchmen, principally for the purpose of training members of the clergy. Until a few decades ago their most important faculties still tended to be those of philosophy and theology.

THE UNIVERSITY REFORM

Beginning at the end of World War I a movement known as the "University Reform" swept across Latin America. It was in essence a revolt of the students and a minority of the faculty against both the nature of the university education being offered and the methods of administration of the institution. The students demanded the introduction into the curriculum of the social and physical sciences and less emphasis on philosophy, classical learning, and theology. At the same time they demanded that the administration of the university be placed in the hands of the faculty and the students rather than of outsiders.

The University Reform was widely successful. Starting in the University of Córdoba in Argentina in 1918, it spread to all of the other Argentine universities, and from there was carried to Chile, Peru, Cuba, Mexico, and other countries. Although the degree of emphasis given to the reforms varied from country to country and from institution to institution, there is no doubt that the University Reform very much modernized and democratized the Latin American universities as a whole.

One effect of the University Reform was to throw the students deeply into politics. In a few countries, notably Cuba, they had already played an important role in general political affairs. After the Reform they tended to do so in virtually all of the Latin American nations. One of the principles of the University Reform movement was that the students and the university as a whole should be in close contact with and should serve the interests of the community as a whole and of the lower economic and social classes in particular. The university should thus become an agent of change in the general society.

There are undoubtedly many reasons for the importance which the university thereafter played in Latin American politics. One of these reasons is certainly the key position which the university-trained person has traditionally had in these countries' affairs. Only members of the ruling class received university educations, so that almost by definition university graduates were future leaders of their countries. Feeling this responsibility even before they left the university walls, the students after 1918 demanded to be heard in their own right. The idealism and vigor of youth were also undoubtedly important explanations of this important role of the university student in national affairs. So was the fact that the young men—and, increasingly, young women—in the universities possessed large amounts of "leisure" time with few worries or responsibilities for earning a living, and could give full freedom to their idealism and political passion. Finally, there is no doubt that after 1918 each generation of students passed on to the next what became a tradition of intense political activity by an appreciable part of the student body.

However, the students are not the only members of the educational community who during recent decades have played a role in political life far beyond their weight in numbers. The teachers, both on a lower and university level, have done this too. It has come to be taken for granted in most Latin American countries that the teachers are in the forefront in the struggle for reforms of all kinds. This tradition, also, has now been passed on for several generations.

CHANGES IN THE UNIVERSITY

As a result of the University Reform, and of the general changes in the nature of Latin American economic and social life, the university has been undergoing many changes. On the one hand, it has been expanding very greatly, in the numbers of students which it has been handling. A university with a student body of 15,000 to 20,000 students is now no novelty.

In the second place, the kind of subjects taught has been changing, although perhaps not as rapidly as the situation demands. The law, medicine, and civil-engineering faculties still remain important parts of the Latin American university, but much more emphasis is being given to the physical sciences. Even more attention would be paid to these if it were not for the very sizable cost of laboratory and other needed equipment. The university has also broadened to take in an increasingly wide range of social sciences. The humanities curricula have been altered to give more importance to modern languages and to contemporary arts and letters, and less to the classics.

Finally, there is a perceptible shift in the influences from abroad which are helping to shape the Latin American university. North American influence has been rising, that of Europe declining. Perhaps this is seen most graphically in the tendency of the Latin American universities to develop "university cities" or campuses, where all or most of the parts of the university are concentrated in one place, instead of being spread around the city, as was traditionally the case. Perhaps also the growing interest in sports and other nonpolitical extracurricular activities is an evidence of this same trend, as is the growing number of students who are working their way through the universities. Finally, the employment of an increasing number of full-time faculty members is also due in large degree to U.S. influence.

PRIVATE SCHOOLS

The great majority of the Latin American educational institutions are owned and controlled (at least financially) by the State. Usually this means the national government, although there are also many lower-echelon schools and some universities which are financed by provincial or even municipal authorities. Private institutions play a secondary role.

The majority of the non-State schools of all kinds are financed and run by the Catholic Church. The Church has parochial primary and secondary schools in a number of countries, and in Brazil it is the dominant factor in the latter category. On a university level there exist one or more Catholic universities in Argentina, Brazil, Chile, Peru, Colombia, Venezuela, and Cuba.[1]

[1] All Catholic schools in Cuba were taken over by the Castro government early in 1961.

There is also a scattering of other private educational institutions. Some of these are run by Protestant denominations, usually on a missionary basis, and some, as in Brazil particularly, are run by private individuals as business enterprises. In the university field there are a few private institutions, perhaps the most notable of which is the Santa María Technical University, originally started by an endowment willed by Gustavo Santa María, Chile's sugar king, but now partly State-subsidized.

VOCATIONAL EDUCATION

Changes in lower schools have been as important as changes in the university in recent years. Of particular importance has been the development of vocational education and technical training. As mass primary education becomes nearer to being a reality in the Latin American countries, it is increasingly realized that only a small percentage of the elementary-school graduates will ever get to the university. Thus there is a growing tendency to mold education to suit the needs of those who will be going to work directly from lower school, as well as for those who will be university students later.

Another reason for the development of vocational training is the growing need for people who can take their place in the ranks of well-trained workers in the new industries and the multiplying offices which are spreading throughout Latin America. The school system is thus being adapted to turn out skilled manual workers and clerks as well as lawyers, engineers, and doctors.

Most of the vocational schools are on the level of secondary institutions. They include schools for training people in certain craft skills, as well as a much smaller number of institutions which train their students in the variety of skills needed in a particular industry. In Mexico, Venezuela, and some other countries both primary and secondary schools in rural areas have been molded so as to train students to be more efficient farmers.

A special type of vocational-training institution, which has been copied in other countries, was established in Brazil in the early 1940s. Twin organizations, Serviço Nacional de Aprendizagem Industrial and Serviço Nacional de Aprendizagem Comercial, give part-time vocational training and general education to youngsters who are already employed in industry or in commerce. All employers are required by law to permit a certain percentage of their workers to attend these schools with the official status of "apprentices." During their attendance of from two to three years the students receive half of the ordinary base pay of full-time workers.

In several countries the secondary-school vocational institutions have been integrated with special universities. Thus, the Universidad Tecnica Santa María in Valparaíso, Chile, trains skilled workers and foremen on the secondary-school level and engineers in its upper division. In the same country the Universidad Tecnica del Estado also includes a combination of secondary- and university-level institutions. During Perón's administration several similar institutions were established in Argentina. In Uruguay there has existed for more than two generations a Universidad del Trabajo in Montevideo, which combines technical training on several levels. Institutions in Mexico and several other countries do the same thing.

SUMMARY

As part of the transformation of the economies and societies of the Latin American nations, their educational systems are also changing. The traditional schools, which were designed only to train the children of the ruling aristocracy, are being dramatically increased in quantity, in an effort to provide mass education for all sections of the community. At the same time the educational system is being quantitatively altered, to train students to be future participants in the more complex society which is evolving in their countries.

Culture

Both North Americans and Latin Americans tend to misunderstand and underestimate the other's cultural achievements. The Latin Americans often think in terms of the "materialistic" Yankee as a semibarbarian, very capable in the production and manipulation of gadgets but without any "soul" and with little or no interest in the finer things of life. For their part, the North Americans tend to regard their Latin American neighbors as "romantic," somewhat shiftless, and utterly unsophisticated. They seldom think of them as having any particular interest or ability in arts and letters, or in the physical or social sciences.

Both of these stereotypes are incorrect. We in the United States certainly have much to be proud of in our high level of literacy and our accomplishments in literature, art, architecture, and music, as well as in science and technology. Although there is still much illiteracy in Latin America, the area has a rapidly expanding educational system, and an exceedingly active interest in arts and letters. Latin Americans have made and are making notable contributions in the fields of poetry and the novel, painting, architecture, and music, and are also beginning to gain recognition in the physical sciences. Indeed, the area may well be at the beginning of a notable cultural renaissance.

The Latin American intellectual tends to be somewhat different from his North American counterpart. The "universal man" is more widely respected in Latin America than in the United States. The Latin American scholar is likely to be "broader" and not as "deep" as his United States opposite number; that is to say, he is more or less informed about a wider range of questions and less specialized than the North American in any one of them. This probably reflects the still strong tradition of classical education in the area, and is tending to become less generally the case.

EARLY LATIN AMERICAN LITERATURE

Latin American literary history goes back to early colonial times. Some examples of these early writings have gained world-wide attention, such as the history and description of the Inca Empire written by Garcilaso de la Vega, descendant of the last of the Peruvian Indian rulers. Similarly renowned is the long epic poem *La Araucana*, written by the Chilean poet Pedro de Ona during the first half of the seventeenth century, recounting the tale of the valiant fight of the Araucanian Indians against the encroaching Spaniards.

Virtually all of the colonies had their representative poets, essayists, local historians, and theological writers during the colonial era. In the last decades of the period the literary efforts of the Spanish colonials were encouraged by the opening of printing presses in several of the colonial capitals, though no such machine was introduced into Brazil until the Portuguese court was transferred to Rio de Janeiro in the wake of Napoleon's conquest of Portugal in 1808.

During the first century or more of independence the Latin Americans tended to follow the fashions of Europe in their literary creations, as they did in so many things. Romanticism was particularly popular, and Latin America had numerous followers of the Frenchman Chateaubriand in writing idyllic but unrealistic epics about the American

Indian. Few of these obtained much international recognition. However, the genre novels of the Brazilian José de Alencar, and *María,* the famous work of Colombian novelist Jorge Isaacs, were read far beyond the homelands of their authors.

More recently Latin American literature has tended to become more self-assertive, and to develop without slavishly following models imported from abroad. Certainly one of the first examples of this trend was the famous poem by José Hernández called *Martín Fierro,* which immortalized the Gaucho, the mestizo cowboy who ranged over the plains of Argentina, Uruguay, and southern Brazil.

The same turn toward indigenous themes and original methods of presenting them was shown by the Brazilian Euclides da Cunha's famous study of life in the interior of his country, *Os Sertões,* translated into English as *Revolt in the Backlands,* which appeared during the first decade of the twentieth century. At about the same time the Nicaraguan poet Rubén Darío won world attention and was regarded widely in Latin America as expressing with peculiar aptness the Latin American personality and mood.

THE NOVELISTS, POETS, AND ESSAYISTS

Subsequently, it has been the novelists who have been especially active and successful in using the life, problems, conflicts, and even the peculiarities of language within the Latin American countries as sources for their material. Probably the most famous Latin American novelist of this century is the Venezuelan Romulo Gallegos, who has often been suggested as a candidate for the Nobel Prize. A series of Mexican novelists have mined the vast resources of the Mexican Revolution for material, which several of them have exploited with great ability. In Brazil, too, a whole series of novelists has produced works on historical and contemporary themes which have gained them hemispheric and even world attention. Among these Jorge

Amado, Raquel de Queiroz, Erico Verissimo, and José Lins do Rego are probably the best known.

There is virtually no Latin American country today which does not have its own novelists, almost all of whom look to their own countries for inspiration and who experiment with a variety of forms in developing their thematic material. Jorge Carrera Andrade of Ecuador, Ciro Alegria of Peru, Jesús Lara of Bolivia, and Manuel Rojas of Chile are among the most distinguished of this number.

Latin American poetry, too, has continued to flourish. Chilean poetess Gabriela Mistral won the Nobel Prize for Literature in 1945. Pablo Neruda, also a Chilean, the Cuban Carlos Guillen, and the Peruvian Magda Portal are numbered among the outstanding poets writing in the Spanish language. Carlos Drummond de Andrade, Jorge de Lima Mulio Araujo, and other Brazilian poets have the same position in Portuguese-language poetry.

Poetry enjoys higher prestige in the Latin American countries than it does in the Anglo-Saxon countries. Politicians, businessmen, and scholars are not afraid in Latin America to admit that they are poets. Characteristically enough, Puerto Rico's longtime governor, Luis Muñoz Marín, is known among both friends and foes as *El Vate*, or "The Bard." The essay also remains a standard means of literary expression in Latin America and is by no means confined to those who make a career of literary pursuits.

An indication of the high regard in which the average educated Latin American holds literature is the prevalence of poetry, essays, short historical pieces, and smaller works of fiction in many of the daily newspapers of Latin America. Virtually every Latin American capital, and some of the provincial cities, possess at least one paper which is comparable to the New York *Times*, and these are a prime outlet for aspiring, as well as established and recognized, literary folk.

As yet, no Latin American has carved an outstanding

place for himself as a playwright. However, there is a good deal of experimentation going on in this field among Latin American writers, and the theaters in the leading Latin American cities which are willing to try out the works of aspiring national writers are increasing in number. This is particularly the case in Brazil.

PUBLISHING

Literary activity received great encouragement in the Spanish-speaking parts of Latin America by the transfer of the publishing center in that language from Europe to the New World in the late 1930s. As a result of the Spanish Civil War and its aftermath, many Spanish publishing houses transferred to America, or at least set up branches there that could publish works which might not appear in Spain. Most of these went to Argentina and Mexico, which became the two most important centers of book publishing in the Spanish language. Although publishing suffered severely in Argentina under Perón, it survived and is once again flourishing.

Not only did well-established European firms migrate to Buenos Aires and Mexico City, but many new local ones were established in these two cities. At the same time an increasing number of publishing firms has been set up in the major cities of the other Spanish American republics, notably in Santiago, Chile.

In Brazil, too, since the end of the Vargas dictatorship in 1945, book publishing has increased by leaps and bounds, especially in Rio de Janeiro and São Paulo. Brazil, not its mother country Portugal, is now the principal center of Portuguese-language publishing.

These Latin American firms not only publish large quantities of new material written in their respective languages, but also translate and issue works which originally appeared outside the area, particularly in the United States.

PAINTING

Latin American painting also gained world-wide recognition during the first half of the twentieth century. This form of art, too, has its roots far back in Latin American history. Semiliterate Indian and Negro painters frequently decorated colonial churches with pictures in which they interpreted in their own fashion the stories of the Christian gospel. The simplicity and lack of cant of some of these early painters is perhaps symbolized by a picture still to be found in an obscure corner of the Cuzco cathedral in Peru, showing a scene with Joseph and Mary sharing a conjugal bed.

In recent decades it has been Latin American mural painting which has attracted most attention outside of the region. Three Mexican painters in particular became world famous. These were Diego Rivera, José Orozco, and David Alfaro Siqueiros, whose great murals picturing incidents of Mexican history, and particularly episodes of the Revolution, cover innumerable walls in Mexican public buildings. Reproductions of them have been sold around the world. Following in their footsteps has been a younger Brazilian painter, Cândido Portinari, one of whose huge masterpieces is to be found in the United Nations Building in New York City.

The day of great Mexican mural painting is now past, and with the exception of Portinari, no new Latin American painters have as yet achieved world fame. However, there are active groups of artists in virtually all of the Latin American countries and some of them may well take their place in the front ranks in the years to come. Some of these artists are much influenced by the example of the Mexicans; others are experimenting in a wide range of forms and media. Only a minority seem to have become abstractionists. An interesting example of the new Latin American artistic groups is that of Puerto Rico, composed of comparatively young men, whose vivid paintings of the Puerto Rican scene, along with etchings, lithographs, and silk-screen paintings, are gaining increasing attention in the United States and Latin America.

ARCHITECTURE

Architecture is probably the art form in which the Latin Americans have made the most vivid impression since World War II. In this field Brazil is the unquestioned leader, though Mexico and some of the smaller countries have made some notable contributions.

The leading contemporary Latin American architects belong to the modern school. Although they follow the general principles laid down by such European masters as Le Corbusier, Gropius, and Miës van der Rohe, they add innovations of their own and experiment with new materials and forms.

Certainly one of the great buildings in the modern genre in the world today is the Brazilian Ministry of Education in Rio de Janeiro, built along lines originated by Le Corbusier, but having the personal touch of its Brazilian architect Oscar Niemeyer. Subsequently, Niemeyer has built many other edifices throughout Brazil and he was a consultant in the construction of the United Nations Building in New York City.

The new Brazilian capital, Brasília, is the most spectacular example of that country's accomplishments in architecture. The basic plan for the city was drawn up by Lucio Costa, dean of contemporary Brazilian architects, after a nationwide contest. He has laid out some of the individual buildings, and Oscar Niemeyer has also done many of them. The whole theme of the city is modernity, not only in the structure of its buildings, but in the layout of its streets and main arteries, its provisions for traffic control, and its concept of what a city really should be like. Whatever one may think about the wisdom of constructing such

a huge city out of nothing—and this wisdom is more questioned outside of Brazil than in that country—there is little
doubt that it is a tribute to the ability of the Brazilians both
as architects and city planners. It will be the object of study
by people from all over the world.

The new architecture has also found its ardent champions in Mexico. The capital city has been largely remod-
eled, and most of the new edifices in the center and in the
richer residential areas have been built along modern lines.
The new campus of the National University, on the out-
skirts of Mexico City, is a brilliant example of the ver-
satility and originality of Mexican professional architects,
as well as of the famous Big Three painters—Rivera,
Orozco, and Siqueiros—each of whom contributed at least
one mural to the University City.

Caracas (Venezuela), Medellín (Colombia), Havana
(Cuba), and San Juan (Puerto Rico) are among the other
Latin American cities which contain notable buildings constructed recently by local architects. Only a few countries
seem to lag completely behind in this renaissance of Latin
American architecture. One of these is Chile, where, with
a few notable exceptions, the architects have seemed un-
willing to venture out of paths which have been well worn
for centuries.

MUSIC

Latin American music is probably one of the most important but least appreciated contributions to the contemporary world cultural scene. There is little doubt that
rhythms and musical forms originating in Latin America—
such as the rumba, the samba, and the tango—are played
and sung the world around. But it is doubtful whether most
people who play them think of them as a contribution to
world culture.

But Latin American achievements in the musical field go
far beyond these popular dance forms. The Latin Ameri-

cans have also made their mark in the world of serious music. In the nineteenth century there was at least one Latin American composer, the Brazilian Carlos Gomes, whose music was played in the concert halls of Europe and North America. Though much influenced by the Italian music of his day, he also wove Brazilian themes into his compositions.

In the present century the growing confidence of the Latin Americans in their own abilities, ideas, and resources, which we have seen reflected in economics, politics, and literature, has also been noticeable in music. The great Brazilian composer Heitor Villa-Lobos has gained world renown for his haunting use of Brazilian melodies and rhythms in his compositions. The Mexican composer and director Carlos Chávez has done the same with Mexican materials and his work has been widely acclaimed and played outside of his own country. Numerous other composers in many Latin American countries have experimented with national materials, though with less recognition for their efforts from outside their native countries.

Latin American orchestral groups and individual musical artists have also gained attention. The national orchestras of Mexico and Chile, the Teatro Colón orchestra in Buenos Aires, and that of the Municipal Theater in Rio de Janeiro are among the best in the world. At the same time individual performers such as Bidu Sayão, a Brazilian member of the Metropolitan Opera; Claudio Arrau, the Chilean pianist; and José Sanromá, the Puerto Rican pianist, are but a few of those who are heard in concert halls throughout the world.

THE MOVIES

In the newest art form, motion pictures, the Latin Americans have also gained considerable prestige. The two great movie centers in the Spanish language are Buenos Aires and Mexico City, and their products are shown wherever Spanish is spoken.

The motion-picture studios of Buenos Aires and Mexico City doubtless have their share of bad pictures, but they also turn out some outstanding productions. They tend to bear the imprint of the two nations in which they originate. Mexican pictures not infrequently have a touch of bittersweet sadness which is typical of many Mexicans. Argentine products are more boisterous and more European, as is Argentina.

Some artists who received their start in Mexican films have migrated to Hollywood. Such has been the fate of the great comic Cantinflas, and such actors as Dolores del Río, César Romero, and Ricardo Montalban. Perhaps distance and unfamiliarity have prevented a similar migration to southern California from Buenos Aires.

Several other Latin American countries in addition to Argentina and Mexico have sought to establish motion-picture industries. Most of the larger countries at least turn out newsreels and other shorts for local showing. In the late 1940s Chile attempted to establish a studio in which to turn out regular full-length features, but it failed financially in spite of liberal government aid. Brazil also has undertaken to set up a film industry on a sizable scale. However, it is as yet in its infancy. The Castro regime has announced its intention of establishing a full-scale motion-picture industry in Cuba.

SCIENTIFIC PROGRESS

Until fairly recently, Latin Americans had made relatively little progress in the physical sciences. This fact was perhaps explainable in terms of both the nature of traditional Latin American society and economy, and the prevalent psychology of the people, particularly the educated people.

The social and economic system which was dominant before industrialization began to have a serious impact in the region was not particularly conducive to scientific progress. It was essentially conservative, and sought to maintain the status quo. There was little economic incentive for technological innovations which might provoke and promote scientific advances. Landlords did not need such innovations because they had at their disposal virtually free labor. The Church in many countries tended to be suspicious of science. The armed forces felt no impelling need for it. Scientific development as a means of achieving greater output and higher standards of living was not yet an important consideration.

There are now economic and political reasons for interest in things scientific and there are increasing numbers of Latin American educated people who are willing to impose upon themselves the self-discipline and concentration necessary to become an expert in a physical science.

Although none of the countries has a sufficiently strong economic base at the present time to permit it to lavish much in the way of resources on such things as atomic-energy research or development of rocketry, several countries have established atomic-energy commissions or similar bodies. Their function is more to try to keep abreast of current developments insofar as possible, and to lay the groundwork for research and development in the future, than actually to undertake the latter at the present time. Latin Americans are getting some experience in rocketry through their cooperation with the United States in tracing the progress of satellites.

Latin America has not yet progressed far enough in the physical sciences to gain much world renown. However, there are some exceptions. At the turn of the century Dr. Carlos Finlay was successful in isolating the mosquito which causes yellow fever, and became world famous. In 1947 the Argentine Bernardo Houssay won the Nobel Prize in Medicine for his study of the pituitary gland.

THE SOCIAL SCIENCES

In the field of the social sciences the Latin American record is more impressive. Brazilian, Mexican, Cuban, and Peruvian sociologists have done outstanding work. Some of their writings, such as the Brazilian Gilberto Freyre's *Casa Grande e Senzala* (translated as *Masters and Slaves*), have gained fame among members of their profession the world over. Mexico and the Andean countries of South America have developed expert groups of anthropologists and archaeologists who have done much to explain the history and nature of the Indian societies of those areas.

History has always been a favorite field for Latin American scholars. Usually they have centered their attention on the history of their own countries, or at least on Latin America as a whole. However, there is now beginning to emerge a group of Latin American historians who are interested in other problems as well. For instance, José Luis Romero of Argentina is recognized as a leading authority on the Middle Ages in Western Europe. Similarly, Germán Arciniegas of Colombia, who has already published one volume on the Florentine thinker and explorer Amerigo Vespucci, is one of the important contemporary scholars of Renaissance Italy.

Latin America has also developed a talented group of top-flight economists. Many of them have been trained in European and North American universities, and they are widely conversant with not only the history of economic doctrines, but with contemporary economic ideas. The Economic Commission for Latin America of the United Nations, with its headquarters in Santiago, Chile, has been the rallying point and practical training ground for many of the more brilliant young Latin American economists. Under the leadership of Dr. Raúl Prebisch of Argentina they have made invaluable surveys of economic problems of individual Latin American countries as well as of the region as a whole, and have made important, if highly controversial, contributions to economic ideas, particularly in the field of economic development.

SPORTS

One aspect of popular culture of Latin America should be noted—sports. The people of the region are ardent fans. There have been no sports of importance which have originated in the area, but the Latin Americans have taken avidly to several imports. Probably, the most popular sport in the region as a whole is soccer, known locally as "football" or *futbol*. In Argentina, Chile, and several other countries this is a professional sport, as well as being very popular with amateurs. Residents of Buenos Aires are as fanatical supporters of "Boca Juniors" or "River Plate" as they are enthusiasts for their preferred political party. Massive crowds turn out for their games. Amateur soccer teams from Uruguay and Brazil have contested for top place in Olympic competition.

Baseball, introduced half a century ago from the United States, is the most popular sport around the Caribbean. Teams from Central America and the West Indies, as well as from Colombia and Venezuela, compete annually in a "little World Series" for Latin America. Individual players from several Latin American countries, including Cuba, Venezuela, Mexico, and Puerto Rico, have won berths on the major-league teams of the United States.

Other sports are of less importance. Polo has long been popular among the Argentine aristocrats, who have produced a number of international champions, and horse racing is widely popular. In Mexico and a few other countries the Basque game of *jai alai* has many enthusiastic fans.

Finally, bullfighting must be mentioned. Public opinion in Latin America is badly divided on this form of sport, if that is what it is. In the majority of the countries bullfighting is not permitted. However, in Mexico, Peru, Colombia, Venezuela, and a few other nations it is permitted and has many *aficionados*. The world's best matadors consider it a sign of success if they are invited to perform in the bull rings of Mexico City or Lima.

SUMMARY

It is certain that the cultural and intellectual flowering of Latin America is only beginning. Its growing wealth will provide larger resources to be devoted to intellectual and artistic pursuits. Its growing self-confidence will make the writers, thinkers, and artists of the area less reticent about giving full rein to their creative abilities and to the spirit of innovation. The clashes and drama growing from the tremendous social, economic, and political changes through which the area is now passing will provide incentive and invaluable source material for creative intellects in whatever field.

The Church

The great majority of Latin Americans are at least formally members of the Roman Catholic Church. Brazil is now the world's largest predominantly Catholic country, and other Latin Americans are also beginning to play an increasingly important role in the hierarchy, intellectual life, and financial affairs of the Church. However, sizable numbers of Latin Americans belong to other branches of Christendom; there are likewise some members of other world religions—Judaism, Islam—and much larger numbers hold pagan beliefs native to America and Africa.

EARLY CATHOLIC PENETRATION

The Catholic Church arrived in America with the conquistadors. While the conquerors used the sword to overthrow the military and political power of indigenous rulers, the priests brought the Cross to destroy the religion and ethos of the conquered peoples, and tried to raise in their place the faith, theology, and morality of Christianity. The accomplishments of these early missionaries were almost as remarkable as were those of the conquistadors themselves. In some parts of the Spanish Empire priests, by their patient and self-sacrificing efforts, were able to win the confidence of Indians whom the armed soldiers had never been able to conquer, and thus to incorporate them into the domains of the Spanish Crown.

In early colonial times the role of the Church and its ministers was a complicated one. On the one hand, they carried on an uncompromising struggle against the outward forms of the pagan religions which had preceded them. It was the priests who insisted on the total destruction of the temple of the Aztecs in Mexico City, and of most of their other public buildings as well. It was the Dominican friars who chose the ruins of the Temple of the Sun in the Inca capital of Cuzco upon which to erect a beautiful church of their own. Indeed, the early Spanish Churchmen in America often sought to obliterate the old gods by building temples to the new one on land which was already holy to the newly converted Indians.

The missionaries' efforts to wipe out the old religion were far from completely successful. Very often the worship of the Christian Deity and the saints became a thin veneer to cover the continued adoration of the preconquest gods. The Church, furthermore, though unbending on matters of dogma, was tolerant with regard to liturgy and other matters of relatively secondary importance. Many a visitor to mass in a South American Indian village has been startled even in the mid-twentieth century by the use of conch-shell horns at important points in the service, and by other survivals from a worship which was old in this area before Columbus was even born.

The missionaries' efforts probably contributed to breaking the spirit of active resistance of the great mass of the Indians to their white conquerors. It is probable that in their zeal to destroy things associated with the pagan faith, the early priests destroyed historical records and other documents which would have thrown invaluable light on the past of the Indians. There is no doubt, too, that the Indian priestly class, which was one of the principal forces transmitting the history, legends, and communal spirit of the Indians from one generation to the next, was largely obliterated, due in large part to the fervor of the Catholic missionaries.

Furthermore, it is impossible to calculate the subtle damage, all but hidden to the white man, which was done to the Indians by the attempt to destroy en masse the very bases of their faith and life, a task to which the missionaries were dedicated. When old gods and systems of belief are destroyed among people with cultures such as those of pre-Columbian Mexico and Andean South America, there is no doubt that the result is much confusion, indecision, and despair.

THE CHURCH AND THE INDIANS AND NEGROES

On the other hand, the early Churchmen in Spanish and Portuguese America played a gallant, useful, and compassionate role as defenders of the Indians against the cruelty and exploitation of the laymen among the conquistadors and their descendants. The example of Fray de las Casas, the Protector of the Indians, was followed by thousands of priests and bishops during the next three centuries. Very frequently the Church used its considerable influence with the Spanish and Portuguese monarchs and their viceroys in the New World to mitigate the conditions of the Indians. They began the efforts to educate at least some of the Indian children, organized charitable enterprises to shelter some of the worst victims of the system, and even brought some of them into the priesthood.

Nor was it only the Indians who felt the helping or comforting hand of devoted clergymen. The Negro slaves, who took the place of the Indians as performers of manual labor in the Caribbean and the tropical coastal areas of South and Central America, likewise became the special charge of such clergymen. One of these, Father Pedro Claver, was one of the great figures of colonial Colombia.

JESUIT *REDUCCIONES* IN PARAGUAY

One of the most striking and famous examples of the Church's tutelage of the nonwhite subjects of the Spanish Empire was that of the Jesuit colonies of Paraguay. Members of the Society of Jesus pushed into remote areas covering parts of the present-day republics of Paraguay, Argentina, and Brazil. Here they established a virtually independent State, albeit one which enjoyed for several generations the protection of the Spanish Crown.

The Jesuits brought the Guarani Indians of this region together in communities. Under the tutelage of the priests the Indians built homes for themselves and churches to the glory of their newly found God. Warehouses, schools, and primitive hospitals were also constructed. The people were taught new techniques in agriculture and grazing as well as numerous handicrafts necessary to the kind of civilized society to which they were being introduced.

These colonies were veritable theocracies. Although they were benevolent despots, the Jesuit priests were the rulers. There was little attempt to prepare the Guarani to govern themselves, there was no intention of training the Indians to be the equals of the priests who were their masters. Nevertheless, these Jesuit colonies remain one of the finest examples of self-sacrificing labor by Spanish clergymen on behalf of the indigenous people in colonial America.

So long as they were allowed to rule their communities, the Jesuits were more or less successful in protecting their wards from depradations by avaricious laymen. Raiders from Portuguese São Paulo, and from Spanish settlements west and south of the Jesuit area, were a constant menace to the theocratic communities, eager as they were to kidnap their inhabitants to serve as docile and well-trained slaves in neighboring colonies. It was only after the Jesuits were expelled from the Spanish Empire in 1767 that these raiders were finally successful. They were so successful that within a few short years nothing remained of the patient and persevering work of the Jesuit fathers.

CHANGE IN THE ROLE OF THE CHURCH

As the colonial period drew to a close, the role of the Church began to change. The missionary fervor and the passionate desire to defend the weaker members of the community from the stronger notably decreased. At the same time the wealth of the Church vastly increased. This development has been graphically described by Helen Phipps:

> The clergy was an economically privileged class from the beginning. The members of it received large grants of land from the crown. Many monasteries, cathedrals and individual prelates were given encomiendas which had more or less the same history as those conferred upon laymen. For the erection of churches, monasteries and residences the royal treasury furnished half the money, the encomenderos or the Spanish population in general furnished the other half, and Indians did the work without remuneration. Ecclesiastical capital was free from taxation—legally in the early days, virtually always. . . . From the outset [the Church] had an economic advantage over even the richest of the encomenderos, who had to build their own houses and provide their own working capital, and had not the resources of income that the clergy had. So with the immense prestige of the Church behind them, it is not surprising that the clergy dominated the Colonial era economically and politically. Nor is it strange that, as the years went on, the early missionary fervor tended to give place to complacent well-being and easy acceptance of priority thrust upon them; that adventurers were to be found in the ranks of the clergy as in all walks of life; that

this easy means of acquiring an honorable position and a comfortable livelihood attracted such large numbers that in 1655 the town council of Mexico City implored Philip IV to send no more monks, as more than six thousand were without employment, living on the fat of the land.[1]

THE CHURCH AND INDEPENDENCE

With the outbreak of the struggle for independence from the Old World the Church in the revolting colonies was badly split. For the most part, the bishops and other top officials of the Church, who had usually been born in Spain and had been appointed by the Spanish king, were generally among those still loyal to the Crown. On the other hand, the lower clergy, particularly the parish priests, many of whom were natives of America and were of mixed blood or even of pure Indian or Negro parentage, were often passionate advocates of independence.

The independence movement in Mexico, for instance, was started by two mestizo priests, Fathers Miguel Hidalgo and José María Morelos. In the sermon with which Father Hidalgo launched the uprising, a sermon which has gone down in history as "The Cry of Dolores," after the town in which Hidalgo was parish priest, he presented the cause of liberation from Spain in the following terms:

My children, this day comes to you a new dispensation. Are you ready to receive it? Will you make the effort to recover from the hated Spaniards the lands stolen from your forefathers three hundred years ago?

[1] Helen Phipps: *Some Aspects of the Agrarian Question in Mexico* (University of Texas, 1925).

THE NINETEENTH-CENTURY
CHURCH-STATE STRUGGLE

During much of the first century of independence the most bitter element of political controversy in the Latin American countries was the status of the Church. The outcome of this long struggle, in the name of which many revolutions and counterrevolutions were carried out and civil wars were fought, was generally favorable to the anticlerical Liberals. Today separation of Church and State exists in Chile, Uruguay, Mexico, Guatemala, and Cuba. In all countries the basic educational system is in the hands of the State, though most nations have a more or less extensive Catholic parochial-school system parallel to that of the government. All of the old universities originally founded by the Church were taken over by the States. In all nations official vital statistics are now the jurisdiction of the State and not of the Church. In all countries most political rights are equal for people of all religions or none, though in a few cases the president must still be a Catholic.

Sometimes the Liberals were able to go further than this. In Uruguay, Chile, Mexico, and Cuba, among others, there are more or less easy divorce laws, which were passed over the strenuous objections of the Church. (In contrast, the Church was powerful enough in Brazil in 1946 to get a prohibition of divorce written into the constitution). In several countries, including Mexico and Guatemala, priests and nuns may not wear their clerical garb on the streets, and the Church may own no property except that strictly needed for conducting religious services.

The attitude of the majority of the people differs as much from country to country as does the legal position of the Church. In mid-twentieth-century Colombia even the Liberals pride themselves on being good Catholics. In contrast, only a relatively small percentage of the population of Uruguay or Cuba actually practice their religion.

In some countries, such as Argentina, there still exists a significant part of the population which is bitterly opposed to the Catholic Church and all its works. In Venezuela, on the other hand, Church-State relations are virtually not an issue in the country's politics.

The role of the Catholic Church in Latin American society and political life has been changing in recent years. In the latter part of the colonial period and during the long Church-State struggle of the nineteenth century and the early years of the present one, the Church generally stood on the side of the status quo. Its hierarchy was usually aligned with the landlords and the mercantile ruling classes. It found no difficulty in living on friendly terms with dictatorial regimes of all kinds, so long as those regimes did not interfere with the Church's own privileges. Seldom was a Church voice raised against the injustices and cruelties of the long list of tyrants who plagued the Latin American countries during their first century of independence.

During this long period the Church in the Latin American countries seemed to be much more concerned with maintaining its temporal status than in answering the needs of its flock. As a result, the Church became alienated from large parts of the population. Any movement for social, economic, or political reform tended to run into Church opposition, and as a result most advocates of such reforms became avowed enemies of the Church. The Church came to have relatively little influence or following among the urban workers, and even less among large segments of the middle class and the intelligentsia.

A contributing factor to this situation was the lack of adequate training and the somewhat lax moral fiber of large segments of the priesthood. The Catholic intelligentsia was at best a small minority and few of its members were clergymen. The fact that the rules of priestly celibacy were frequently violated was almost taken for granted in many parts of the region. The prestige of the clergy as individuals did not measure up to the importance of the Church as an institution, and hence helped to reduce that importance.

One result of this situation was that it was very difficult to recruit enough candidates for the priesthood in the Latin American countries to meet the Church's needs. So there was a sizable importation of foreign priests, particularly Spaniards, to fill the vacant parishes, and in many cases the foreignness of the priest has added an additional barrier to communication between the Church and its faithful.

CHANGING CHURCH ATTITUDES

All of this has been changing in recent decades. The discipline of the clergy, particularly in moral matters, has been considerably tightened. Some of the foreign priests, both European and North American, have tended to jolt the local clergy out of their complacency. At the same time the opening of Catholic universities in a number of countries, such as Chile, Brazil, Cuba, Colombia, and Argentina, has been indicative of a renewed interest in intellectual affairs on the part of the Church in Latin America. Likewise, it has helped to provide a new Catholic intelligentsia, which is beginning to make its weight felt in Chile, Argentina, Brazil, and some other countries. Many of these Catholic intellectuals are followers of such progressive Catholic thinkers as Henri Bergson, François Mauriac, and Jacques Maritain.

The growing industrialization and urbanization of Latin America have set in motion two conflicting trends within the Church. On the one hand, as more people have moved into the urban working and middle classes, an increasing number of faithful Catholics has tended to be subject to the religious skepticism or indifference which is so characteristic of city populations throughout the Christian world. On the other hand, urbanization has brought to the cities hundreds of thousands of peasants from the more isolated parts of Latin America, who have hitherto been virtually outside the reach of the ministrations of the Church. In the cities it has been much easier for the Church to minister to their needs and reinforce their faith.

At the same time the Church has tended to shift its emphasis from defense of the economic, social, and political status quo and of its own privileges, to a more critical attitude toward the Latin American society to which it is ministering. This new attitude is reflected in the development, particularly since World War II, of both Catholic trade-union movements and Christian Democratic parties.

Even before the Second World War groups of Catholic priests and laymen had begun to become concerned with the labor movement in a number of Latin American countries, including Argentina, Chile, Ecuador, and Uruguay. Subsequently, Catholic elements took the lead in establishing what became the largest central labor organizations in Costa Rica and Colombia, while smaller Catholic labor confederations existed in Ecuador, Uruguay, and Chile. In Chile, Brazil, Venezuela, Cuba, and Argentina laymen and priests organized strong pressure groups in existing united labor movements. In 1955 a number of the Catholic labor groups of the hemisphere were brought together to form the Confederación Latino Americana de Sindicalistas Cristianos, regional organization of the International Federation of Christian Trade Unions.

This work directly in the trade-unions was "nonconfessional"; that is, it was concerned directly with the problems faced by Catholic workers in their jobs and their labor organizations, rather than with questions of religious dogma or practice. However, during the last several decades the Church in most of the Latin American countries also has undertaken to set up groups known as Young Catholic Worker circles and federations. These organizations have the dual task of training their members in the Catholic faith, and of preparing them to act as Catholics in the community at large. In a number of cases the Young

Catholic Worker organizations have set up training schools to prepare their members for leadership positions in the labor movement. This work has been particularly significant in Cuba, Venezuela, Brazil, and Argentina.

The Catholics do not represent a major force in the labor movements of most of the Latin American countries. However, by 1960 they had begun to make their weight felt in several of them. There was little question that elements of the clergy and laity of the Church had become deeply concerned with the problems of urban workers, and that they were beginning to win the confidence of a growing group of these workers, who had heretofore felt that the Church was uninterested in them or in anything which concerned them.

CHRISTIAN DEMOCRATS

A new type of Catholic political activity has also emerged as a significant force since World War II: the Christian Democratic parties. Although at least two such parties, the Unión Cívica of Uruguay and the Falange Nacional of Chile, existed before the Second World War, the Christian Democratic movement became a hemisphere-wide phenomenon only after 1945. In the following ten or a dozen years Christian Democratic parties were established in Argentina, Bolivia, Paraguay, Brazil, Venezuela, Peru, Cuba, Haiti, and Guatemala.

These parties took their place on the moderate Left in Latin American politics, in contrast to the Church parties of the nineteenth century, which had generally been exceedingly conservative. The emphasis of the Christian Democrats has been on social justice and political democracy. They have sought to apply Catholic social doctrines to the conduct of public affairs, rather than to defend the temporal position of the Church. They have been in the forefront of the fight against the dictatorships of Perón in

Argentina, Odría in Peru, Pérez Jiménez in Venezuela, and Batista in Cuba.

This change in the social and political orientation of the Church has undoubtedly had encouragement from the Vatican. Although the initiative for work in the trade-unions and for the organization of moderate Left Christian Democratic parties has usually come from laymen and lower-ranking clergymen, it has frequently received at least the tacit consent of the hierarchy in the various countries, including that of several of the Latin American cardinals. A number of religious orders, particularly the Jesuits, have taken a great interest in social and political problems.

However, the change in Church policy on social and political matters has not gone unchallenged within the Church. There have been priests and bishops as well as many of the more conservative laymen who have been strongly opposed to the trend. Many of these people find it hard to understand how the Church can support organized labor and basic social reform, which they tend to equate with Communism and atheism. In part, their astonishment is explainable in terms of the role which has traditionally been played in the trade-union movement and Left Wing politics in Latin America by elements opposed to the Church; in part it is explainable in terms of these people's own self-interest.

As the Church's role in Latin American public affairs has been changing in recent years, so has the role of Latin American Catholics in the Church as a whole. Every new consistory since World War II has seen the creation of one or more new Latin American cardinals. By 1959 there were nine princes of the Church from this area, the largest number in history. Of these, two were from Argentina, three from Brazil, and one each from Chile, Cuba, Ecuador, and Colombia. Venezuela received its first cardinal in 1960.

Several factors have served to increase the importance of Latin America within the world Church. Sizable seg-

ments of the faithful in Eastern Europe have been at least
partially cut off from contacts with Rome. On the other
hand, the fact that Latin America as a whole has the
world's most rapidly increasing population means that the
numerical importance of Latin American Catholics within
the Church is increasing. The growing wealth of the area
has also meant that the financial contribution made to
Rome by Latin American Catholics has been of increasing significance.

PAGANISM OF THE INDIANS

In spite of the nominal membership in the Catholic
Church of the Indian and Negro masses of several of the
Latin American countries, many millions of these people
in fact remain pagans. This is certainly the case in Guate-
mala, Bolivia, Peru, Ecuador, and the remoter parts of
Mexico, as well as in Haiti and in large areas of Brazil.

The conversion to Catholicism of many of the Indians
was purely formal. Partly as a result of the early missionaries' eagerness to claim converts to Christianity, the
Indians tended to continue to worship the old gods under
the names of Christian saints, or even of Christ himself.
A not untypical example of this is found in the ancient
Inca capital of Cuzco, which has in its cathedral a dark-
colored figure of Christ upon the cross. This is known as
Our Lord of the Earthquakes, and for the simple Indian
peasants who worship it, this figure is little more than a
reincarnation of their own ancient god of the earthquake.

With simple observation a visiting tourist can still see
the persistence of this paganism in the Guatemalan town
of Chichicastenango. There, on market days, the Indians
come not only to sell and to buy, but to worship according
to their own ancient ways in the town's colonial Christian
church. This edifice, rising at one side of the town square,
sits upon a pyramid-like platform, not dissimilar to the

temples of the pre-Conquest ancestors of the Mayas, who still inhabit the area.

At the bottom of the pyramid an Indian tends a small flame which is used to light the incense which the Indian worshipers put in small braziers rented from the fire-tender before going into the church. On each step of the pyramid the worshipers swing their containers of incense, and pray in loud voices. Their prayers, uttered in their own language, are not directed to the Christian God, or to his saints, but rather to their own ancient deities of the east wind, the rain, and so on.

Once inside the church the worshipers' attention is cen-tered upon the stations of the cross, which are marked down the middle of the church floor. However, here too the Christian form covers pagan substance. Each Indian man squats next to one of the stations of the cross, throws a handful of rose petals upon it, and prays to the souls of his dead ancestors.

Furthermore, the Christian sacraments are held in little regard by the Indian parishioners of Chichicastenango. Only baptism is regularly received at the hands of the local parish priests. The other sacraments honored by this flock —marriage and burial—are received at the hands of Indian priests, dully camouflaged as leaders of *cofradías.* These *cofradías,* each of which is supposedly organized to do honor to a Christian saint, are the real heart of pagan wor-ship in the community. It is their leading officials who are in fact the pagan priests, and who make the wedding bond "legal" in the eyes of the Indians. Only to them will the Indian trust the task of giving his soul the proper intro-duction to the Other World. The local Catholic parish priest dare not even approach these sacred Indian ceremonies.

Early in the 1940s the Indians of Chichicastenango wanted to pay great honor to their local Catholic clergy-man upon the occasion of the fiftieth anniversary of his ordination in the priesthood. After due consultation among themselves they decided that they would do so by abiding by what they considered his idiosyncrasies and having him wed half a dozen of their young couples according to the Christian rites of marriage. Only on such occasions were they willing to make effective their supposed belief in the Christian religion.

NEGRO PAGANISM

However, it is not only the Indians who have maintained their ancient religions. The same thing has occurred among Negroes in Brazil, Cuba, Haiti, some of the British West Indian islands, and elsewhere. The Negro cults are basically African in origin, though they frequently represent a mixture of beliefs of various African tribal groups, and have assimilated ideas and creeds from Christianity and even from the American Indian pagan religions.

Speaking of the prevalence of African cults in the Brazilian city of Recife in recent decades, René Ribeiro has written:

> With the expansion of the city and the settling of the poor population in the periphery of the urban area one finds the cult temples in the outlying wards in 1934. There were five in Fundao, four in Campo Grande, two in Encruzilhada and Arruda; Agua Fria, Tegipic, and Pina each had one. Most of these groups represented a merging of Yoruban and Dahomeyan beliefs. . . . Priests, officials, and worshippers include all the degrees of racial mixture common in Brazil, including pure whites, and in all of these groups the fusion and reinterpretation of elements of the African, Amerindian, and European religions is evident. . . .
> It is difficult to determine with certainty the age of each of the groups now functioning in Recife. The most traditional, with the longest history, goes back to the last quarter of the last century, the rest being of much more recent organization. All indications are

that . . . the cults function in small groups, with private rituals, only occasionally holding public ceremonies. It is very understandable how this was made necessary by police reprisals, pressure of the Catholic Church, and the hostility of the part of the population more identified with European culture. This is so true that the priest of one of the groups dissolved during the last organized persecution—that of 1937— did not reorganize his group thereafter, preferring to carry on his magical-divine practices in private, in spite of official guarantees of recognition and freedom then offered to everyone.[2]

Most of the Negro cults profess a belief in a supreme god, known in Brazil as Oshala or Orishala, who presides over a number of lesser deities. In some of the cults three of these lesser deities are equated with the Holy Trinity of the Christian faith. In other cases one of the pagan deities is identified with the Crucified Jesus. Such identification is found not only in Recife, but in Baía, and in the African cults in Cuba as well.

The belief in these African deities is by no means confined to people of African descent. The author has heard of cases of important members of the Brazilian congress, men of largely European ancestry, who have consulted priests of one or another of the Afro-Brazilian cults before voting on important legislation coming before them for consideration.

The African cults involve the use of sacrifices, usually of chickens or some other domesticated animal. They are also marked by rhythmic dancing, and in some cases by artistic painting of some considerable, if primitive, beauty, done by the priests of the cults. In Haiti the government's Art Center was very active after World War II in trying to discover these peasant artists, regarding their work as an

[2] René Ribeiro: *Cultos Afrobrasileiros do Recife,* Boletim do Instituto Joaquim Nabuco, Numero Especial, 1952, pp. 35–36.

important contribution to the nation's culture. At the same time officials of the local Protestant Episcopal cathedral invited a number of these pagan "voodoo" artists to paint their conception of the Christian story on a wall of the cathedral.

The attitude of the authorities toward the African pagan religions in the New World has varied a great deal from time to time and place to place. During much of the colonial period in Brazil the Portuguese colonial officials gave semiofficial recognition to the cult leaders among the slaves as people whose cooperation was very important in maintaining order among the people of African origin or descent. At other times the Portuguese, and later the Brazilian officials, tended to suppress the African cults. The same variation in official attitudes has been found in Cuba, Haiti, and the British Caribbean areas. In recent decades a general attitude of tolerance has prevailed, except in rare cases in which extremist cult elements have engaged in ritual murders.

THE PROTESTANTS

Protestants constitute a small minority among the Latin Americans. In some areas, such as southern Brazil, the southern part of the Central Valley of Chile, and certain parts of Argentina, where sizable numbers of Germans have settled, there exist what may be called "indigenous" Protestant churches, particularly Lutheran. There are also scattered groups of people of British descent, especially in Brazil, Uruguay, Argentina, and Chile, who have maintained their traditional Protestant faith. In the British and Dutch West Indies, too, Protestant groups owe their origin to settlers there. The rest of the non-Catholic Christians of the area have been converted to Protestantism largely by the activities of missionaries, most of them from the United States.

Most of the recognized Protestant sects are represented

in Latin America. For instance, in Brazil the Lutherans are most numerous, followed by the Methodists, Presbyterians, Baptists, and Episcopalians. Some of the more extreme Protestant groups also carry on very active missionary work in the area. These include the Pentecostals, the Four Square Gospel Church, the Jehovah's Witnesses, and the Seventh-day Adventists. The last of these groups has done particularly impressive medical missionary work in a number of the Latin American countries.

The appeal which the Protestant sects have to different groups of Latin Americans varies considerably. Some of the more extreme fundamentalist sects recommend themselves to people who might be sympathetic to some of the African pagan cults, since both groups practice very emotional forms of worship and believe in one's being "possessed" by the Holy Spirit. On the other hand, the author has been informed in both Haiti and Brazil that the Episcopal Church has a considerable appeal to upper-class people who resent the fact that the Roman Catholic service is not conducted in their own language. They sometimes tend to look upon Episcopalianism as being more or less a version of their old faith practiced in their native tongues.

Relations are sometimes uneasy between the Protestants and the predominant Catholic group, in spite of the fact that all of the Latin American constitutions guarantee freedom of religion. In some instances the more fundamentalist Protestant groups tend to provoke reprisals by their particularly vigorous denunciations of the Catholic Church. In other instances there has been actual persecution of virtually all Protestant groups, as in Colombia during the late 1940s and early 1950s.

On the other hand, there have been times during struggles between State and Church in Latin America when governmental authorities have enthusiastically welcomed Protestant missionaries. This occurred in the latter part of the nineteenth century when strongly anticlerical governments dominated Guatemala. It also happened in the 1920s when relations between Church and State were particularly un-friendly in Mexico.

It is probably true that the activities of the Protestant missionaries in Latin America have helped to provoke the renovation in the Catholic Church which we have already noted. Faced with the fact that at least some of the workers and peasants with whom they had lost contact were being converted to Protestantism, and in many cases as a result were becoming militantly anti-Catholic, many priests were inspired to try to do something about the situation.

In any case, there is probably no Latin American coun-try in which the Protestants amount to more than 10 per cent of the total population. The rise of nationalism, tinged with antipathy toward the United States, is likely to hamper future development of Protestant missionary activities in the area. Many of the nationalists tend to regard foreign missionaries as "agents of Yankee imperialism."

OTHER RELIGIONS

There are some small groups of Moslems to be found in Latin America and the Caribbean. The most important group is in Trinidad, British Guiana, and Surinam, among the descendants of immigrants from India and Indonesia. There are also some Moslems among the small but wide-spread and influential group of Arab origin to be found in many Latin American countries, though most Arabs were Christians when they arrived in America or became so soon after their arrival. Also, there are remnants of Islam to be found among some Brazilian Negroes, though they practice a very adulterated form of this world reli-gion.

Finally, there are important groups of Jews in several of the Latin American nations. The largest Jewish populations are in Buenos Aires and Mexico City, though there are also important Jewish colonies in Chile, Brazil, Bolivia, El Sal-vador, and Jamaica in the West Indies. Some of these, particularly in Jamaica, are Sephardim, who trace their families' residence in America back to Spanish times, though most Latin American Jews are Ashkenazim, whose arrival in the New World dates from the late nineteenth and early twentieth centuries.

SUMMARY

There seems little likelihood that the predominantly Catholic nature of the Latin American population will change in the foreseeable future. The nature of the Catholic Church in the area is likely to alter very greatly as it becomes increasingly concerned with the social and economic problems of the people and attempts to regain the allegiance of many who have abandoned the Church in the past. Catholicism is likely to make considerable gains as the Indian and Negro masses of a number of the countries are increasingly incorporated in the general life of their respective nations. On the other hand, at least some of those who now are pagans may become members of one or another of the Protestant sects. In general, it is likely that as the impact of industrialism and urbanism becomes increasingly great in the area, the relative indifference to religion which seems to characterize large segments of the population of the highly industrialized nations of Western Europe and North America will become an increasingly important factor in Latin America as well.

Latin America and the World

Latin America is playing an increasingly important role in world affairs. At the same time, as part of the revolutionary transformation which is taking place in the area, its relations with various areas of the world are undergoing basic changes.

As we have noted in the foregoing chapters, Latin America has in the past been wont to ape the ways and ideas of Europe and North America. In politics the Latin Americans for a century patterned their constitutions and political parties after those in other parts of the world. In economic policies they were long prone to adhere to the doctrines of "free trade" because these were popular in England and elsewhere, no matter how inappropriate they might be to their own situation. In cultural affairs, too, in their works of literature, painting, and architecture, they tended to follow the fashions of Europe, though frequently with a somewhat Latin American accent.

However, in recent decades the melding of the indigenous and the imported elements in the Latin American society and culture has increasingly brought the development of a new national self-consciousness in the countries of the region. This merging is seen in virtually every field. There is the physical mixing of the races which has resulted in the emergence of the Indian-white mestizos and Negro-white mulattoes as the predominant groups in most of the Latin American nations. Political ideas and institutions borrowed from abroad have been modified and adapted to the Latin American scene. Economic policies have been decided upon increasingly in terms of national self-interest. New cultural institutions have developed, and Latin American architects, musicians, painters, and novelists have expressed themselves with increasing originality.

The growing integration and maturing of the people of Latin America has led to an increasing awareness of their own distinctive personalities in all of these countries. One political expression of this development is the growth of nationalism, but it is shown in other ways as well. It has led to an increasing fraternity of feeling and action among the people of the Latin American nations. This feeling of unity is expressed both in relations with the world outside of Latin America, and in the relationships among the countries of the area.

LATIN AMERICAN SOLIDARITY

Toward the outside world there is an increasing tendency on the part of the Latin Americans to present a united front. There is a feeling that the Latin Americans must control their own economies. There is also a growing determination among them to help themselves, which is given concrete form in the moves of the Central Americans to form a common market and of a number of South American countries and Mexico to establish a free-trade area.

This trend toward Latin American solidarity is a revival of a theme which has persisted since the area generally achieved its independence a century and a half ago. Simón Bolívar and other fathers of Latin American independence believed in and preached the eventual political unification of the areas which had been parts of the Spanish and Portuguese empires. More recently, the Apristas and other political movements have had such unity as a fundamental element in their philosophy. It is likely that there lurks in the minds of many of those who have been pushing the idea of Latin American economic unity the possibility that this may eventually lead to political unification of the area as well.

It does not seem likely to the author that political unification of Latin America as a whole will be achieved during the remainder of the twentieth century. The differences and interests of the various countries of the region are still too great for that. However, the possibility that regional federations within the area—such as in Central America, or possibly among the Bolivarian countries of northern South America (Venezuela, Colombia, and Ecuador)—may be achieved in the foreseeable future should by no means be overlooked.

LATIN AMERICA AND THE UNITED STATES

Moves toward economic unity among the Latin American nations, and the possibility of some degree of eventual political unification as well, present interesting problems in connection with Latin America's relationship to the United States. To a certain degree, it is undoubtedly true that moves toward unity within Latin America are motivated by the desire to put the area in a better bargaining position vis-à-vis its powerful northern neighbor.[1]

Many of the Latin Americans have a schizophrenic attitude toward the United States, their most powerful neigh-

[1] The well-known economist Stacey May of the Rockefeller Fund is one of several North Americans who have suggested the need for forming a hemisphere-wide common market, to include both the United States and Latin America, in order to prevent the proposed moves toward economic unity within Latin America from becoming the source of future conflict between the two parts of the New World, and so that the hemisphere as a whole can present a common front to an economically united Western Europe.

bor. On the one hand, there is a widespread feeling of admiration for the material, technological, and economic accomplishments of the great northern country. Among many, too, there is appreciation of the democratic creed in which the citizens of the United States believe, though they do not always practice it. There is a widespread desire among Latin Americans to emulate the achievements of the United States in these fields.

On the other hand, there is also widespread jealousy and dislike of the United States. These feelings are often held by the same people who admire and desire to emulate many things North American. The resentment is engendered by the very size of the United States and by its power in the Western Hemisphere, particularly the influence of U.S. business enterprises in the Latin American economy. It is also fomented by memories of past misbehavior by the United States in its relations with its southern neighbors, some of this misbehavior having transpired in the quite recent past.

CAUSES OF ANTI-U.S. SENTIMENT

The dislike of the United States has grown catastrophically since World War II. The aura of good feeling which had been engendered by the Good Neighbor Policy and the alliance of virtually all the hemisphere in the struggle against the Axis powers has disappeared since 1945.

This has been due in part to what the Latin Americans conceive to have been the neglect of their area, as compared with Europe, Asia, and Africa, by U.S. policy-makers in the decade and a half after the Second World War. They feel that this neglect was particularly obvious in the economic field, where the United States did not give aid to Latin American economic development on the scale which they believe they were promised during the war. This fact, as well as U.S. reticence for many years to discuss the problem of maintaining prices of the agricultural and mining export products upon which Latin America depends for its foreign-exchange income, led many Latin Americans to feel that the United States was opposed to the industrialization of Latin America, to which the area itself is totally committed.

Finally, Latin American resentment against the United States was fostered by mistaken political policies pursued by the United States in Latin America for many years. This country, unfortunately, gave almost universal support to the dictators who have ruled so many of the countries of the area between 1945 and 1961. This support was moral and political, as evidenced by the presentation of this country's highest decorations to several of the tyrants. It was economic and it was military, as in the case of the United States providing most of the arms with which General Fulgencio Batista tried to prevent the overthrow of his dictatorship.

CHANGES IN UNITED STATES POLICY

The Kennedy Administration during its first year in office took steps to rectify these past mistakes. After taking office President Kennedy made clear his belief that the problems of Latin America were of greatest concern to this country, and he frequently took occasion to reiterate this belief. In the Alliance for Progress program put forward by Kennedy, the United States was placed strongly behind a joint hemispheric effort to step up the pace of economic development and raise living standards in Latin America. On a political level the Kennedy Administration made clear in word and deed that its sympathies lay with those regimes and groups which were trying to bring about long-overdue social changes in a democratic fashion, and that the U.S. government does not approve of dictatorships of either Right or Left.

As this is being written it is too early to know whether this fundamental change in policy has come in time to stem the growing tide of frustration and hatred toward the United States among the Latin American people. However, the precedent of the Good Neighbor Policy of Franklin D. Roosevelt, which transformed almost universal hostility toward the United States in Latin America into widespread friendship and confidence, indicates that an intelligent policy by this country may be able to turn the tide which has been running against it in the hemisphere since World War II.

Certainly, to be effective the alterations in specific policies made by the Kennedy Administration will have to be accompanied by a fundamental change in attitude by the United States, which may be more difficult. This is made increasingly necessary by the development of the Latin American countries. Although it is perhaps trite to say so, Latin America is "coming of age." The region now carries much more weight in world affairs than has ever been true in the past, and its importance will increase.

We have already noted the potentialities of Brazil for becoming one of the Great Powers within the foreseeable future. Other nations of the area are also developing beyond the state of economic, political, and psychological dependence which has hitherto been the role of the Latin American countries. Mexico, with half of Brazil's population, a rapidly developing economy, and extensive resources, may well become a country of at least secondary importance in the balance of world power. The same may be said of Argentina, while several other countries, including Colombia, Venezuela, and Peru, will also be nations of measurable importance in world affairs.

In the face of these developments the time is fast passing when the United States can any longer treat its Latin American neighbors in the spirit of the "big brother." Even presuming that the change in U.S. policies undertaken by President Kennedy is successful in stemming the anti-U.S. tide of the post-World War II period, this country will have to deal on more nearly equal terms with the nations with which it shares the hemisphere. In their approach to the problems of the New World, President Kennedy and his chief aides have indicated that they are aware of this need for a change in attitude as well as in deeds in the inter-American field.

This country must expect in the future that the nations of Latin America will increasingly seek to limit their economic and political dependence on the United States. Some of them, without necessarily becoming hostile toward the United States, may seek to develop closer association with the neutralist or uncommitted countries of Asia and Africa than they have had hitherto. A number of governments, perhaps led by Brazil, may be expected increasingly to take positions on world issues which differ from those adopted by the United States.

Neutralist sentiment may well grow. Although this has its disadvantages for the United States, such a development may seem logical to many Latin American leaders. Their focus on world affairs may be somewhat different from that of the North Americans. They may well not see the East-West struggle as the world's most pressing problem, as we do, and indeed may tend to see it as preponderantly a Russia-U.S. fight in which they are only tangentially involved. To them, the problems of economic development and even the struggle of the remaining colonies against the old imperial powers may seem of greater over-all importance. Some Latin American governments may well take different positions from the United States on specific issues in these fields.

Above all, there will tend to be a growing tendency on the part of Latin American governments to judge all issues in international affairs from the position of what they interpret to be the best interests of their particular country. Latin American government leaders may often see their nations' best interests in a somewhat different light than that in which they are seen in Washington.

These changes in attitudes of the Latin American countries will undoubtedly present serious problems to U.S. policy-makers. They may find themselves annoyed at the attempts of various Latin American governments to break the leading strings of the United States. They may resent opposition from Latin American governments on problems outside of the hemisphere. They may find it hard to accept movements in the neutralist direction by some of these governments.

However, if the United States wishes to maintain friendly relations with Latin America over the remaining decades of this century, it must be willing to accept these changes in Latin America. It must become accustomed to dealing with at least the more important of the Latin American nations with the same degree of frankness and equality with which it treats the countries of Western Europe.

On the other hand, in certain respects the unity of the Americas may well be strengthened in the years to come. If Latin America's traditional belief in democracy begins to conform to a greater degree than in the past to the facts of the region's politics, most of the nations of the hemisphere will really share a common political ideology and have common ideals to fight for. Furthermore, the frontier spirit which is becoming an increasing element in the psychology of several of the more important Latin American nations should be something which we can understand, and should be a bond of unity between us and our southern neighbors. The economic trends observable in both the United States and Latin America will assure that in the decades to come the mixed economies of the two parts of the hemisphere will become increasingly similar.

LATIN AMERICAN RELATIONS WITH EUROPE

Latin American relations with Europe have also been undergoing fundamental changes in recent decades, and will be likely to change even more in those immediately ahead. The ties between the two areas have traditionally been very close. The countries of Latin America were all originally colonies of one or another European power. For almost a century after independence, most of the foreign trade of Latin America was conducted with Europe. Investments by Europeans were largely responsible for developing the railroads, public utilities, and even some of the early banks, factories, and commercial enterprises of Latin America.

Culturally, too, most of the Latin American nations remained virtually colonies of Europe for many decades after receiving their political independence. Fashions in ideas as well as in clothes and buildings tended to be copied from the Old World.

Much of this changed during the first half of the twentieth century. The United States took the place of Europe as the principal provider of trade and investment, and its cultural influence, too, tended to become more important than that of Europe.

However, there is still an important role for the Europeans to play in the future growth of Latin America. Since the recovery of Europe from the effects of World War II, the Latin Americans have looked increasingly to the countries and investors of that area for economic aid in their development. This trend is likely to be intensified in the immediate future. Ties of language, religion, and temperament will also continue to bind the Latin Americans to at least the southern countries of Europe.

A disturbing factor in European-Latin American economic relations in the years immediately ahead will be the tendency toward European economic unification, particularly the Common Market. This Market has provided for opening the six European countries—France, Germany, Italy, Belgium, Luxembourg, and the Netherlands—to the products of the former members of the French Empire in Africa which recently received their independence. If the United Kingdom finally enters the Common Market, the

British former colonies in Africa may also get the same preference.

These nations of Black Africa grow many of the same products exported heavily by Latin American countries: coffee, cacao, sugar, bananas, etc. Their inclusion within the Common Market will give them a considerable competitive advantage over the Latin Americans. The Latin Americans' own efforts to establish a Common Market or at least a Free Trade Area, are in part a reply to European economic unity.

The maturing of the Latin American nations will undoubtedly bring further changes in their relations with Europe. In some cases dramatic alterations have already occurred. For instance, for some decades at least, Brazil has been the senior partner among the Portuguese-speaking parts of the world. Likewise, several Spanish-American nations, notably Mexico and Argentina, have taken the cultural leadership in the Spanish-speaking world. These two nations are the principal source of literature and motion pictures in the language, and in other fields, too, the Spanish-American nations have taken the leadership away from their erstwhile mother country.

LATIN AMERICA AND OTHER UNDER-DEVELOPED REGIONS

The relations of the Latin American nations with the economically underdeveloped nations of Asia and Africa have been growing closer since World War II and are likely to become a good deal more important in the closing decades of this century. The people of these areas share many common problems and ideas.

Like the nations of Africa and Asia, those of Latin America are exceedingly anxious to get rapid development of their economies. They are thus equally concerned with finding ways and means of getting the already industrialized nations to increase their aid to the growth of the underdeveloped economies. However, there is a considerable degree of rivalry between the underdeveloped nations of the New World and the Old in the distribution of this aid from the industrialized countries.

The Latin American nations and those of Asia and Africa also share the headaches of being principally producers of raw materials and foodstuffs for export. Since World War II they have frequently joined hands in international economic conferences and other ventures to try to get the big industrial countries, particularly the United States, to agree to measures to stabilize the prices of these exports. In some instances they have worked together in cartels to this end—as in the case of the tin cartel to which Bolivia in South America and several Asian and African nations have belonged. Venezuela has taken the lead in trying to interest the oil-producing countries of the Middle East in establishing some kind of cartel arrangement in that field as well, through the Organization of Petroleum Exporting Countries (OPEC) which was set up in 1960.

Such cooperation on concrete problems is likely to increase in the future. It is reinforced by a growing feeling of solidarity in the Latin American countries with the underdeveloped nations in other parts of the world. Perhaps it may also be strengthened by the development of at least some trade—which hitherto has been all but nonexistent— between the Latin Americans and the Asians and Africans. However, although it can be expected that even broader programs of cooperation between these countries will be sought in the coming decades, this may be hampered to a degree by the undoubted rivalry which exists between Latin American raw material and foodstuff producers and those elsewhere in the underdeveloped parts of the world.

RELATIONS WITH COMMUNIST COUNTRIES

Latin American contacts with the nations of the Communist bloc have traditionally been very limited. Although several hundred thousand immigrants from Russia and Eastern Europe came to Latin America during the early decades of the twentieth century, and smaller numbers of Chinese also settled in these countries, these groups make up only a small proportion of the total population of the area.

Trade between Latin America and the Communist countries, too, has been limited in the past. Until the advent of the Castro regime in Cuba in 1959, only Argentina, Uruguay, and Brazil engaged in any appreciable commerce with these nations. Such trade made up less than 2 per cent of the total trade of the Latin American countries.

Even diplomatic recognition of the Communist countries by the Latin American nations has been very limited. Although a considerable number of countries recognized the Soviet Union during World War II, by 1959 only Argentina, Uruguay, and Mexico had diplomatic relations with the U.S.S.R. A few other countries had such relations with one or another of the East European satellites. No country recognized Communist China.

However, the Castro regime has somewhat changed this picture. This government has not only re-established diplomatic relations with the Soviet Union, but has exchanged embassies with the East European satellites and has recognized the government of Communist China. Furthermore, its policies have resulted in Cuba's trade being altered so that instead of being overwhelmingly with the United States it has come to be almost exclusively with the Communist countries.

Soviet help offered to the Castro regime since 1960 has been part of the intensification of the efforts of the U.S.S.R. and other Communist countries to gain influence in Latin America. Sizable offers of aid were made to several other Latin American nations, notably a suggestion by the Soviet Union that it was willing to finance the construction of a tin refinery in Bolivia, an offer which Bolivia has not finally accepted as this is being written. These offers indicated that the Soviet Union and its satellites now have available an important new weapon in their campaign to gain influence in Latin America, a campaign which heretofore has been confined largely to propaganda and the activities of the Communist parties.

The Administration of President Jânio Quadros during its seven months in power in Brazil in 1961 also recognized the Soviet Union and several East European satellites, as part of its proclaimed "independent" foreign policy. The Quadros regime also sought to increase greatly the commercial relations of Brazil with these countries, and signed agreements for an annual exchange of approximately $1 billion worth of products.

Whether other Latin American nations will follow Castro's example in establishing very close relations with the Communist bloc, while virtually breaking off all contact with the United States and Western Europe, will depend on many factors. Fundamentally, it depends on the trend of internal politics in these countries. If it proves impossible to obtain the long-overdue social and economic changes and the rapid economic development so generally wished for through democratic processes, the Castro policies in both internal affairs and international relations will become increasingly attractive. If U.S. support of the effort to get these changes democratically and to encourage rapid economic development is not successful, it is inevitable that the Latin American nations will look with increasing sympathy upon the use of Communist methods at home and on help from the Soviet Union and its associates.

SUMMARY

It is clear that Latin America's role in world affairs is going to be much more important in the decades to come than it has been in the past. With its fast-growing population, which is increasing at a more rapid rate than that of any other part of the globe, it will make up a proportionately larger part of mankind. It is farther advanced on the road to economic development than are most of Asia and Africa, and development showed an ability in the decade after World War II to increase with great rapidity. Its economic weight will therefore be felt much more in the future than heretofore. At the same time it will be an important part of that two-thirds of mankind which is seeking help from the wealthier one-third to raise its production levels, its standards of living, and its strength. Its leaders have shown in recent decades an ability to innovate both in ideas and institutions, insofar as economic-development problems are concerned.

All of this amounts to saying that Latin America will no longer remain what it was during the nineteenth century and much of the first half of the twentieth—an isolated area more or less off the stage upon which the future of the world was being determined. It is moving out of the wings and onstage.

This changing role of Latin America is of peculiar importance to the United States. This country has always tended to regard Latin America as its own back yard, as a reserve upon which it could draw in times of need, but as an area which could more or less be taken for granted in the interim.

Such is no longer the case. It is clear that Latin America is increasingly inclined to play a more independent role. The Castro case indicates that the possibility of one or more of the Latin American countries joining our enemies is no longer to be discounted. In any case, though they may decide to continue to cast their lot with the United States on the world scene, most Latin American countries will do so only after considering the problem on its merits and deciding that such an alignment is in their own best interest. They can no longer be taken for granted by this country.

Bibliographical Note

For those readers who wish to carry their studies of Latin American affairs beyond the confines of the present slender volume, there is a mass of readily available material. Although the general public and the United States government tended to pay little attention to Latin America for several decades, the scholars and journalists in the field have been busy exploring the most diverse aspects of life in the area.

The works which we recommend below are available in English, and deal with general subject headings for Latin America as a whole. We have made no attempt to list studies in any field which deal with only one or a small group of countries. Such a task would be virtually interminable. However, anyone who would delve into even a small proportion of the books which we have noted would be richly rewarded in terms of a broadening of his perspective concerning the other countries of our hemisphere.

A number of good over-all surveys of Latin America have been written. Certainly the veteran of them all was *South America,* written by the famous English historian James Bryce (New York: Macmillan, 1916), which is still readily available in many libraries. More recent works of this kind are William Lytle Schurz's *This New World: The Civilization of Latin America* (New York: Dutton, 1954) and *Latin America: A Descriptive Survey,* by the same author (New York: Dutton, 1949). Also of interest are two small volumes by Lewis Hanke entitled *South America* and *Mexico and The Caribbean* (New York: Anvil Books, 1959).

For those who want to learn more about the geography of the area, two volumes are particularly recommended: *Economic Geography of South America* by R. H. Whitbeck and Frank E. Williams (New York: McGraw-Hill, 1940); and Preston James's *Latin America* (New York: Odyssey Press, 1959).

Several books are available which deal with material we have discussed in our chapter on "The People." These include the March 1958 volume of *The Annals* of the American Academy of Political and Social Sciences, edited by Kingsley Davis and entitled "A Growing Hemisphere: Population Change in the Hemisphere." Of a rather different nature is Frank Tannenbaum's *Slave and Citizen: The Negro in the Americas* (New York: Knopf, 1947).

There is a wealth of material on the economies of the Latin American countries. General surveys on the subject include Simon Hanson's *Economic Development in Latin America* (Washington, D.C.: Inter-American Affairs Press, 1951); and Wendell Gordon's *The Economy of Latin America* (New York: Columbia University Press, 1950). Also, both excellent and brief is W. S. Woytinsky's *United States and Latin American Economy,* published in 1958 by the Tamiment Institute.

Two excellent studies of the problems of industrialization have appeared. These are Lloyd Hughlett's *Industrialization of Latin America* (New York: McGraw-Hill, 1947), which deals with the problem industry by industry; and George Wythe's *Industry in Latin America* (Columbia University Press, 1949), which discusses it country by country.

Finally, in the economic field one might mention the series of excellent studies of the economies of various individual countries which have been published by the International Bank for Reconstruction and Development through the Johns Hopkins University Press. Such studies have been forthcoming on the economies of Cuba, Mexico, Guatemala, Nicaragua, Colombia, Venezuela, and Chile.

Labor relations is a field which has received relatively little attention. The present author published a pamphlet on the subject entitled *Labour Movements of Latin America* (London: Fabian International Bureau, 1947). A Chilean and an American professor, Moises Poblete Troncoso and Ben Burnett respectively, joined hands to write *The Rise of the Latin American Labor Movement* (New York: Bookman Associates, 1960).

Changes in Latin American society, and particularly in class relationships, are discussed in "Social Change in Latin America Today" (*Harper's* magazine, 1960), and in an older book by David Efron, George Soule, and Norman Ness entitled *Latin America in the Future World* (New York: Rinehart, 1945). John Johnson also deals with this problem and its political implications in his *Political Change in Latin America: The Emergence of the Middle Sectors* (Stanford University Press, 1958).

Several excellent studies of Latin American government and the forces working upon it have been made in recent years. The two most thorough are William W. Pierson's and Federico Gil's *Governments of Latin America* (New York: McGraw-Hill, 1957); and Harold Davis' (editor) *Government and Politics in Latin America* (New York: Ronald Press, 1958). Very handy is R. A. Gomez' small paperbound volume *Government and Politics in Latin America* (New York: Random House, 1960). Somewhat older is Asher N. Christensen's collection of articles entitled *The Evolution of Latin American Government* (New York: Holt, 1951). Finally, for those who want to refer directly to the constitutions of the Latin American countries as of 1948, Russell Fitzgibbon's *The Constitutions of the Americas* (University of Chicago Press, 1948) is readily at hand.

The politics of Latin America has also been dealt with in some detail by recent writers. Still excellent is *The State of Latin America* (New York: Knopf, 1952), written by Germán Arciniegas, Colombian historian and political leader. Also excellent is a special number of the *American Political Science Review* edited by W. W. Pierson in March 1950 and entitled "The Pathology of Democracy in Latin America." The volume edited by Fredrick Pike entitled *Freedom and Reform in Latin America* (Notre Dame University Press, 1959), stresses the forces at work below the surface in Latin American political life.

One might also recommend two books by the present author: *Communism in Latin America* (Rutgers University Press, 1957) and *The Struggle for Democracy in Latin America* (New York: Macmillan, 1961), the latter written in conjunction with Charles O. Porter. Finally, of particular interest is the issue of *The Annals* of the American Academy of March 1961, edited by Robert Burr and entitled "Latin America's Nationalistic Revolutions."

There exists so far only one thoroughgoing study of the Latin American military. This is Edwin Lieuwen's *Arms and Politics in Latin America* (New York: Praeger, 1960).

A number of scholars have turned their attention to the educational systems and the cultural achievements of the Latin Americans. In the former category are a series of pamphlets issued by the United States Office of Education between 1940 and 1947, and written by Cameron D. Ebaugh, on the educational establishments of various of the Latin American nations. Much older is *Education in Latin America* by Henry L. Smith and Harold Littell (New York: American Book Company, 1934). The International Labor Organization issued a rather pedestrian study of vocational education in the region entitled *Vocational Training in Latin America* (Geneva, 1951).

Several studies of Latin American literature are of interest. These include Germán Arciniegas' *The Green Conti-*

nent: A Comprehensive View of Latin America by Its Leading Writers (New York: Knopf, 1944); and Pedro Henríquez Ureña's *Literary Currents in Hispanic America* (Harvard University Press, 1945). Architectural achievements of the Latin Americans have been discussed by Henry Russell Hitchcock in his *Latin American Architecture Since 1945* (New York: Museum of Modern Art, 1955).

The problems of religion and the Church have been treated by various authors. Worthy of mention are Lloyd Meacham's *Church and State in Latin America* (University of North Carolina Press, 1934); George P. Howard's *Religious Liberty in Latin America?* (Philadelphia: Ambassador Books, 1944); and John Considine's *New Horizons in Latin America* (New York: Dodd, 1958).

Finally, there have been many works written about the relations of the Latin American nations with the outside world. Most of these have dealt with the area's relations with the United States. However, Walter M. Daniels' *Latin America in the Cold War* (New York: Wilson, 1952) and J. Fred Rippy's *Latin America in World Politics* (New York: Appleton Century, 1938) are rather broader.

Among the works dealing particularly with inter-American relations, the following may be mentioned:

Joseph B. Lockey's *Pan Americanism: Its Beginnings* (New York: Macmillan, 1920).

Samuel E. Bemis' *The Latin American Policy of the United States,* (New York: Harcourt, Brace and Co., 1943) a classic in the field.

Carlos Davila's and Clarence Senior's *Latin America and the Good Neighbor Policy* (New York University Press, 1943), written by a leading Chilean statesman and an American sociologist.

Lawrence Duggan's *The Americas: The Search for Hemispheric Security,* (New York: Henry Holt & Co., 1949) by one of those principally responsible for United States policy during the Good Neighbor era.

Arthur Whitaker's *The Western Hemisphere Idea: Its Rise and Decline* (Cornell University Press, 1954), for an over-all view of the subject.

J. Fred Rippy's *Globe and Hemisphere* (Chicago: Henry Regnery, 1958), for a very jaundiced view of inter-American relations in recent years.

Anyone wishing to keep up-to-date on events in Latin America should certainly look at *Hispanic American Report*, issued by Stanford University each month, containing detailed information on events in each one of the Latin American countries. Of special interest, too, is the periodical *Hemispherica*, published monthly by the Inter-American Association for Democracy and Freedom, in New York City which deals particularly with political questions.

Some general newspapers and periodicals do a reasonably good job of keeping up with Latin American affairs. Outstanding in this regard are the New York *Times*, the Washington *Post*, and the *Christian Science Monitor*. Increasingly, general news magazines have also begun to devote more attention to Latin American events. Finally, the journals of opinion of both Right and Left have in recent years begun to comment more frequently on the problems and events of the hemisphere.

Although it may take somewhat more diligence to keep oneself reasonably well informed on Latin American affairs than upon those of the nations in Western Europe, behind the Iron Curtain, in Asia, and in Africa, it is possible to do so. Anyone who does keep informed will find himself rewarded by his ability to understand the fast-changing panorama of what is, after all, part of our own hemisphere.

Index